PRESENTING

—— WITH ——

CREDIBILITY

PRACTICAL TOOLS AND TECHNIQUES
FOR EFFECTIVE PRESENTATIONS

Bruna Martinuzzi

Presenting with Credibility
Practical Tools and Techniques for Effective Presentations

Publisher's Cataloging-in-Publication data

Martinuzzi, Bruna.
   Presenting with credibility : practical tools and techniques for effective presentations / Bruna Martinuzzi.
   p. cm.
   ISBN 978-1-935667-12-4

1. Public speaking. 2. Business presentations. 3. Sales presentations. 4. Communication in management. 5. Persuasion (Psychology). 6. Oral communication. I. Title.

HF5718.22 .M328 2012
658.4/52 --dc23   2012931853

Printed and bound in the United States.
First printed April 2012.

The paper used in this book meets the minimum requirements of the American National Standard for Information Services—Permanence of Paper for Printed Library Materials, ANSI Z39.48-1992.

Book design by Alex Miles Younger

Six Seconds Emotional Intelligence Press
San Francisco, CA

The poem "Come to the Edge" has been reprinted with permission from Christopher Logue, copyright © 1969 by Christopher Logue.

PRESENTING
—— WITH ——
CREDIBILITY

*PRACTICAL TOOLS AND TECHNIQUES
FOR EFFECTIVE PRESENTATIONS*

Bruna Martinuzzi

Six Seconds Emotional Intelligence Press
San Francisco, CA

*To my husband, Saul, who flung the door wide open
and taught me to enter by myself.*

Come to the edge.
We might fall.
Come to the edge.
It's too high!
COME TO THE EDGE!
And they came
and he pushed
and they flew...

—Christopher Logue

CONTENTS

"I try to leave out the parts that people skip."
—Elmore Leonard

Acknowledgments   xi

Introduction   xv

Part One: Expertise and Competence

Chapter 1   *The Cornerstone of Credibility: Your Expertise*   2

Chapter 2   *Before You Hit the Road: What Do You Want to Accomplish?*   23

Chapter 3   *Grab Their Attention: Getting Them Interested Instantly*   31

Chapter 4   *Leave Them Wanting More: Ending Memorably*   52

Chapter 5   *Final Touches: Editing Your Presentation*   60

Chapter 6   *Task Tenacity: Preparing for Questions*   63

Chapter 7   *A Golden Opportunity: Presenting to C-Level*   77

Chapter 8   *And Now for Something Totally Different: Your Keynote*   86

Chapter 9   *Teaching or Torture: Your Workshop*   103

Chapter 10   *PowerPoint Is Not Evil: Bozo Users Are*   122

Chapter 11   *A Long-Distance Affair: Virtual Presentations*   133

Part Two: Authenticity

Chapter 12   *Making It Real: Your Authenticity*   146

Chapter 13   *The Crown Jewel of Credibility: Your Trustworthiness*   157

Part Three: Personal Presence

Chapter 14   *When You Enter a Room: Your Personal Presence*   164

Chapter 15   *Step Out of Your Comfort Zone: Adaptability*   180

Chapter 16   *Performance Anxiety: Your Survival Toolkit*   186

Chapter 17   *When Things Go Wrong: Don't Go with Them*   206

Chapter 18   *Difficult Audiences: Don't Let Them Pull Your Strings*   215

Part Four: Dynamism

Chapter 19   *Are You a Ventriloquist to the Slides?: Your Dynamism*   226

Chapter 20   *The Icing on the Cake: Metaphors and Analogies*   245

Chapter 21   *Get Them to Lean In: Storytelling*   257

Part Five: Over to You

Chapter 22   *Your Frequently Asked Questions*   264

Epilogue   **281**

Resources

A.   Transitions   284

B.   A Speaker's Library   289

C.   Speaking Blogs   294

D.   Other Useful Websites   296

E.   A Compendium of Presentations   306

F.   A Planning Template   308

Notes   **313**

Index   **343**

About the Author   **361**

ACKNOWLEDGMENTS

"Each of us has cause to think with deep gratitude
of those who have lighted the flame within us."
—**Albert Schweitzer**

One of my favorite Emerson quotes is, "Be an opener of doors for such as come after thee, and do not try to make the universe a blind alley." I have been blessed with a large number of people who have held many doors open for me at every step of my circuitous journey from Cairo to Canada. I am grateful to Jean Alouche for the hours he spent in my teenage years, tutoring me to write speeches to imaginary audiences, continually reminding me of the perils of "becoming a barbarian." I will be forever grateful to Avi, wherever in the universe you are, my friend, for pushing me, none too gently, through a portal and into the sky so long ago. I am also particularly indebted to all those who had a positive influence on my education and career path, angels who opened narrowing gates—too many to mention.

I have deep gratitude for my publishers, Joshua Freedman and Anabel Jensen, for twice believing in me. I am also thankful for Jenny Wiley, Program Manager at Six Seconds, for consistently going the extra mile and for her 24/7 kindness.

I am deeply indebted to my copyeditor, Brookes Nohlgren. An author could not hope to find a more conscientious and thorough editor. She encouraged me and maintained the intellectual integrity of the book by painstakingly checking each quote and link, down to the minutest detail. Brookes has that rare ability to skillfully edit without eroding the author's voice or ethos.

Special thanks to Alex Miles Younger, who worked with talent and heart to marry form and content to come up with a beautiful cover that catches the intent of the book. I am also thankful for his patience, responsiveness, and skilled attention to all the other design details in the book. I would like to thank Robert A. Saigh for his excellent index. Thank you also to Natalie Giboney-Turner for her considerable effort in obtaining permissions for the book.

I express heartfelt gratitude for Ron Crossland, who opened up a gateway for me into brain science. He sparked my interest in authentic leadership communication and continues to inspire me with his teachings.

This book is about credibility. I am blessed to have encountered in my life more than my fair share of people who never gave me cause to doubt their credibility—leaders worth following.

I am especially indebted to my students, accomplished men and women in the corporate and academic worlds whom I have had the honor to teach over the years. They have given me the opportunity to practice my craft and have inspired me to write this book, which is for them. I have learned from their questions and challenges.

I am profoundly grateful for Saul, my husband and mensch. Every day, for the past four decades, he has inspired and encouraged me.

Lastly, this book builds on the rich body of work already produced on this topic by giants in the field, who led me down research paths I never even knew existed.

There are not enough years left in my life for me to give back the equivalent measure of the gifts I continue to receive in my journey.

INTRODUCTION

"Ideally a book would have no order to it,
and the reader would have to discover his own."
—**Mark Twain**

"To be believable," broadcast journalist Edward R. Murrow said, "we must be credible." Credibility is the most important aspect of presenting. It's a well-established fact in communication theory that people are more likely to be persuaded by a speaker who is credible. Anyone with low credibility is less likely to convince others, even when presenting the same arguments as someone with high credibility.[1] If you have no credibility as a communicator, your audience will not believe what you are telling them. If they don't believe you, they will not buy your product, support your project, or adopt your ideas.

The Edelman Trust Barometer® for 2011 asked the following question: "If you heard information about a company from one of these people, how credible would that information be?"[2] Only 70 percent would believe information from an academic or expert, and less than 65 percent would believe a technical expert within a company. Only half would believe a CEO. Globally, we have a deficit of credibility.

This book is about developing the expertise and confidence to be a credible presenter. Many books have been written on credibility's role in influence and persuasion, communication, and leadership. The leaders of the modern-day credibility movement are James Kouzes and Barry Posner, who have conducted extensive studies on leadership credibility.[3] This book is about applying the established principles of credibility to presentation skills, covering everything from platform presence to presentation anxiety to presentation technology.

Credibility is the holy grail of presenters. It is the foundation for effective presentations. Making a presentation without credibility is like steering a car that is stationary: you can go through the motions, but you won't go anywhere. It is crucial to do everything you can as a speaker to gain credibility first. Once you have achieved credibility, you will have eliminated a lot of the issues that may prevent you from delivering a successful presentation. Developing credibility as a speaker will also go a long way toward reducing your presentation anxiety.

If you picked up this book in the hope of finding tips that will make you look good *without* doing the hard work of learning your core material, then this is not the right book for you. All the recommendations, tips, and techniques outlined in this book are geared toward enhancing your credibility so that you can deliver your message as an authentic person. They are an adjunct to knowledge and expertise, not a substitute for them.

So what is credibility exactly? Credibility is defined as the quality of being believable or trustworthy. It is not a characteristic that we can claim for ourselves. Rather, it is a quality that others attribute to us: our audience decides whether or not we are credible.[4] Therefore, whenever we speak of credibility as a speaker, we are referring to perceived credibility—something every presenter must be concerned about.

More than 2,500 years ago, Aristotle stipulated that the source of a message, or its "ethos" as he called it, contributed to the credibility of that message. Modern-day researchers have conducted studies proving this to be true.[5] McCroskey and Teven undertook one of the most complete of these studies in 1999.[6] They identified three key components of source credibility for a communicator: competence, trustworthiness, and goodwill (the extent to which the audience believes that the individual cares for them and has their best interests at heart). Earlier research had identified expertise, trustworthiness, and likability as components of credibility.[7] Another study that is often quoted identified the following keys to credibility: safety (trustworthy, friendly), qualification (competent, experienced), and dynamism (energetic, bold, emphatic).[8]

The overlap in these studies is clear: expertise (sometimes referred to as competence or qualification) and trustworthiness surface as major components of source credibility. Two other components of source credibility are dynamism and likability. Credibility as a communicator, then, is made up of several dimensions. How can we, in today's world, use this research to help us become credible—and dynamic—presenters?

This is what I have set out to do in this book. I have developed a model for presenting that combines the essence of credibility with additional components that are particularly important in our zeitgeist. Today more than ever, to deliver a successful presentation, a speaker needs not only expertise and trustworthiness but the ability to engage an ever-distracted and impatient audience. As far back as Roman times, the orator Quintilian had defined credibility for a speaker as "a good man speaking well." Speaking well in our fast-paced, multimedia-rich world requires personal presence and dynamism, the other elements of our model.

When we put into practice all of the elements of this model for presenting, we end up with a winning combination of credibility, confidence, and authority on one hand; and warmth, likability, and empathy on the other hand.

Just as a quadrilateral pyramid is made up of four triangular faces, your credibility as a speaker is made up of the following four essential dimensions:

- Expertise and competence
- Authenticity
- Personal presence
- Dynamism

See Figure 1.

Figure 1

You will find the model easy to remember and learn. But it will take your entire career to practice it. When you understand and incorporate all of the components of the model into your presentations, you rise like a pyramid—and like a pyramid, you are on solid footing. For the duration of this reading journey, I would encourage you to keep this image of the pyramid in your mind. Metaphorically, it represents the solidity that credibility gives you in terms of your performance as a speaker.

The primary aspect of your credibility as a presenter is your expertise: your perceived knowledge and clarity about your speaking topic and your competence at the front of the room. Expertise includes your ability to handle a variety of speaking situations, from the simplest to the most challenging, such as presenting to C-level (highest level of executives) or delivering a keynote. Part One of the book covers **expertise** and **competence**. These are nonnegotiable components of credibility.

Part Two covers **authenticity**. Authenticity is about being the best version of the real you: it's your genuineness, trustworthiness, and goodwill. It's how truly likable you are to the audience. You cannot have credibility without authenticity. While your expertise is dependent on your cognitive intelligence, your authenticity is based on an emotional interaction: how do people *feel* about you? Tuning up your emotional intelligence is essential for mastery in this area.

Part Three deals with **personal presence**. This is something that people notice about you when you enter a room or start to speak. It includes several components that together signal self-confidence as a speaker. It is your composure and your aplomb—your capacity to adapt your communication style to meet the needs of your audience and your ability to stay cool under fire. The presence of mind and strength to confidently deal with whatever comes your way during a presentation are the mark of a credible presenter.

Part Four of the book deals with **dynamism**. This is the energy that you bring to your presentation—your vitality. It is energy not only in your comportment but also in your language—your facility with the pearls of communication (metaphors, analogies, and story-telling). Above all, it is your passion and your emotional engagement with the audience and with your material.

As the title of the book promises, each chapter will provide you with practical tools and techniques to help you develop and strengthen your skills as a presenter. These are the blocks of stone that make up the pyramid. Just as the whole structure of the pyramid is perfectly oriented to the points of a compass, so the building blocks of presentation skills in this book are oriented to developing your credibility as a presenter worth listening to.

The book has useful information for anyone who wants to take their presentation skills to the next level. Even seasoned presenters can benefit from reading it. As the writer and critic George Santayana said, "The wisest mind has something yet to learn." Each chapter is written so that it can stand alone. The book will appeal to the busy professional who doesn't normally read books about presentation skills. It's a presentation skills workshop on the run—a one-stop shop that is a gateway to many of the best resources on the topic.

The last section of the book includes **frequently asked questions** regarding presentation skills. There is also a generous **resources** section. Please don't skip this section, as it opens a portal to some of the best books and blogs on the topic. You can use these materials to further develop the essential skill of standing in front of a group and speaking confidently and competently, with genuineness and warmth about what matters to you and your organization. Investing time to enhance your presentation skills will pay dividends for your career. As *The McKinsey Mind* puts it, "Presentation is the 'Killer Skill' we take into the real world. It's almost an unfair advantage."[9]

References to helpful online resources appear not only in the Resources section but throughout the book. Links to these sites can be found at http://www.clarionenterprises.com/links. On this Web page, you can click to go directly to the URLs in the book.

In my career spanning several decades in the business world, I sat through hundreds of presentations by speakers who, in Alfred Hitchcock's words, seemed "to want to make the audience suffer as much as possible." I have also attended presentations that were so informative and engaging that they profoundly inspired me and forever changed my outlook on many issues.

In your career path, you come across innumerable opportunities to deliver presentations to a variety of audiences: formal presentations to your board, professional associations, conferences, and trade shows; important presentations to clients and other stakeholders; and in-house presentations to your superiors, staff, and colleagues. These are all opportunities to showcase your leadership abilities— to sell your product, your company, and yourself. The stakes are too high to leave presentation skills to chance. It is my sincere wish that this book will be a valuable tool for you in your quest to become a speaker worth listening to. Let's start our journey together.

PART ONE

EXPERTISE AND COMPETENCE

CHAPTER 1

THE CORNERSTONE OF CREDIBILITY: YOUR EXPERTISE

"Smooth ice is paradise for those who dance with expertise."
—**Friedrich Nietzsche**

"Does he know what he is talking about?"[1] This is the fundamental question that underlies **expertise**—the primary aspect of the credibility model for presenting. Expertise is your perceived qualifications, experience, and knowledge of your content. It is also your perceived **competence** at the front of the room.

Your audience will judge you on your knowledge of the *core* material—that part of the presentation that addresses their needs, the reason they came to listen to you. They are not there to evaluate how smart you are or how much knowledge you have accumulated on the topic. Avoid information overload.

We may spend days crafting the PowerPoint slides for a presentation, but slick slides don't increase credibility—knowledge does. Nothing erodes your credibility faster than signaling to the audience that you are dependent on your slides. To boost your credibility, you need to be able to deliver your content without having to use the slides as a teleprompter. This is only possible if you know your material very well.

This chapter provides six best practices for boosting your credibility through your expertise and competence.

ADOPT MEMORY-BOOSTING PRACTICES

We will start by looking at some of the best practices for maximizing your ability to remember your material so that you can internalize the sequence of ideas and be able to announce a slide before showing it, rather than have to wait until the slide appears to know what you must say next. These memory-boosting strategies, then, are intended to help you remember the key concepts that you want to talk about—not to memorize the script. The only two parts of your presentation that you should memorize word for word are your opening and closing comments and catchy phrases.

THE EIGHT-SECOND CONCENTRATION RULE

To form and retain information, the brain goes through the three processes described in Figure 2.

Acquisition »	Consolidation »	Retrieval
New information enters your brain along pathways between neurons in the appropriate area of the brain. The key to encoding information into your memory is concentration; unless you focus on information intently, it goes "in one ear and out the other."	If you've concentrated well enough to encode new information in your brain, the hippocampus sends a signal to store the information as long-term memory. This happens more easily if it's related to something you already know, or if it stimulates an emotional response.	When you need to recall information, your brain has to activate the same pattern of nerve cells it used to store it. The more frequently you need the information, the easier it is to retrieve along healthy nerve cell connections.

Figure 2
Source: *Ellen Jaffe-Gill, M.A.; Amara Rose; Gina Kemp, M.A.; and Suzanne Barston,* Helpguide, *Helpguide.org.*[2]

Memory experts tell us that it takes about eight seconds of focus to process a piece of information. To remember something, you need to encode it in your brain, and you cannot encode it if you don't concentrate for the eight seconds that it takes for the piece of information to be processed through the hippocampus and into memory.

Consider your habits when you are preparing for a presentation. If you are like most people, more than likely you are not fully concentrating on the task of getting the information from the PowerPoint notes into memory. In this digital age, in which everyone is in a multitasking pressure cooker, people often work on a presentation while checking email, reacting to each Blackberry ding, or answering the phone. The most crucial step in remembering your information is to *carve out dedicated, uninterrupted time for knowing your material.* Find a quiet place where you can receive the information, unencumbered by other tasks.

THE 20-20-20 RULE
Memory experts recommend going over the details of a presentation for 20 minutes, then repeating the same material twice more. If material is not repeated within 30 minutes, it does not enter long-term memory.[3]

MIND MAPPING
Mind maps are powerful graphics that allow you to lay out all of your presentation material in a visual shape rather than in list form. The visual shape or image is imprinted in your brain and might make it easier for you to recall the information than a linear list of

items would. Here is a succinct explanation of how to create an effective mind map for dramatically improving the amount of material that you will remember.

1. Write the topic of your presentation in the center of a plain sheet of paper.

2. Draw branches from the center topic just as you would when drawing a tree.

3. On each branch, write pertinent information about your central topic.

4. Keep creating branches for as many pieces of information that you come up with. This is your own brainstorming session; keep going until you have exhausted the ideas you want to speak about.

5. Go back to the map and add some color and images to make the information more graphic—which will make it easier to remember.

For example, let's say you are creating a presentation on the topic of blogging. Your linear list might look something like the one presented in Figure 3.

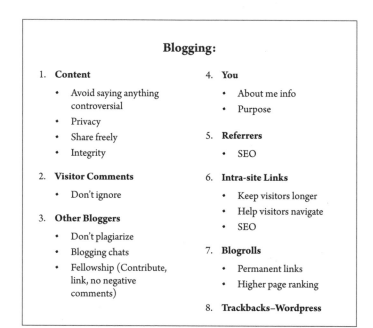

Figure 3

Now contrast this with a mind map of the same information, shown in Figure 4.

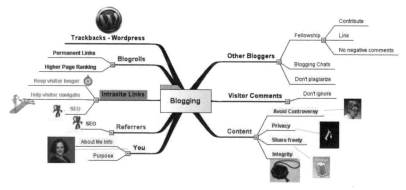

Figure 4

If you are visually inclined, you might find a mind map more helpful than a linear list in remembering your material. You can consider purchasing mind-mapping software. The program I used to create the sample map in Figure 4 is MatchWare: MindView. For a list of mind-mapping applications, see the Resources section of this book.

POWERPOINT NARRATION

A useful yet often overlooked tool is the PowerPoint function for recording narration. You can record yourself giving your speech and then play it back many times. This practice will help you re-member the material better, as you now have two memory aids: the visual and the auditory. If you are not familiar with this fea-ture, see the step-by-step video "How to Record a Narration for a PowerPoint Presentation for Dummies" at http://www.youtube.com/watch?v=QZp3jumnWUg.

SIMULATION

Along the same lines as recording your presentation in PowerPoint and listening to it, consider rehearsing your presentation by actu-ally going through the same movements you will use on the day of the presentation: stand up, move around, and talk out loud. Go through all the motions just as though you were in front of an audi-ence. Studies have shown that memory improves by 10 percent for things said out loud.[4]

These tactics enhance your ability to remember information by creating links in your brain through your kinesthetic and auditory memory. Actors who need to memorize their lines are instructed to rehearse them out loud, to hear the sound of their voice fill the space. This is sound advice for presenters, as well.

REHEARSAL BEFORE BEDTIME

Brain researchers have found that sleep enhances the consolidation of recently acquired information in the hippocampus-dependent memory system. In other words, if you review and rehearse material just before going to sleep, the mind will rearrange the information in a systematic way during your slumber and you will remember the material more easily.[5]

MUSIC

Music helps us retain information. If you listen to music while rehearsing your presentation, the memories you create are linked to the musical pathways created in the brain. A large body of research shows that the music of Mozart is the best for enhancing memory; there is even a well-known term for it, the "Mozart Effect." However, baroque music with sixty beats per minute is also very effective in helping us absorb and remember large amounts of information. This type of music activates the left and right brain; this simultaneous action of both hemispheres maximizes the retention of information.

According to The Center for New Discoveries in Learning, the potential for learning can be increased a minimum of five times by using this sixty-beat-per-minute music. Dr. Georgi Lozanov, the renowned Bulgarian psychologist, developed a methodology for teaching foreign languages that used baroque music with about sixty beats per minute. Students not only learned in a fraction of the normal time, but they had an average of 92 percent retention. The same applies to retaining your presentation material.[6]

THE PALACE METHOD

The palace method, also known as mind palace, is an ancient memory technique. It was revisited in Joshua Foer's book *Moonwalking with Einstein: The Art and Science of Remembering Everything*.[7] It is highly effective for remembering a long list of concepts. It involves three steps:

1. Assemble a sequential list of concepts that you want to cover in your presentation.

2. Visualize your house, office, or any other place that you know well.

3. Place each of your concepts in a different room (or in a different part of one room). The key is to visualize each concept in an unusual framework.

For example, say you are delivering a speech on the most important features of Google+, and you want to remember the following three points. (You can extend this technique to dozens of points.)

1. The Google+ community creates extensions to fix any problems.

2. It has a feature called Sparks, which identifies links from individuals or organizations that might be of interest to you.

3. When you mention someone, they will be notified.

For the first point, you might visualize, in the middle of your living room, Google's Chrome logo with a wrench embedded in it. For the second point, you might visualize, in the center of your dining room table, fireworks enclosed in a chain-link fence. For the third point, you might visualize a friend's face, circled in red, drawn on your kitchen window.

This works because neuroscientists have now discovered that there is a very deep connection between the way we remember an event and the space in which it occurred. The brain system that is important for memory is also important for space; in other words, we remember things on the basis of spatial locations or "spatial scaffolds." Josh Foer describes this method in the video "To Remember Better, Build a Mansion in Your Mind."[8]

The ability to remember your material without having to read your notes or use the slides as a teleprompter is a boost to your credibility as a presenter. Following are additional pointers.

SPEAK FROM THE HEART

Don't rely on your formal credentials. They may give you authority, but they don't necessarily earn you credibility. Go beyond the formulaic introduction of yourself, and convey to the audience your passion for your topic. Tell them specifically how you acquired expertise in your particular subject area. For example, let's say your presentation is about the use of multimedia on the Web. Instead of talking about your formal credentials, speak with energy and drive about your impressive track record in multimedia programming. Tell them how long you have been interested in the field, what fuels you about it. Mention your personal experience, for instance:

- "I have been a contributing member of the U.S. Multimedia Information Processing Group for the past ten years."

- "To prepare for the presentation I am making today, I spent the last six months researching what our closest competitors are doing in the rapidly changing and advancing field of multimedia development."

This is not bragging but confidently speaking about your knowledge base. You have done the hard work, so don't be reticent to let the audience know.

GUARD AGAINST FAULTY LOGIC

Columnist and author Burton Hillis said, "There's a mighty big difference between good, sound reasons and reasons that sound good." Back your points with solid and well-thought-out evidence. Guard against badly structured arguments and common fallacies, such as the following:

- Hasty conclusions
- Ambiguous assertions
- Generalizations
- Irrelevant material
- Inconsistencies
- Internal contradictions
- Outdated information
- Ignoring key issues
- Faulty analogical or causal reasoning
- Bandwagon arguments

No matter how much knowledge you have on your topic, if an audience member catches a fallacious argument, you instantly lose credibility. It pays to go the extra mile and think things through very carefully.

KEEP UP WITH THE TRENDS IN YOUR INDUSTRY

Not keeping up with changes and developments in your industry will create a small leak in your credibility as a speaker. "An investment in knowledge pays the best interest," Benjamin Franklin said long ago.

Find out where the conversations about your current field of expertise take place, and participate—whether you attend conferences, become a member of a professional association, subscribe to trade journals and blogs, or read recently released books in your field. Consider social networking with a purpose:

- Join industry-specific groups on LinkedIn.
- Join communities on Ning, where members share information in their field.
- "Like" Facebook pages specific to your academic or industry discipline.

Consider using additional online resources for staying on top of current events. Google Reader, for example, is a powerful, free tool that lets you subscribe to feeds from your favorite sites and blogs; any content from these sources automatically appears in your reader. There is a wealth of sites from which to choose, from the largest newspapers and magazines to specialized sites on topics ranging from technology to trading, product management to public relations. It's all there. It takes just minutes to set up Google Reader, and doing so will save you a lot of time in your quest to stay current. Take a look at the video tour for Google Reader, "Google Reader in Plain English."[9]

A secondary source to consider for general information is Refdesk.[10] This free source for articles and speeches indexes and reviews quality, credible, current Web-based resources on a wide variety of topics.

Google Alerts™ is another tool that you can use to stay up-to-date. This feature of Google allows you to monitor articles and news stories about your topic of choice, to keep current on a competitor, industry, or topic. Google sends you an e-mail when new content related to your search terms appears online.[11]

Ultimately, expertise is about continuing to learn. Author Seth Godin put it aptly: "If you're doing important work..., then you owe it to your audience or your customers or your co-workers to learn everything you can."[12] Staying ahead in your field is a strong credibility booster.

QUOTE THE GIANTS IN YOUR FIELD

Showing that you know and understand the thoughts and contributions of experts on your particular topic boosts your own credibility by association. This is one time that name-dropping is good. It pays to make the extra effort to cite some of the leading voices in your field to support and strengthen your assertions. By adding this type of validity to your argument, you in turn validate your own expertise.

LEARN HOW TO BE PERSUASIVE

Author and speaker Zig Ziglar said, "The most important persuasion tool in your entire arsenal is integrity." You can have a great product or a great idea, but if you don't have the expertise and competence to speak about it in a persuasive manner, your presentation will fall flat. Learning to be persuasive with integrity and responsibility earns us respect and credibility and increases our likelihood of success.

Persuasion and influence are often associated with making voluble claims, or being somewhat psychologically fraudulent—the actions of a flamboyant deceiver, someone who makes you believe something that is not true. While persuasion tactics can be used for this purpose, we need to accept that learning such tactics for a responsible use is not something to denigrate. Persuasion can be used for good or evil: we have Jim Jones using his influence to induce 900 people into a mass suicide while we also have Gandhi, who influenced the masses to adopt nonviolence in the struggle against oppression. In *The Art of Woo: Using Strategic Persuasion to Sell Your Ideas,* Richard Shell and Mario Moussa talk about persuasion as the ability to "win others over" to your ideas without coercion, using relationship-based, emotionally intelligent persuasion.[13]

Following are fifteen best practices to increase your expertise in making strong, persuasive presentations.

GIVE A REASON

Outline for your listeners all the valid reasons your ideas merit a nod. In *Yes! 50 Scientifically Proven Ways to Be Persuasive,* Robert Cialdini, the master of influence, tells us that the single word *because* drastically increases the likelihood that you will be successful in persuading your audience.[14] It appeals to your audience's need for rationality or logic. Appealing to logic is a powerful persuader. One of the most famous examples was Johnnie Cochran's line at O. J. Simpson's trial, "If it doesn't fit, you must acquit."

DON'T RELY ONLY ON FACTS

Remember that, notwithstanding our empiricist inclinations, we don't always make decisions based solely on evidence. While the facts are important, our intuitive judgment plays a role. For some people, intuition constitutes primary data.

So where does intuition come from? It derives from an individual's experience in a given field. Physicians use it to make decisions; even engineers are prone to use intuition as special insight.[15] So if you use facts alone to persuade someone, you may fail, as their own past experiences—often translated in hunches and gut feelings—will be a greater influence.

Ron Crossland and Boyd Clarke developed a powerful model for persuasive presentations.[16] It addresses the challenge of speaking only on the "factual channel," as they call it. Their model involves speaking on two other important channels:

- **Symbolic channel**, tapping into the power of storytelling and symbols.
- **Emotional channel**, stating your own emotions (how you feel about your topic) as well as addressing the emotions your presentation might elicit in the audience. To reach an audience, you need to be aware of their emotional reaction

to your message and let them know that you recognize these emotions; that you understand their world.

It's a fact that a presentation that doesn't evoke emotion will not generate commitment and action. What do you want your audience to *know, feel,* and *do* as a result of your presentation? Established communication theory encourages us to determine what the audience needs to feel at the start, middle, and end of a presentation. In order to generate these feelings, what do *you* need to feel? I asked Ron Crossland to comment on this, and here is his response:

A speaker must convey his or her interior emotional landscape in a deliberate manner or risk others inferring that landscape from other sources. As good as we are at detecting others' emotions, we can be wrong, and as a leader, for example, you need to declare your emotional state, not ask others to decipher it. There are positive consequences for understanding your personal feelings and conveying them in appropriate ways. First, your credibility will be higher because you've risked vulnerability. There is a direct relationship between disclosure and credibility. Secondly, making others try to guess your genuine feelings distracts that part of their mind and encourages it to fill in the gaps of this part of the message with guesses. Distraction is not your ally. Too many still believe that holding cards close to the chest, using power rather than vulnerability, and feigning confidence through polished mannerisms yield greater alignment and motivation than simply and honestly communicating their feelings.

My advice is to work through your emotional states as thoroughly as you do your strategic choices. With some sensitivity to decorum, a leader should then be prepared to declare his or her emotions in a manner that will gain greater attention to the message and create the possibility for greater alignment and movement against the message.

Neuroscientists have now uncovered the vital role that emotions play in our thinking process. They are a vital component of reason, and you cannot hope to persuade others without appealing to their emotions. On the positive side, speakers can appeal to

- A sense of pride
- Hope for the future
- Happiness
- Contentment
- Peace of mind
- Security
- Gain
- Success
- A sense of achievement
- Opportunities

On the negative side, we can appeal to

- Loss
- Fear of risk or failure
- Regret at missed opportunities
- Anger

Always craft your argument on a foundation of authenticity. Appeal to emotions if they indeed represent a real factor in what you are proposing. Appealing to emotions dishonestly, in order to manipulate others, is the showy behavior of a huckster. People want to be inspired and influenced, but they certainly don't want to be manipulated or compelled.

BECOME FAMILIAR WITH BIASES IN DECISION MAKING

Spend some time studying factors or prejudices that can shape how we view information and make decisions. Studies have shown that appealing to someone's aversion to loss, for example, is more powerful than appealing to their potential for gain. How you frame information can have an impact on whether or not you can persuade your audience. Become familiar with the different biases in decision making to help you frame your proposal effectively. Wikipedia offers a comprehensive list of cognitive biases to consider.[17]

BE THE FIRST TO BRING UP OBJECTIONS

Consider bringing up any potential objections to your proposal or ideas yourself, before anyone else does. This transforms the objection into a discussion point and makes it much easier to handle.[18] Answer each objection by showing why counterarguments are incorrect. Transition words and phrases such as "although," "despite," "nonetheless," "however," "but," and "on the other hand" add particular strength in this regard. These transitions signal that you have carefully reflected on all the angles and that you take a firm stand. This is a powerful strategy for convincing others of the worthiness of your ideas.

SIMPLIFY YOUR ARGUMENT

Spend time reducing your ideas to their simplest form. You are likely to have lived with your ideas for a while, so they are totally clear to you—but others will be hearing them for the first time. If your argument or idea is not clear, it will create confusion and hesitation in the audience—and persuading is much harder if you need to overcome confusion and doubt. Work diligently at removing any sediment from your thoughts so that your explanations are crystal clear. Test your ideas out on a smart layperson in your entourage. If that person gets it, you can scale it to an expert audience. If not, you need to go back to the drawing board.

In addition, keep explanations short. The more convoluted the explanation, the lower your chance of persuading people. Simplicity prevents the audience from being sidetracked by splinter issues.

AVOID SURPRISE REVELATIONS

This idea comes from *The McKinsey Mind*, where it is called "prewire everything."[19] It entails presenting your recommendations to key decision makers in your organization to request comments prior to the presentation. *The McKinsey Mind* advises, "Walk the relevant decision makers in your organization through your findings before you gather them together for a dog and pony show." You are more likely to convince your audience if you know their thoughts ahead of time and if there are no shocking revelations for them.

SECURE COMMITMENTS

Many a proposal has failed when a speaker believes that they have a go-ahead based on receiving acquiescence from one person.

"Research shows that in most organizations, a minimum of eight people will need to sign off on even simple ideas. The number goes up from there."[20] Secure both individual and organizational commitments. For example, if you are making a proposal in your organization and you have acquiescence from the marketing director to go ahead, you might find that your proposal will be derailed by other stakeholders in the finance department who have not been brought into the persuasion process. As a Wharton University professor says in *The Art of Woo: Using Strategic Persuasion to Sell Your Ideas*, "One of the most common mistakes people make in selling ideas is to think that their job is finished once they succeed in getting someone to say 'yes' to their proposal. That's only the beginning."[21]

SHOW FAIRNESS AND OBJECTIVITY
If you are presenting different possibilities, treat all options fairly, without undue bias for your favorite option unless it is clearly the best one. Don't make facts fit your desired solution. Don't omit facts to make one option look better than another. This is treading on a slippery slope and is a quick way to lose credibility.

USE CONCRETE LANGUAGE
Concrete language is more persuasive than vague language. Go over your presentation and, as much as possible, replace generalizations with specific language. As Emerson said long ago, "Put the argument into a concrete shape, into an image, some hard phrase, round and solid as a ball, which they can see and handle and carry home with them, and the cause is half won." For example, replace "heavy" with "weighs five tons"; instead of saying "bad weather," be precise and say "rain and sleet."

AVOID BEING VAGUE

Vagueness is a death knell for a persuasive presentation. Be precise in delivering your ideas or proposal. Many a presentation has been derailed by too many questions from the audience trying to clarify the meaning. It dilutes the energy from the decision making.

EMPHASIZE THE BENEFITS

Do a final audit of your presentation to find out how many statements you make about features as opposed to benefits. Balance in favor of benefits. Unless the audience members are engineers, benefits are of greater interest to them than features.

BE POSITIVE

Focus on maintaining a positive tone, even if the overall context of your presentation or proposal is negative. While you must acknowledge the negatives, do so by limiting the references to negativity and focusing on your solutions to the problems. A sense of hope, combined with a well-thought-out proposal, is more likely to instill confidence in your presentation.

TELL THE AUDIENCE WHAT YOU WANT THEM TO DO

Be explicit with your request or recommendation. This is the same as asking for the sale at the end of a sales presentation. One reason we may hesitate to ask explicitly for the audience's action is that we are afraid of rejection. This fear puts a dint in our credibility.

REPEAT, REPEAT, REPEAT

Don't expect your audience to remember what you want them to do. Introduce the main point in the beginning, explain it in the middle, and reinforce it in the end. And always conclude by summarizing the benefits of your idea. Studies show that people have the maximum trust in an idea after it has been repeated at least three times. People even consider assertions that have been repeated just once as more credible than things they've heard for the first time. (The research shows that individuals even rate statements as more credible when the person saying them has been repeatedly lying!) Familiarity, it seems, breeds liking.[22]

INSPIRE WITH A STORY OR METAPHOR

One of the most effective tools in your persuasion arsenal is telling a story. People can disagree with your facts, but they can't disagree with a personal story. Other powerful persuasion tools are metaphors, symbols, and analogies. Chapters 20 and 21 are devoted to these topics.

In the end, your expertise includes not only your qualifications and experience, but also your perceived competence. That's your apparent ability to perform successfully or efficiently. For example, no matter how much expertise you have on your topic, if on the day of the presentation you are seen to fumble with the technology (e.g., getting used to a new remote or struggling to adjust the sound of videos midstream), this will chip away at your credibility. When you are up front speaking, you are on exhibit. Take charge of what is within your control. In Chapters 10 and 17, I outline how to prevent some of these things from happening.

CHAPTER 2

BEFORE YOU HIT THE ROAD: WHAT DO YOU WANT TO ACCOMPLISH?

"I am rather like a mosquito in a nudist camp;
I know what I ought to do, but I don't know where to begin."
—Stephen Bayne

An insidious problem with presentations, especially those delivered by technical people and knowledge experts, is the tendency to think that one needs to impart everything one knows on the topic. Imagine the person who tunes into a TV channel to check the weather. The forecast calls for windy conditions. The viewer expects to hear that it is windy and does not want to hear how and why air flows around the globe.

Dumping data on the audience most often happens for two reasons, as Ron Ashkenas suggests in the *Harvard Business Review* article, "In Presentations, Learn to Say Less."[1] The first reason is that we often deal with problems that have no right answer, which propels us to collect a lot of data. Eventually, when the deadline arrives for delivering the presentation "and we still don't have a clear answer, we end up presenting stories, facts, figures, and other interesting tidbits hoping that someone else will be able to make sense out of this ambiguity." The second reason is a lack of self-confidence: even if we are able to analyze the information we have collected and arrive at a conclusion, many managers, for example, often "lack the self-confidence to state it and stand behind it." Individuals often worry what will happen if a senior person disagrees with their message or if the message upsets someone on the team. "With these doubts in mind," states Ashkenas, "many of us hedge our bets, avoid uncomfortable discussions, and surround the message with so much fluff that the real conclusion is barely visible."

Dumping data on your audience is a sure way to create a disorganized presentation, one that will detract from your perceived competence. Being well organized and stating your points concisely are some of the easiest ways to boost your credibility as a speaker. Following are some pointers.

HAVE A CLEAR OBJECTIVE

It has been said that "knowing your destination is half the journey." Before you write one word, determine your objective. You can do this by answering the following simple question: "If my presentation is successful, my listeners will know, feel, and do what?"[2] Specifically, ask yourself the following:

- **Know.** What's the one key issue, concept, or piece of information that I want people to know, understand, learn, or question?

- **Feel.** How do I want my audience to feel at the conclusion of my presentation?

- **Do.** What action do I want people to take as a result of what I present to them?

Statistics show that when people research and analyze data, most spend 80 percent of the time researching and only 20 percent of the time analyzing. In preparing presentations, we spend the majority of our time gathering information and a lot less time stopping to carefully consider each item. After thoughtful reflection, include only those items that will help you meet the objective of your presentation.

Think of yourself as a gemologist, examining each piece of information to assess its value. Look at each item of data that you add to your presentation. Is it just glass? If so, discard it and resolve to keep only the diamonds; that is, what people need to hear. Your presentation will shine. And so will you. As motivational speaker Jim Rohn put it, "What is powerful is when what you say is just the tip of the iceberg of what you know."

If there is background information that falls in the category of "nice to have," distribute it in a handout. Focus only on what will help you achieve one, or all three, of the "know, feel, and do" objectives.

HAVE A CLEAR ROAD MAP FOR YOUR TALK

A presentation without a clear structure becomes like a messy ball of yarn: it forces your audience to untangle your main points. It requires too much effort to get to the core of what you are saying.

Consider that your presentation is the concrete embodiment of your thinking. If your presentation is not well organized and does not follow a logical structure, it will cast doubt on the clarity of your thought process. A lack of clear organization weakens your credibility, no matter how much knowledge you have.

Before creating even a single slide, carve out time to plan your presentation. The Resources section of this book includes a template for planning your presentation.

Following are some pointers to organize your material.

FOLLOW THE RULE OF THREE

The famous rule of three suggests that the optimal number of points to include in a presentation is three, because your listeners are likely to remember only three things. Multitudes of articles have been written on this topic, citing examples from diverse areas:

- Religion: Father, Son, and Holy Spirit
- History: "Life, Liberty and the pursuit of Happiness" (the Declaration of Independence)
- Literature: "Friends, Roman, countrymen" (Shakespeare's *Julius Caesar*)
- Philosophy: Logical, pathetic, and ethical (Aristotle's three types of speech for appealing to audiences)
- Psychology: Freud's id, ego, and super-ego

The literature on the power of the number three is abundant.

In a lecture at Google, Dr. Daniel J. Siegel, M.D., talks about the dorsal lateral prefrontal cortex, which is responsible for keeping information in what he calls "the chalkboard of our mind."[3] The old research said that we can hold seven items, plus or minus, in our working memory; but brain science has now proven that, in daily life, we can hold three items.

If the rule of three is indeed so powerful, then it's nowhere more important than when you present using PowerPoint slides. Why is that? Because there is a limit to how much we can absorb when we visually scan information. An example of this was shown in eye-tracking studies, comparing interactions on Yahoo!®, Google, and Microsoft Search. The study determined that we scan three to four listings at a time; these are temporarily loaded in our memory slots. From that first group of three to four listings, we make a determination if any of them are relevant to the query we have just launched.[4]

Think, as well, about how the rule of three shows up in marketing. In an interesting study at the University of Minnesota, it was found that providing consumers with a third, less attractive option (called the decoy marketing option) simplifies and speeds up the decision-making process.[5] Our brain seems to favor threes.

So, in order to make it easier for your audience to remember the points on a slide before you move on to the next slide, consider keeping your bullets per slide to a *maximum* of three. This single rule will improve the clarity of your information.

Let's look at some examples from powerful speakers. In his annual speech to shareholders in 1981, Jack Welch, then CEO of General Electric, organized his content using the rule of three:

*I have three subjects to cover in this ten-minute report. **First,** I want to give you a brief perspective on your company at the beginning of a new administration... **Second,** I want to discuss the rationale behind the company's recent major moves in* *electronics... And **third**, I want to talk about one of my basic objectives for this company over the decade ahead.*

Even if your presentation is in the form of storytelling, you can use the rule of three. Here is a brilliant example, from Steve Jobs's commencement address at Stanford University in 2005:

*Today I want to tell you three stories from my life. That's it. No big deal. Just three stories... The **first story** is about connecting the dots... My **second story** is about love and loss... My **third story** is about death.*

Here is a simple, powerful template that consultants often use:

1. **Why** there is a problem
2. **What** the client must do about it
3. **How** you are uniquely positioned to solve the problem

If you must have more than three main points in your presentation, organize all the points in three global buckets and include sub-points. Here is an example of how this works. The Six Seconds Emotional Intelligence Model is organized as three major components with eight sub-components. The rule of three, applied here, takes a body of complex information and distills it into three major pursuits that are easy to remember.

1. Know Yourself
   • Enhance emotional literacy
   • Recognize patterns

2. Choose Yourself

- Apply consequential thinking
- Navigate emotions
- Engage intrinsic motivation
- Exercise optimism

3. Give Yourself

- Increase empathy
- Pursue noble goals

Not all great presentations adhere to the rule of three, but they have a clear, easy-to-follow structure. For example, Guy Kawasaki, author of *Enchantment: The Art of Changing Hearts, Minds, and Actions*, uses a top-ten format to structure his talks.[6] To make this approach effective, clearly announce your structure at the start of your talk to guide the audience.

CHOOSE AN ANTICLIMAX ORDER FOR YOUR MAIN POINTS

In structuring a presentation, anticlimax order (working from the most important point to the least important point) is generally preferred over climax order (going from the least important point to the most important point).

Once you have clarified your objective and structured your presentation, you need to decide how you will communicate information in a way that will reach your audience.

ANSWER TWO CRUCIAL QUESTIONS
ABOUT YOUR AUDIENCE

To get some objectivity, imagine for a moment that you are part of the audience. Visualize yourself sitting amongst them and ask yourself these two fundamental questions:

- Is this information relevant to them/me?
- How does this information help them/me?

It is safe to say that people are generally alike in their reactions. So if you have a hunch that your information is tedious and humdrum, you can be sure that your audience will perceive it the same way. If you think something is novel and practical, more than likely it will land that way with the majority of your audience. Go the extra mile to make information more appealing and more interesting to you, and it follows that it will appeal to most of your audience.

Any effort you make to organize your thoughts by using the ideas in this chapter will pay dividends in raising the clarity index of your presentation. This material gives you a set of coordinates that will help you on the road toward an organized, structured presentation.

CHAPTER 3

GRAB THEIR ATTENTION: GETTING THEM INTERESTED INSTANTLY

"The beginning is the most important part of the work."
—Plato

It takes an editor only a few pages to decide if he or she will like a book enough to consider publishing it. The reader, in turn, decides within the first paragraph or two whether or not to buy the book. As a speaker, you have even less time to convince the audience to like you or your presentation. *Beginnings are too crucial to your presentation's success to be left to chance.* You should not aim for a good opening—you should aim for a *superb* opening. The beginning of a presentation is a powerful moment for engaging the audience and establishing your credibility.

Following the five-step formula presented in this chapter will help you deliver a successful opening every time—it's the mental equivalent of GPS for your audience. It will create a good first impression and leave the audience with the feeling that they are in good hands, that they are listening to a professional who will not waste their time. As a special dividend, following this five-step template will reduce your presentation anxiety and enhance your self-confidence, as it gives you a clearly laid out path to follow.

The five-step opening is like a straight line to your destination, instead of a curved line that wastes time and fails to immediately grasp the audience's attention. Although individual attention spans can vary significantly, depending on age, education, interest in the topic, and other variables, we know that the attention of an audience is at its highest at the beginning of a presentation. For some, it can take as little as 30 seconds to 2 minutes before their attention starts to wane and their minds wander. Consider that many, if not most, members of your audience will fall into this category.

Our minds are flooded with novel experiences and bits of knowledge on a daily basis. We are information junkies—getting quick fixes from browsing the Internet, participating in social media sites, tweeting, viewing YouTube videos, and test-driving new software applications, to name a few activities. Imagine that when people sit down to listen to you, you are competing with the fast pace and stimulating nature of these digital communications.

People have become used to processing large amounts of complex information in seconds. You must adapt your presentation to this fact—or perish. Add value right away, as soon as you speak, and you will be valued as a credible presenter. Waste time in a long, trite preamble, and the audience will quickly decide that they are in for another tedious presentation that they have to endure. First impressions are crucial; even if the rest of your presentation improves, it will be tainted by the original negative impression.

Think of yourself as a racehorse, a fine thoroughbred, rather than a tired old workhorse. Racehorses are schooled to start running as soon as the gate springs open and to maintain a steady pace. How can you do this as a presenter? Figure 5 shows a formula to help you.

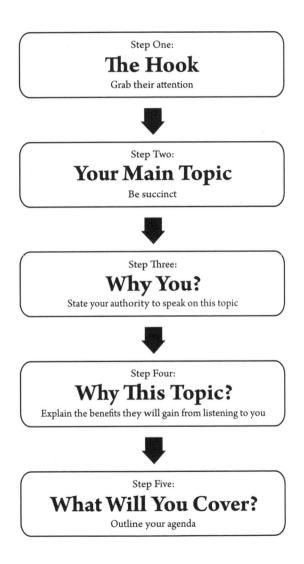

Figure 5

STEP ONE: THE HOOK

Some audience members are somewhat distracted in the first few minutes of a presentation, before they mentally prepare to settle down, quiet their minds, and listen attentively. The hook grabs everyone's attention right away.

One of the "brain rules" in John Medina's *Brain Rules: 12 Principles for Surviving and Thriving at Work, Home, and School* is, "We don't pay attention to boring things."[1] Brain research shows that novelty and emotional stimulus are the two biggest attention getters. For a presenter, this means that you will be more successful if you start your presentation with an unusual item or something that will elicit an emotional reaction from the listeners.

If your audience is older, you will grab their attention if your beginning taps into what they find relevant and useful. If your audience is predominantly young, you will grab their attention if your beginning has an entertainment factor. Whatever you do, don't waste those precious few minutes of maximum audience attention with standard platitudes ("I am very pleased to have the opportunity to...", "Thank you for having me...") or excuses ("I was only told yesterday that I was to make this presentation, so I am only going to provide what I was able to...", "I have just come back from vacation today, so bear with me while I get organized here..."). These are credibility destroyers!

Following are eighteen best practices for starting your presentation with a hook.

START WITH A QUESTION

Starting with a question not only grabs the audience's attention, it sets a trend: you condition the listeners for interactivity throughout your presentation. Getting them to respond to a question right at the start has the effect of moving them away from being passive spectators and toward being active participants.

Following are some pointers for starting with a question.

Avoid Trite or Obvious Questions

Trite or obvious questions insult the audience's intelligence and will fall flat. For example, don't ask, "How many of you would be unhappy to hear that your house is worth less than you paid for it?" A better question would be, "With a show of hands, how many of you thought that your home would be your safest investment?"

Start with Several Linked Questions

Use a variety of connected questions that relate to your topic. For example, you might open with the following sequence of questions:

1. How many pixels are needed to match the resolution of the human eye?
2. How many pixels can you see at once?
3. So what's your optimal display size?

Start with an Emotional Question

Steven K. Scott, author of the book *Mentored by a Millionaire: Master Strategies of Super Achievers*, started a presentation by asking the audience, "How many of you have been hurtfully criticized at least once this past week?"[2] Language charged with emotion is an attention magnet.

Start with a Rhetorical Question

A rhetorical question involves the audience and creates immediate interest. Success expert Richard St. John started his TEDTalk "Success Is a Continuous Journey" with the following rhetorical question: "Why do so many people reach success and then fail?" Then he answered it immediately by saying, "One of the big reasons is we think success is a one-way street."[3]

A rhetorical question is the easiest way to grab the audience's attention at the beginning of your presentation. It can also embed an implied answer that is meant to provoke a thought. American stand-up comedian and satirist George Carlin was a master at this type of rhetorical question:

- "How did a fool and his money get together?"
- "Why is it that doctors call what they do 'practice'"?
- "Why is the man who invests your money called a broker?"

Start with a Provocative Question

For example, if a representative from Goodyear was delivering a presentation on the importance of tires in auto safety, they might start with a rhetorical question that provokes a thought: "How much is your child's safety worth to you?" You can use this technique for any presentation.

START WITH A CONTRADICTORY STATEMENT

This hook is most effective when we cite a universally accepted concept and then contradict it. For example, market trader Oliver Velez talks about the commonly held advice that one should buy low and sell high. "It's terribly wrong," he states. "Why? Because buying low typically entails purchasing a stock that is going in the opposite direction (down) from the most desired direction (up)."[4]

My grandfather used an old expression that falls into the category of contradictory statements: "I am not rich enough to buy cheap" (on quality versus price). Other examples include "Speed will slow you down" (on the hazards of frenetic multitasking) and "Uncertainty is your friend" (on learning to be adaptable to change).

START WITH A STARTLING ASSERTION

Seth Godin started a presentation with this startling fact: "In India, the way the government measures the severity of the drought is by measuring how many farmers commit suicide."[5]

Imagine talking about identity theft. You might start by saying that identity theft is a fast-growing crime—or you could energize your opening with a startling statistic: "Every 79 seconds, an identity-theft crime is committed."[6] It is worthwhile to spend time finding a startling statement that is pertinent to your topic.

A startling fact on its own is a good attention grabber; however, a series of related startling facts has an even more powerful impact. It has a slight shock effect and creates a sense of urgency by painting the big picture for your audience. Let's say that you are giving a speech on health and eating disorders. You might begin by outlining a series of startling facts.[7] Say to the audience, "Did you know that ... ?," followed by these statements:

- One out of four college-aged women has an eating disorder.
- In one national survey in the United States, women feared being fat more than dying.
- Americans spend more than 40 billion dollars a year on dieting and diet-related products. That's roughly equivalent to the amount the U.S. government spends on education each year.
- Forty-six percent of nine- to eleven-year-olds are sometimes or very often on diets.

START WITH A QUOTATION

Study how political figures and high-profile executives pepper their speeches with quotes that catch our attention. Quotations are memorable, and they are accepted at face value. No one contradicts a quotation, especially one by a famous person. To use quotations to great effect, however, make sure that they are fresh. Don't use a quotation such as, "A journey of a thousand miles starts with a single step." It has been heard a thousand times before.

A manager in a sales presentation started his talk by using professional speaker Orvel Ray Wilson's quote, "Customers buy for their reasons, not yours." So much was said with just these seven words.

Well-chosen quotes are like an index of the mind. They give people an indication that you are witty or well read—or at least that you have made an effort to be interesting to listen to. The right quotation can sum up your main point and make it stand out.

Following are three types of quotations, with examples, to consider for your presentations.

Humorous

- "Man invented language to satisfy his deep need to complain." (Lily Tomlin)
- "The shortest distance between two points is under construction." (Noelie Altito)
- "The secret to creativity is knowing how to hide your sources." (Einstein)

Business

- "In the business world, the rearview mirror is always clearer than the windshield." (Warren Buffett)
- "When your work speaks for itself, don't interrupt." (Henry J. Kaiser)
- "If change is happening on the outside faster than on the inside, the end is in sight." (Jack Welch)
- "Your most unhappy customers are your greatest source of learning." (Bill Gates)

Sports

- "Winning is everything. The only ones who remember you when you come second are your wife and your dog." (Damon Hill, British Grand Prix racing driver)

- "Whoever said, 'It's not whether you win or lose that counts,' probably lost."(Martina Navratilova, Czech-American tennis player)

- "Champions keep playing until they get it right." (Billie Jean King, American tennis player)

- "Champions aren't made in the gyms. Champions are made from something they have deep inside them—a desire, a dream, a vision." (Muhammad Ali, American boxer)

START WITH A REFERENCE TO A HISTORICAL EVENT

In a TEDTalk, Dave Logan asked the audience if they remembered what happened on February 3, 2008.[8] He then proceeded to discuss why that date was of momentous importance and how it tied in to his topic.

To get ideas for interesting historical events that you can reference in your presentations, visit the extensive "Today in History" calendar at WorldofQuotes.com.[9]

START WITH A FOREIGN PROVERB

A way to add interest to the start of your talk is to use a proverb from another culture. These are sure to surprise your audience with their novelty. Here are some examples:

- "Don't look where you fell. Look where you slipped." (African)
- "You'll never plow a field by turning it over in your mind." (Irish)
- "Act quickly, think slowly." (Greek)
- "Our last garment is made without pockets." (Italian)[10]

START WITH A PERSONAL STORY OR ANECDOTE

One of the most powerful ways to start a presentation is with a brief personal story or amusing anecdote that immediately engages your listeners' attention. Check out this example from Google co-founder Larry Page's commencement speech at the University of Michigan in 2009:

A long time ago, in the cold September of 1962, there was a Stevens co-op at this very university. That co-op had a kitchen with a ceiling that had been cleaned by student volunteers probably every decade or so. Picture a college girl named Gloria, climbing up high on a ladder, struggling to clean that filthy ceiling. Standing on the floor, a young boarder named Carl was admiring the view. And that's how they met. They were my parents, so I suppose you could say I'm a direct result of that kitchen chemistry experiment, right here at Michigan. My mom is here with us today, and we should probably go find that spot and put up a plaque on the ceiling that says, "Thanks, Mom and Dad!"[11]

START WITH THE WORD IMAGINE

The word *imagine* is an action verb that attracts attention. From John Lennon's song "Imagine" to Nintendo's "Imagine" video game series to the *Re-imagine!* volume of management guru Tom Peters, the word carries special appeal. It asks the audience to form a mental image of something—to envision or create something in their minds. It's an invitation, for a moment, to use their imagination, to conjecture, to play. It is especially effective when you add a pause, right after you say the word, as in "Imagine..."

Bryan Dyson, CEO of Coca-Cola, gives us a great example of a speech (for the commencement at Georgia Tech in 1996) that starts with "Imagine":

> *Imagine life as a game in which you are juggling some five balls in the air. You name them—work, family, health, friends, and spirit... and you're keeping all of these in the air.*
>
> *You will soon understand that work is a rubber ball. If you drop it, it will bounce back. But the other four balls—family, health, friends, and spirit—are made of glass. If you drop one of these, they will be irrevocably scuffed, marked, nicked, damaged, or even shattered. They will never be the same. You must understand that and strive for balance in your life.*
>
> *How?*
>
> *Don't undermine your worth by comparing yourself with others. It is because we are different that each of us is special.*[12]

START WITH A REFERENCE TO CURRENT EVENTS

An easy way to grab attention is to bring the day's newspaper and refer to a story related to your topic. As a bonus, using a visual rivets the audience's attention to the news item. You can briefly read a part of the item, or just the headline, or you can simply point to the paper in your hand while talking.

You can use an article to agree with your position or to establish a contrarian opinion. Let's say you are making a presentation on Internet security. You might start your talk by pointing to an article on the topic and agreeing with it: "There is no doubt that cyberspace security is an emerging battlefield." Or you might disagree: "Am I the only person who thinks that the cyber threat is overblown?"

Here is another example. Let's say your presentation is about stimulating creativity. You might start your speech by saying, "In the current issue of *Fast Company*, which I am holding in my hand, there is a feature article called 'The 100 Most Creative People.' What can we learn from these dazzling new thinkers, these rising stars?"

START BY SHOWING A PICTURE

In a speech on breaking a speed record for a trek to the South Pole, Ray Zahab showed a visual of a sign in the snow indicating the geographic South Pole. Pointing to the sign, he said, "A month ago today, I stood there: 90 degrees south of the top of the bottom of the world, the geographic South Pole."[13]

In a TED presentation, inventor John La Grou started by showing an image of a smoke alarm:

This is a world-changing invention: the smoke alarm. It has saved perhaps hundreds of thousands of lives worldwide. But smoke alarms don't prevent fires. Every year in the U.S.A., over 20,000 are killed or injured with 350,000 home fires, and one of the main causes of all these fires is electricity. What if we could prevent electrical fires before they start? Well, a couple of friends and I have figured out how to do this.[14]

This is a brilliant start, which makes use of three hook strategies: an image, a startling statistic, and a question.

You could also distribute a picture relevant to your topic and ask the audience what they see in the picture. Then tie their responses to your topic. If handing a picture to everyone is not logistically feasible, you can simply show the picture on a slide on the screen. A speaker I know shows a poster of a diverse group of people, with varying functions, dress, ages, and pursuits, in what seems like a chaotic potpourri of humanity. He asks the audience how this image might metaphorically describe what is going on in their organizations. He then ties this thought to his central topic: "Only three things happen naturally in organizations: friction, confusion, and underperformance. Everything else requires leadership."[15]

START WITH SOMETHING PERSONAL AND DIFFERENT
Here are two ideas from professional speaker and speech coach Patricia Fripp:

- "As a young man, my father gave me this valuable advice..."
- "Of all the questions I am most frequently asked..."[16]

START WITH A FAMOUS MOVIE LINE

Use a movie quote to introduce yourself or your topic.[17] Here are some examples of lines that will resonate with the audience:

- "First rule of leadership: everything is your fault." (*A Bug's Life*)
- "Houston, we have a problem." (*Apollo 13*)
- "Show me the money!" (*Jerry Maguire*)

START WITH A REFERENCE TO AN IMPORTANT PAST EVENT

Referring to a past event is a good way to bridge lessons or examples from the past with current issues. Here is an example from Lord Browne's speech at Stanford University in 2007: "I stood here 10 years ago, almost to the day, and first talked about the risk of climate change and global warming."[18] And another example: "Five years ago this month, we launched our first product amidst a great deal of uncertainty."

START BY ASKING THE AUDIENCE
TO REMEMBER SOMETHING

Asking the audience to reminisce about something in the past is another way to attract and retain their attention. Make sure that the prompt engages the audience's intellect. For example, "Do you remember when Pentium 75 was state-of-the-art?" Or appeal to their emotions:

Can you remember a time when you accomplished something that you were very proud of? Do you remember how great this felt? How excited you were? The sense of accomplishment you had? Now imagine that you have an opportunity to repeat this feeling by becoming involved in XYZ project.

START WITH SOMETHING UNUSUAL OR A GIMMICK

People enjoy a gimmick, if it is clever and pertinent to the topic. A speaker at a motivational presentation for emerging consultants handed out a gift-wrapped box and asked one of the participants to open it on behalf of the entire group. When she unwrapped the box, we saw that it contained a can. The facilitator used the object as a bridge to his speech motif, "You can..." And the can, at the center of the table, became a visual representation of his message throughout the speech.

In a presentation, Seth Godin grabbed the audience's attention right away with a balloon and a candle. Take a look at the video online to see how he pulls it off.[19]

START WITH A VIDEO

There is a wealth of video clips that you can now download from YouTube and other sources. Make sure the video clip you use is no longer than two or three minutes. To use a video effectively at the crucial beginning of a presentation, embed it in your PowerPoint file, test the sound in advance, and enlarge the clip to fill the screen so that it all works flawlessly when you click the remote.

START WITH A SONG

Songs are encoded in our memory and often elicit an emotional response. Quoting or playing a piece of a song that is pertinent to your topic is, therefore, a powerful way to start. Here are some popular song lyrics with messages:

- "Doesn't anybody stay in one place anymore?" (Carole King)
- "Every single day, every word you say, every game you play, every night you stay, I'll be watching you." (The Police)
- "You got to know when to hold 'em, know when to fold 'em, know when to walk away, and know when to run." (Kenny Rogers)
- "I'd rather be a hammer than a nail." (Simon and Garfunkel)

START WITH A CARTOON

Cartoons are an effective form of visual humor. They are guaranteed to attract attention. The Resources section of this book contains a list of sources for cartoons that you can purchase.

These eighteen techniques are guaranteed to start your presentation with energy and a promise that what is to follow is likely to be interesting. It's your killer headline, your powerful opening paragraph.

STEP TWO: YOUR MAIN TOPIC

Immediately after you deliver your hook, state your main topic. You might say, "I have been asked to give you a briefing on ..." or "Today I will focus on..."

You should be able to articulate your topic in three or four sentences. If you can't distill it into a few sentences, it means that you don't have the necessary clarity about your topic. If you ramble on at this point, you risk confusing the audience and sabotaging your credibility. Be succinct. Practice tightening your statement.

This concept is similar to that of an elevator pitch, a short statement that quickly and simply defines what you are talking about. A tool to help you create such a statement when you want to succinctly present your vision, goal, or business is Harvard Business School's "Elevator Pitch Builder."[20] This ingenious, interactive tool gives you one minute to explain your goals, your business, or your passion through a series of five questions (such as what you would most want your listeners to remember about you and why you are unique). The system creates the statement and then helps you analyze and edit it. You can use a similar process to create an opening thesis statement for your topic.

STEP THREE: WHY YOU?

The third step conveys your authority to speak on the topic and is a key step for establishing your credibility.

This is the time to introduce yourself to the audience, to provide a brief description of your company, and to establish your credentials as an expert on your presentation topic. Your title gives you the authority to speak, but it doesn't automatically give you respect as an expert. For this, you need to explicitly draw the audience's attention to your right to speak on the particular topic. (If you are talking to an internal audience, you don't need to introduce yourself and your company; however, you still would benefit from reinforcing your expertise on the topic by stating some salient facts about your preparation for the presentation.)

Examples of credentials to boost your credibility include the following. Be brief in describing your credentials.

- Your work and accomplishments
- Research you have conducted or are in the process of conducting
- Articles you have written
- Months or years you have spent analyzing case studies
- Having just attended a conference on your topic and hearing experts speak
- Having canvassed a particular number of competitors, vendors, clients, or other entities pertinent to your topic
- High-profile clients you have helped
- Having hired an advisor or expert on your topic
- A personal experience. For example, if you are advocating for the benefits of exercise to avoid heart disease: "Ten years ago, my husband had a heart attack. This event changed the way we live our lives. The doctors had warned him for several years that his stressful lifestyle, unhealthy eating, and lack of exercise were going to take their toll. Embarking on an exercise program has saved his life."

STEP FOUR: WHY THIS TOPIC?

In the fourth step of your opening, provide a brief description of why your presentation is important: what benefits the audience will derive from listening to you. Clearly articulating a few of the tangible takeaways for the audience is a sure way to peak their interest and ensure that they will be fully engaged in listening. Don't rely on the assumption that the audience knows the benefits of listening to your presentation. Connect the dots for them. Here are a few examples of how to do this:

- "By the end of my presentation, you will have everything you need in order to make a decision on XYZ project."
- "This presentation will give you a complete understanding of the challenges that led to this problem and a three-part strategy for solving the situation before the end of Q2."
- "You will walk away with ten practical tools and tips on XYZ."

STEP FIVE: WHAT WILL YOU COVER?

The fifth and final step of your introduction is your agenda: the road map for your presentation. It tells the audience what to expect. Like any good meeting, all presentations need to have an agenda. There are three points that I want to cover regarding agendas.

USE ONLY KEY WORDS IN YOUR AGENDA

List only a few words for each item on the agenda, so that you can add value rather than recite what is on the slide word for word. For example, instead of "Update on Upfront and Maintenance Costs," your agenda item on the slide should simply be "Costs." You then add value to the slide when you elaborate that you will be providing an update on upfront and maintenance costs.

CREATE HYPERLINKED AGENDA ENTRIES

Prepare an agenda slide on which each line item in the agenda is hyperlinked to a group of related slides in your presentation. Each group of slides is called a "custom show." When you click on an item on the agenda slide, it displays the related set of slides and then automatically takes you back to the agenda. This structure helps you and your audience stay on track and is particularly useful for long presentations. Refer to the video "How to Create an Agenda Slide to Organize a PowerPoint Presentation" for technical guidance.[21]

DESIGN A VISUALLY ATTRACTIVE AGENDA

A visually attractive agenda is a detail that creates a great first impression on the audience. For agenda examples, see the following:

- "Before and After: A New Spin on the Old Agenda Slide," *Presentation Advisors*, http://www.presentationadvisors. com/powerpoint-before-and-after-a-new-spin-on-the-old-agenda-slide
- "How to Do an Agenda Slide," *Speaking About Presenting*, http://www.speakingaboutpresenting.com/design/ garr-reynolds-agenda-slide/
- "PowerPoint Agenda," *SlideShop*, http://slideshop.com/ PowerPoint-Agenda-Green

Starting your presentation by following the five-step template will help you make a positive first impression. The audience gets an interesting, competent, organized presenter—one who signals to them that they are in good hands and that their time will not be wasted.

CHAPTER 4

LEAVE THEM WANTING MORE: ENDING MEMORABLY

"Finally, in conclusion, let me just say this."
—**Peter Sellers**

Often, a great presentation is tarnished when the speaker ends abruptly or in a low-energy manner. A weak ending can lessen the strength of even a powerful presentation, just as a weak spot compromises the stability of a pillar. This blunder is always the result of not planning how you will conclude. A presentation just comes to a sudden halt—or worse, the speaker rambles on before stopping suddenly, as if out of breath or relieved that the whole ordeal is over. No matter how good your presentation was, this type of conclusion makes you appear less competent and erodes what scholars call "terminal" credibility.

A cognitive bias known as the "recency effect" comes into play. It means that audiences have a tendency to remember what came at the end of a presentation more vividly than what happened in the middle. Take advantage of this effect by leaving them with a positive memory of your talk. If you find yourself running out of time, don't eliminate your prepared, powerful conclusion. Instead, shorten your talk midstream. Avoid sacrificing the conclusion.

MEMORABLE ENDINGS

Following are four best practices for crafting a powerful ending to your presentation.

SIGNAL THE END

Seasoned presenters never end their presentations suddenly. They always signal the end. Here are sample signals:

- "I have one more point to cover and then we will wrap up."
- "I will outline XYZ and then I will open it up for discussion."
- "We have one more item on the agenda and then I will take your questions."

SUMMARIZE

A mistake some presenters make is to provide a tediously elaborate summary that consumes too much time. The aim here is not to summarize the entire presentation but only the key message and supporting points. Consider creating three visually powerful slides for your three key points.

EMPHASIZE THE WHY

If the purpose of your presentation is to influence the audience to do something, then you need to remind them of the actions you want them to take: not only *what* they need to do next but *why* they need to do it. This means reminding them of the benefits of your recommendation or request.

We often omit the call to action because we are afraid of rejection. We don't want to risk hearing a "no" answer. Wayne Gretzky said,

"You miss 100 percent of the shots you don't take." Including this crucial step powers your presentation and solidifies for the audience that you are strongly convinced of the merits of your ideas.

Your call to action will depend on the objective of your presentation. As Rhonda Abrams states in *Winning Presentation in a Day: Get It Done Right, Get It Done Fast*, your call to action can be one of the following:

- **Something you want your listeners to do:** "I urge you to donate to the ASPCA immediately."
- **Something you want your listeners to feel:** "We have what it takes to make this our best sales month ever."
- **Something you want your listeners to think:** "This policy will dramatically improve our profit margins."
- **Something you want your listeners to remember:** "Our company is the leader in wireless technology."[1]

END MEMORABLY

Most importantly, end with a memorable statement. Such a statement is akin to a tagline: it is something powerful that will be remembered. The memorable statement in your conclusion is equivalent to the hook at the beginning of your presentation.

Here are two good examples of memorable statements:

- "So here's the mantra I like to live by: 'Win like you're used to it. Lose like you enjoy it.'"[2] (Innovation expert Jeremy Gutsche, in his presentation "Culture Eats Strategy for Breakfast")

- "Stay Hungry. Stay Foolish." (Steve Jobs, Stanford commencement address in 2005)

The memorable statement can take many forms that are limited only by your creativity. Let's explore some of these.

Book-end Closure

You can start with a quote and end with the same quote. Or you can start with a story, and end by recapturing the thread of the same story. Here is an example from Holocaust survivor and Nobel Laureate Elie Wiesel in his speech "The Perils of Indifference":

Start: *Fifty-four years ago to the day, a young Jewish boy from a small town in the Carpathian Mountains woke up, not far from Goethe's beloved Weimar, in a place of eternal infamy called Buchenwald. He was finally free, but there was no joy in his heart. He thought there never would be again.*

Liberated a day earlier by American soldiers, he remembers their rage at what they saw. And even if he lives to be a very old man, he will always be grateful to them for that rage, and also for their compassion. Though he did not understand their language, their eyes told him what he needed to know— that they, too, would remember, and bear witness.

End: *And so, once again, I think of the young Jewish boy from the Carpathian Mountains. He has accompanied the old man I have become throughout these years of quest and struggle. And together we walk towards the new millennium, carried by profound fear and extraordinary hope.*[3]

Line from a Movie

Seth Godin ended his speech "Standing Out" by referring to a famous line from the movie *Field of Dreams*: "I don't know about you. But if they build it, that's where I am going to go."[4]

Line from a Poem

Here is an example from Elizabeth Lesser, co-founder of Omega Institute. In her inspiring TEDTalk "Take 'the Other' to Lunch," she used a line from the Persian poet Rumi: "Out beyond ideas of wrong-doing and right-doing, there is a field. I will meet you there."[5]

Rhetorical Question

You might end a presentation with a rhetorical question, followed by an opposite question or a one-liner response. Here are some examples:

- "Can we afford to bail out the banks? Can we afford not to?"
- "What is personal in this digital era? Nothing. Your life is in full display."

Trademark Sign-off

If you deliver a lot of presentations to the same groups, you can adopt a one-liner that becomes your own trademark. For example, news anchor Walter Cronkite always ended his broadcasts with "And that's the way it was." Radio show host Jimmie Fidler also had a trademark sign-off: "Good night to you, and you, and I do mean you!" Find something that suits your personality and that would sound authentic. The trademark sign-off could also be your company's tagline, such as "Think different" (Apple) or "Just do it" (Nike).

A Song

I witnessed a manager making a presentation to his team about a failed project. The team had met to hear a talk about abandoning the project because there was no longer any merit in continuing. The speaker ended with the lyrics of "The Gambler": "You've got to know when to hold 'em, know when to fold 'em."

Slides with Your Take-away Message

Powerful slides containing your take-away message need to be attractive visuals with very little text. Designer Tim Brown ended his presentation "Creativity and Play" with three beautiful slides that summed up what he called a series of behaviors that we learned as kids and that are useful to designers:

- First slide: "Exploration: Go for quantity"
- Second slide: "Building: Think with your hands"
- Third slide: "Role play: Act it out"[6]

To view the slides, watch the video of this presentation at http://www.ted.com/talks/tim_brown_on_creativity_and_play.html.

Reference to Your Speech's Title

The title of Neil Pasricha's TED speech, "The 3 A's of Awesome," refers to attitude, awareness, and authenticity.[7] The award-winning blogger ended the speech by saying, "If you live your life with a great *attitude*, ... living with a sense of *awareness* of the world around you, ... and being *authentic* to yourself, ... then I think you will live a life that is truly awesome." This was an effective manner in which to bring the title into his final statement.

THE QUESTION PERIOD

Now we come to the question-and-answer part of your presentation. Do you open up this time *before* the memorable statement or *after*? It depends. In an ideal scenario, the memorable statement follows the question period. You would say, "At this point, I will take any questions and then I will formally wrap up." This signals to the audience that there is more to come after the questions.

In some cases, however, audience members who don't have questions see this as an opportunity to collect their materials and exit. You are then left with a small group and no opportunity to deliver your memorable statement. The question-and-answer period could also take too long, by which time most people are somewhat anxious to leave—and your memorable statement might not land as powerfully on a distracted audience.

If you deliver your memorable statement and then end with the question-and-answer period, the effect of the ending could be weak. Questions are unpredictable, and the discussion could take a different turn, with objections, tough questions, and doubts being raised. The power of the memorable statement would be lost because people will remember most what ensued in the question-and-answer session.

So where does this leave you? If you know that audience members will not depart before you conclude your presentation, plan to deliver your memorable statement after the questions and answers.

On the other hand, if you sense that your audience is edging to leave, then deliver your memorable statement before the question period and reinforce it again, in different words, at the end of the question period. For example:

A lot of interesting points were raised. Thank you for this very healthy and lively debate. I'll wrap up by reminding everyone that, as we have seen from past projects that failed, "out of the box" doesn't always work. We need to preserve what works and only change what doesn't. Thank you.

THE FINAL POWERPOINT SLIDE

The final slide of your presentation should include your contact information. For an internal presentation, where everyone knows you, add your name and local telephone number. For an external audience, add your full contact information.

TEMPLATES FOR CONCLUSIONS

Consider the following templates for ending a presentation, depending on its purpose.

SPEAKING TO INFORM

1. Signal the end.

2. Summarize the key message and supporting points.

3. Take questions.

4. Make a memorable statement.

SPEAKING TO PERSUADE

1. Signal the end.

2. Restate your recommendation.

3. Remind the audience of the benefits of your recommendation.

4. Take questions.

5. Make a memorable statement.

CHAPTER 5

FINAL TOUCHES: EDITING YOUR PRESENTATION

"Rewriting is like scrubbing the basement floor with a toothbrush."
—**Pete Murphy**

Painstaking editing makes the difference between careful and careless, between meticulous and perfunctory. It's about quality—and quality is always a signpost for trust and credibility.

Here are twelve important questions to ask yourself when you review the draft of your presentation:

1. Is each item I mention important for the audience to know—or is it there to show how smart I am? If it is the latter, remove it.

2. Are my metaphors, symbols, analogies, stories, quotations, examples, and other supporting materials relevant, and do they bolster my points? If not, replace them with more powerful, pertinent ones.

3. Is there anything in my presentation that could even remotely dishearten or cause embarrassment to anyone in the audience? If so, remove it or reword it.

4. Does my presentation sound like an off-the-shelf piece of communication that I am just reciting? If so, integrate evidence of your own opinions and feelings about the topic.

5. Is the audience included in my presentation? Have I used words such as *we* and *us*? Look through your presentation and see how many "I"s and "you"s you can eliminate.

6. Have I made my points with a minimum of verbiage? Be ruthless in removing anything superfluous. Perform verbal surgery until you have a focused message.

7. Are there any platitudes or overused expressions? Weed them out and take the time to replace them with more eloquent turns of phrase. The same applies to convoluted language. Aim for simplicity and a conversational tone.

8. Have I included sentences that use the passive voice rather than the active voice? Rewrite them to use the active voice. For example, you would replace "The beta test was conducted by the end users of the software" with "The end users of the software conducted the beta test."

9. Have I forgotten to mention anyone in my talk? Do I need to credit, thank, or acknowledge someone?

10. Does my presentation have the "wow" factor? To borrow one of Tom Peters's terms, is it "gaspworthy"? As Tom says, "I sincerely believe that damn near anything can be made… 'gaspworthy.'"[1] If you think this adjective doesn't apply to your material, then you have not worked hard enough to create a compelling presentation.

11. Do some phrases need to be rewritten? Could I have used a better word? A helpful tool to compare different ways of wording something is http://phras.in/. Just enter your word or phrase as well as an alternative, and the system will indicate the less popular choice and the more popular choice (along with examples of each).

12. Am I helping my audience visualize the numbers in my presentation? For example, in referring to the more than 550 million members of Facebook, journalist Lev Grossman said, "If Facebook were a country it would be the third largest, behind only China and India."[2]

Editing and rewriting your presentation is hard work. Not many go the extra mile to include this final step to polish their presentations, but the effort is guaranteed to pay dividends. It will condense your information, help you focus your points, and ultimately make the work better. It's akin to a craftsman honing his art. Presenting is an art form!

CHAPTER 6

TASK TENACITY:
PREPARING FOR QUESTIONS

*"When someone says, 'That's a good question,' you can be sure
it's a lot better than the answer you're going to get."*
—Unknown

Someone once said, "Good luck happens when preparedness meets opportunity." The question-and-answer part of your presentation is a great opportunity to boost your credibility and showcase your knowledge and ability to think on your feet. If you are not prepared, it can also erode your credibility very quickly. Fortunately, there is a lot you can do to successfully manage this part of your presentation and garner points in the eyes of your audience.

This chapter will explore the best practices for handling questions.

PREPARING TO ANSWER QUESTIONS

Following are some tips for planning to deal with questions that may arise during your presentation.

BE METHODICAL

Prepare for potential questions by keeping four things in mind:

1. The subject of your presentation

2. The major points you are making

3. Your goal in giving the presentation

4. Your audience's expectations, needs, and background

We must anticipate questions that address weaknesses in our argument or controversial aspects of our presentation. We often don't spend the time to prepare for these questions; we avoid them in the hope that the audience will not detect the weak spots. However, you can be sure that if there is a weakness, someone will perceive it and question you on it. To borrow Churchill's phrase, these questions target your presentation's "soft underbelly." Why make yourself vulnerable in this way? Do your homework to strengthen your argument—or, at the very least, have viable answers.

If there are members of the audience with whom you happen to have some issues, keep in mind the words of sports coach John Heisman: "When you find your opponent's weak spot, hammer it." It is an unfortunate reality of life. So why give anyone that opportunity? It is always bewildering how people spend days being anxious about possible questions at an upcoming presentation when they can devote that energy to thinking about what questions might come up and rehearsing answers.

EXAMINE MAJOR POINTS IN YOUR PRESENTATION

For each of your major points, prepare for questions that might require you to give examples, clarify, or expand.

Be prepared to answer questions about your personal opinion or interpretation of the facts that you are presenting. Think about how you *feel* about your message. Even if it is an informational presentation, we rarely speak just to recite information. If this were the case, we would simply send a written report. What is your personal interpretation, opinion, or thought? This is taking your presentation one level deeper, to show that you have greater knowledge than just what is on the slide.

If you have done a thorough analysis of your audience, their needs, and their reasons for attending the presentation, it will be easy for you to guess what their concerns might be. Some of their questions will be directly related to these concerns.

PREPARE A FEW SLIDES FOR YOUR ANSWERS

For complicated questions, consider preparing a few slides ahead of time that might contain a diagram, chart, data, detailed analysis, visual, or anything else that will serve to explain your point. Note the numbers of these slides so that you can go to them quickly while you are answering the question.

PREPARE A HANDOUT FOR YOUR ANSWERS

For some questions, you might even have a handout prepared in advance. You can present the material as follows: "You brought up an important point on a complex issue. I am often asked this very same question, so I have prepared a one-page explanation that I will distribute at the end of the presentation."

REHEARSE YOUR ANSWERS

Once you have gathered all of the information that you need to answer any questions, take some time to rehearse answers to important questions—just as you rehearse the actual presentation. This is hard work, but for high-stakes presentations, it will pay dividends. Also consider enlisting the help of a colleague or a friend. Have them ask you some difficult questions; rehearse the answers thoroughly with that person.

SET UP A CORPORATE DATABASE

If you are delivering a corporate presentation on topics that recur, consider setting up a database of questions and answers. Enlist the help of key people in the organization to answer the questions and post them on your intranet for everyone's reference. Encourage presenters to keep adding new questions they receive from customers and other stakeholders.

ANSWERING QUESTIONS

The following guidelines will help you address questions from the audience during the course of your presentation.

LISTEN ATTENTIVELY

In his book *In the Line of Fire: How to Handle Tough Questions… When It Counts*, Jerry Weissman puts this beautifully: "Heed the advice of the Zen master: empty your cup. Empty your mind of all thoughts so that you can fill it instead with those of the questioner."[1] Concentrating on the question rather than your answer will result in a more thoughtful answer.

FOCUS ON THE TRIGGER WORD

While listening to the question, focus on the trigger word that will dovetail with your mental database of anticipated questions. Then confidently draw from your practiced answer to deal with the question.

For example, say you receive a question like this: "I don't believe that there is sufficient evidence to support the benefits you mention." The trigger word is *evidence*; you can go on a tangent and start repeating the benefits. Talk about the research and evidence that support your point and that dovetail with the answer you had prepared about research and evidence.

VARY THE ACKNOWLEDGMENT

It's surprising how many presenters feel compelled to say, "That's a good question." It is a cliché, and it is also somewhat condescending to the audience. Also, it forces you to say it to every person who asks a question! Here are a few alternatives:

- "Thank you. You've raised a key point."
- "I am glad you brought this up, as it is central to the XYZ issue."
- "Yes, this is an important issue that I need to address."
- "This is a question that comes up often."
- A mere "thank you" or "yes" also suffices.

REPHRASE OR REPEAT THE QUESTION

Rephrase or repeat a question if you have an audience of forty or more people, or if the person asking the question spoke in a soft voice. Use your judgment: if you sense that others did not hear the question, repeat it. It is irritating for people to hear an answer to an unknown question. Even seasoned presenters forget this presentation etiquette. If the question was long and rambling, rephrase the question succinctly. For instance, "The question was about price."

Don't repeat an accusatory or negative question word for word. For example, instead of saying, "The question is about the mess we caused with our new system," reword the statement to soften it: "The question is about the past issues with our new system."

ALWAYS GIVE THE SHORT ANSWER FIRST

Provide the quick answer first; then elaborate if the audience asks for more. Most of the time, they won't. This tactic will force you to give less detail and will eliminate your chances of rambling on.

USE EYE CONTACT JUDICIOUSLY

Look at the person asking the question while you start your answer. At the midpoint, look at the audience so that they also feel included. End by looking at the questioner. If the question was argumentative, don't end by looking at the questioner, as this will encourage the person to continue on the negative path. Instead, end by looking at the audience and ask if there are any other questions. Move slightly away from the negative questioner as you do so.

KNOW WHEN TO STOP

Belaboring the answer becomes pedantic. It can also make you appear less confident and in need of moral support. Answer concisely and move on. If the person needs further clarification, let them ask you.

CONFIRM THAT YOU ANSWERED THE QUESTION

Follow your response to a complicated question by asking something like the following:

- "Does this answer your question?"
- "Is this clear for you?"
- "Have I given you what you need?"

Then move on to the next question. Don't follow up with someone who monopolizes time or with a confrontational individual, as doing so will continue to engage the person in argumentation and waste everyone else's time.

SET UP Q&A RULES

Setting up rules is particularly important if you tend to have difficulty managing the question-and-answer period of a presentation. At the start of your talk, state that you will take questions following each section or at the end of the presentation. Then, if a participant interrupts the flow and hijacks the presentation, you can remind everyone of the rules: "Thank you. As I mentioned, I'll take questions at the end so that we have time to cover everything that we need to address. I'll ask you to please hold on to the question and I'll get to it at the end."

If you are concerned that a member of the audience may monopolize the conversation by asking repeated questions, you can address this in the Q&A rules, as well: "In the interest of time and to make sure that we can cover all the material, I will take one question per person. If there is time at the end of the presentation, I will take more questions from everyone." If a person asks repeated questions, then you can invoke the rule by saying, "Thank you. As I mentioned at the start, I need to take only one question per person for now so that we can stay on track. I'll be happy to take many more questions at the conclusion."

HANDLE IRRELEVANT QUESTIONS EFFECTIVELY
You can choose to answer an irrelevant question or not. Here is a suggested response: "Thank you. Our particular purpose today is XYZ issue. I'd be happy to discuss this with you after the presentation." If the question is totally irrelevant, you can candidly, and in a friendly tone, say, "This is beyond the scope of this presentation." Then break eye contact to look at someone else. If you choose to address an irrelevant question, you can say, "The topic today is XYZ, but the short answer to your question is..." Then give a very short answer and move on.

RECOGNIZE A MONOLOGUE
Sometimes a person will raise their hand to ask a question but then proceed to deliver a small speech. Listen carefully; if there is no question, and you sense that the person is simply airing some views, let them finish, thank them, and move on. However, if their comments are overly long, find a moment when they pause between statements and simply interject, "Thank you. This is interesting. In the interest of time, we'll move on to the next question."

UNTANGLE MULTIPLE QUESTIONS
Before you start your answer, address the fact that you are hearing several questions. This helps you and the audience, who may

otherwise be confused by the answer. For instance, "I heard three questions. One is on price, another is on the problem we had with the last shipment, and the third is about the transportation issue. I'll answer your question on the last shipment first."

MANAGE THE CONVERSATIONS IN THE ROOM

If someone is speaking to a neighbor while another audience member is asking the question, it is up to you to put an end to the distraction. You might offer a simple, "Let's all hear what Jack is saying, please." Or give the following reminder in a friendly tone: "One conversation at a time, please."

MAKE EVERYONE FEEL INCLUDED

Make sure that you take questions from people sitting at the far end of the room or out of your line of vision, e.g., on the sides. Make an effort to see everyone in the room, in case someone has raised their hand. It is frustrating for someone to be missed when the presenter seems to be wearing blinders.

BE AWARE OF YOUR BODY LANGUAGE

Some presenters unconsciously take a step back or move away when someone is asking a question. Or they might frown or raise their eyebrows as they try to understand what the person is saying. Unaware of the expression on their face, they may look grim. Some cover their mouth with their hand. They might break eye contact and briefly look at the window, door, or floor as the person asks the question. They may cross their arms or put their hands in their pockets. Some fumble with papers or their laptop while listening. Others even start disconnecting their equipment and packing papers while asking if there are any questions. Do any of these behaviors describe you? These are all negative signals.

While we don't deliberately set out to exhibit negative body language during the Q&A session, we need to be aware of what we are doing subconsciously because of anxiety or tiredness. Self-awareness precedes self-management.

An emotionally intelligent presenter works on giving positive body signals, such as moving slightly toward the questioner rather than away. They might smile encouragingly—or at least they are aware of their facial expressions and don't frown or look grim. Pay close attention to the person asking the question and don't appear to be preoccupied with anything else. Maintain a neutral, open physical stance. Don't signal impatience by nodding your head repeatedly because you know what's coming. Stay connected with your audience, with grace, to the very end.

Jerry Weissman tries the following exercise with his clients:

> Stand up and ask a seated colleague to ask you a long, rambling question on any subject… Ask the person to keep their eyes fixed on you as they ramble. Shortly after they start, thrust your hands into your pockets and settle back on one foot. Watch what happens. Usually the person's ramble will start to sputter and slow down.

Your slouch is very likely to signal to the person that you are not interested, that you may be bored. "When a presenter sends this kind of message to the audience, the effect can be devastating."[2]

When you practice positive behaviors, you give the message to the audience that you are confident and at ease, and that the person asking the question is important. Acting with grace garners you points with the audience. When you are answering questions, just as when you are actually presenting, you are on display.

DON'T BE AFRAID TO ADMIT
IF YOU DON'T KNOW THE ANSWER

It is okay to say that you don't know the answer to a question that a member of the audience asks, and to offer to get back to them after the presentation. If the question is central to what you are presenting, however, not knowing the answer could put a dint in your credibility—so it is imperative to prepare diligently. You also need to know everything that is on your slides, even if it is information provided by other parties.

If the question is in an area that is clearly not your specialty or is obviously outside the scope of your presentation, simply say so: "I don't have the answer to your question. It's outside the scope of our topic today." And then move on to the next question.

BE PREPARED IF THERE ARE NO QUESTIONS

Ending a presentation without any questions from the audience might detract from the talk's overall effect. Be prepared for this possibility, so that you are not caught off-guard. To preempt the situation, ask for questions in a way that motivates the audience to ask questions. This includes receptive body language—smiling, and moving *toward* the audience, with a slight lean forward. If you are speaking from a podium, step away from it.

Rather than simply saying, "Are there any questions?," consider including a tone of expectancy: "So, what questions do you have for me?" or "Who wants to go first?"

If these or similar questions don't work, have a few one-liners ready: "A question that usually comes up is…" or "Well, I wish you had asked me about…" Then proceed to answer your own question.

Consider, as well, omitting from the presentation some details that you know are of interest to the audience.

Depending on the type of audience, and the nature of your topic, encourage them at the start of the presentation with statements such as, "I am quite comfortable with interruptions, so please feel free to ask questions as I go along. It is up to me to manage the time." This is especially important for complex or technical information, where audience members need to understand points as you go along.

If you have a quiet group and you sense that there will not be any inquiries, ask for questions at the very beginning: "What particular questions would you like me to answer during my presentation?" This is more likely to get a response than at the end. Briefly jot down the questions, or use a flipchart to mark keywords. Most of the time, the questions they want answered will be covered during the presentation, even if in a different format or order. This is also helpful if you are particularly nervous about the Q&A session: it will buy you time to think about the answers as you go along.

CLOSE THE Q&A PERIOD WITH APLOMB

If you have many questions from the audience and limited time, it is courteous to signal the closing rather than to end abruptly and disappoint people. The classic "We have time for three more questions" is an empathetic way of handling Q&A. Also let the audience know when you are taking the final question: "Last question?"

If an extensive discussion arises during the Q&A period, with new information or issues brought to light, some audience members may leave the presentation without a clear understanding of the main issue or goal of your presentation. Always take control of the presentation by pulling all the threads together. Instead of just the perfunctory "That's it; thank you," consider saying, for example, "Thank you, everyone, for this lively discussion. We have uncovered a few important issues. Let me recap that the purpose of the presentation has been to inform everyone of the budget cuts that are going to take effect on February 15. As agreed, we will reconvene next month to address some of the concerns that were raised today."

TAKE CHARGE OF THE CLOSING

You are responsible for ending your presentation at the appointed time. This extends to the question-and-answer period. If the Q&A session takes you beyond your allotted time, you need to bring it to a close. Don't let the organizer do this for you or let departing audience members give you the message to conclude your presentation. These subtle occurrences detract from your credibility at the front of the room. Be in charge.

PROVIDE ALTERNATIVE WAYS OF ASKING QUESTIONS

This is particularly applicable for a training session. Hand out cards for people to jot down their questions. Set up a question board or the proverbial "parking lot" on the wall and provide sticky notes for participants to post their questions. Or in advance of the training session, ask participants to email you their questions.

How you handle the question-and-answer period is crucial to your credibility. Be authentic, don't make up answers, admit if you don't know an answer, be in charge, and be helpful. Answer the questions to the best of your knowledge, with care and enthusiasm, and offer to find the answers if they are not readily available. If you follow all of the guidelines in this chapter, you will be well on your way to mastering the Q&A session in a competent, credible manner.

CHAPTER 7

A GOLDEN OPPORTUNITY: PRESENTING TO C-LEVEL

"If it has a staple in it, it doesn't get read. Never walk into any presentation without a one-page summary."[1]
—Bill Jensen

If there is one audience that unnerves presenters most, it is an audience of executives. If you are in a management role or aspire to climb the ladder, you need to develop your credibility in order to successfully present in front of this group. This chapter will help you do so.

Before I give you guidelines for presenting at a meeting of executives or a board of directors, I need to paint a typical scenario so that you can take my comments and tips in context. Having this frame of reference will help you better understand the world of senior executives and will, I hope, help you not take many of the behaviors that occur in these meetings personally.

It is useful to understand that *all* executive audiences behave the same way. It doesn't matter what industry or what country, their requirements and their agendas are similar. These individuals are always very busy and have little time allotted for your presentation—which is usually one of several that they have to listen to in a given meeting. It is safe to say that in most circumstances, you are not the main course; you are a side dish. Most of them will be impatient—especially when confronted with hesitation, incompetence, lack of preparation, and irrelevance. They don't want you to waste any of their time, and they will let you know if you do.

Generally, they have big—though not necessarily inflated—egos that come from confidence and trust in themselves. They will be openly adversarial if they disagree with what you say. They will challenge you and may very well adopt what might appear to you as an offensive attitude.

Even though they may not say so, they will notice if you are well prepared, know your stuff, don't waste time, and can hold your own. Presentations to executives are great opportunities for them to see your potential. You can be sure that if you do a good job, someone will take note—and it will boost your credibility in their eyes.

The rest of this chapter provides the road map for success in presenting to this group.

PLAN FOR A DISCUSSION

Prepare to have a discussion rather than *deliver* a presentation. If you are given thirty minutes to speak, prepare to present formally for ten minutes and leave twenty minutes for discussion. This is a group that will have many questions, and they expect you to be able to speak about your issue and not be a slave to your slides. I remember a CEO I reported to who explicitly told the company, "I don't want someone to show up here with dozens of slides. We want to talk about this and explore the viability of it for our company, not view a one-hour PowerPoint show."

Be comfortable with being interrupted a lot, as this group will ask a lot of questions. Your greatest chance of being derailed is probably in the question-and-answer part. It pays to spend as much time as possible anticipating all important questions. Meet with those who are close to the group, and enlist their help. They will be a good source to help you find out what the executives' possible concerns are, and how the issues of the day might impact your topic.

PLAN TO ADDRESS THE BIG PICTURE

Do some prework on the big-picture implications of your presentation. Be prepared to discuss the impact of your proposal or views on areas besides your immediate concern.

If you are making a proposal or need approval for something, try to meet with a few group members ahead of the formal meeting to do some preparatory work. Having a few people who are already on your side when you enter the room is smart. Even having one person whom you can count on to be a supporter helps to relax you.

KEEP SLIDES TO A MINIMUM

Limit the number of slides you use. While you should normally limit your slides, nowhere is this more advisable than when you speak to an executive group. Don't derail yourself by creating slides with bullet points. This audience doesn't need to read bullet points in order to follow what you say.

Remember, you are approaching this as a conversation. Your slides should be limited to visuals. A visual might be a graph, chart, diagram, spreadsheet, pricing table, map, photo, product image, structure, or whatever else is applicable. You will talk to everything else.

You can leave the executives with a document containing all the verbiage. This can be a written report; a précis; an executive summary; or even detailed PowerPoint slides with bullet points, entire sentences, and quotations (as long as you don't use this set of slides to present).

PREPARE A SHORTER VERSION

Be prepared to speak for a shorter period of time than initially allotted. You may be told that you have thirty minutes to make your presentation, but when you arrive at the meeting, you may very likely be informed that you now have only ten minutes. Many unexpected events can trigger such a change; for example, other important issues may surface after the agenda is distributed.

To be ready for this potentiality, first prepare your regular set of slides for the full-length presentation. Then prepare a shortened version that will include only two or three crucial slides. To create these, think about the goal of your presentation (addressed in the next section).

Once you are clear on why you are speaking, ask yourself the following question: "If I only have ten minutes, what is the core of my message—the most important thing that I need to present in order to accomplish my goal?" Use this information to form the content of your two or three crucial slides.

Being prepared to speak for a shorter period will go a long way to quiet your anxiety. It is an opportunity to showcase your adaptability, which is a prime leadership quality.

BE VERY CLEAR ABOUT YOUR OBJECTIVE

Be very clear about why you are speaking to this group. This will help you structure the presentation accordingly. For example:

- Do you want a decision from them?
- Do you want permission or approval?
- Do you want advice?
- Do you want to give them an update?
- Did they ask you to provide them with some information?
- Did they ask for your opinion or recommendation?

BE VERY CLEAR ABOUT YOUR POINT OF VIEW

Have a clear point of view. This idea comes from Scott Eblin, author of *The Next Level: What Insiders Know About Executive Success.*[2] In a study, he showed that the people the CEO listened to the most "had an informed and clearly held point of view. They weren't wishy-washy in the way they teed things up." Be very clear about where you are going, why you want to go there, and what will happen when you get there.

PROOFREAD PAINSTAKINGLY

Check your material (slides, handouts, etc.) very carefully. Even the minutest of errors can create a negative impression of you. Small mistakes in calculating numbers, inconsistencies, misspellings, and other omissions will be noticed. These missteps can make the audience doubt your competence. They will wonder what else you may have missed that is important.

AVOID CLIPART

While clipart may be effective for other groups, for a senior audience, it is an unnecessary distraction. Aim for serious graphics. Everything on a slide needs to have a purpose, to clarify and move your presentation forward.

SAVE THE HANDOUT FOR THE END

Distribute the handout, if you have one, *after* the presentation. As Jerry Weissman states in *Less Is More: The Proper Use of Graphics for Effective Presentations*, "If you distribute them before…your audience members will flip through them while you speak and they won't listen to what you have to say."[3] This is particularly true of executive audiences, who will quickly read your handout, skipping ahead. You will not be able to present as planned. "If you're asked to provide a copy of the presentation in advance, as so often happens in the venture capital and financial sector," states Weissman, "politely offer to provide a business plan or executive summary as a document."[4]

CLARIFY YOUR PURPOSE

Begin your presentation by telling the executives succinctly what you are looking for. If it is a decision that you are seeking, say so right away. If it is their advice that you need, then say that. If you are just there to flag an important issue or a new development that they need to be aware of, then state so at the outset. Don't rely on the fact that an agenda has been circulated describing your issue. Some of these busy executives may not have had time to read the information before the meeting.

If you are there to make a recommendation or to give your opinion or expert advice, always begin with a succinct statement about your conclusion or point of view—and then drill down with details. The order of your presentation will, therefore, be counterintuitive:

1. Your conclusion

2. Facts regarding your conclusion

3. Material to substantiate your facts

4. A brief restatement of your conclusion

5. Query about whether they need more information

By structuring your talk this way, you save time and avoid a lot of divergent questions and rambling discussion.

FOCUS ON THE WHY

Don't waste too much time focusing on how you arrived at your conclusions. Focus, instead, on what you are proposing and why. As Scott Eblin says in *The Next Level: What Insiders Know About Executive Success*:

> *A common mistake new executives make is to focus too much on how they came to their conclusions. To do this is to risk getting labeled as someone who, when asked for the time, explains how to build a watch... Focus much more on your recommendations and their implications than on the mechanics of how you arrived at them.[5]*

Explaining the *how* diminishes your credibility. If they want to know, they will ask.

PUT THEIR NEEDS FIRST

When we make a sales presentation (for example, to an executive group), there is a tendency to want to speak about our product and our solution right away. Even though you are excited to talk about what you know best, always start with a discussion and questions about the executives' needs. Then follow with your solution.

SPARE THEM THE DETAILS

Be conservative with details. Remember that most members of this group are big-picture thinkers. That's one of the strengths that got them promoted to their level. Part of their mandate is to see the broad implications of issues. So as you speak, they will be taking a helicopter view of what you are saying—looking at the forest, not the trees. Don't analyze each tree. Again, if they want details, they will ask you for them.

SPEAK IN QUANTITATIVE TERMS

Give them the numbers. "Best case, base case, and worse case scenarios…add clarity and credibility."[6] Show them expected ROI, gross margins, percentage of market share, and other quantifiers that may be applicable to your recommendation.

BE SMART ABOUT EYE CONTACT

Spread your eye contact equally amongst all those present, with *slightly* more eye contact with the most senior person in the room. If you unwittingly ignore someone, they will notice.

Often, there may be one overly aggressive member who will engage you more than the others. It is easy to focus a disproportionate amount of eye contact exclusively on this individual. If you do this, you run the risk of alienating the other executives.

WATCH FOR BODY LANGUAGE

This is a group that gets impatient with long-winded explanations. They will give you plenty of signals if they are running out of patience; heed these signals and make any necessary changes. In a long presentation, if you detect impatience or a loss of attention, stop and ask the executives how they would prefer for you to proceed: "At this point, would you like me to outline the costs, or would you prefer that I discuss benchmarks of competitor companies?"

USE THE PLAN TEMPLATE FOR BRIEF PRESENTATIONS

Consider using the PLAN template to deliver information to busy executives. The laser-like focus of this template works well in presentations, especially for quick meetings. Here are the components:

- **P:** Tell the audience in concise terms what the **problem** or the issue is.

- **L:** Briefly explain the **liabilities** (repercussions, consequences, or what they should be concerned about).

- **A:** Outline what **actions** they need to take (your advice or recommendation).

- **N:** Provide any **necessary** background information. (The emphasis here is on "necessary," which means not overburdening the discussion with lengthy details.)

CHAPTER 8

AND NOW FOR SOMETHING TOTALLY DIFFERENT: YOUR KEYNOTE

*"You aren't untouchable on stage,
and it no longer means you get instant credibility."*[1]
—**Michael Fienen**

During the course of your career, you will likely be asked to deliver a keynote presentation at an important event, such as an academic conference, an industry convention, or your company's sales retreat. This invitation gives you a unique opportunity to showcase your knowledge but also to position yourself as a speaker worth listening to. It's a chance to boost your credibility with your professional network.

If the approaching event causes you anxiety, remind yourself of this: being invited to give the keynote means you have the knowledge you need—and the organizers' confidence that you can pull it off.

What exactly is a keynote, and why do we call it that? In music, the keynote is the first note of a scale; it's the note upon which the pattern of notes that governs a musical piece is based. Similarly, in public speaking, it's the presentation or speech that heralds the main theme of a large gathering, such as a conference or retreat.

This chapter will give you some pointers for preparing and delivering a professional speech that will establish you as a credible speaker on the keynote circuit.

CUSTOMIZE YOUR SPEECH

Just as an article's first paragraph should hook the reader and provide a clear overview of the article's main points, a keynote speaker needs to convey the tone and purpose of the event. Therefore, before you write the first word, you must understand the conference's overall theme as well as what the organizers are hoping to achieve.

By grasping the big picture, you will be able to craft a message that resonates with the audience and taps into their needs. By focusing on the conference's theme, you will be able to judge what to emphasize and what to omit. While you might get away with a cookie-cutter approach for a typical presentation, this will not work for a keynote. You must tailor your message to the event.

KEEP YOUR MATERIAL UP-TO-DATE

People can tell if you are using slides for a talk you delivered several years ago. Keep updating and using fresh material. Stay on top of developments in your topic or field, as your audience most likely is up to speed. One keynote audience member described an event this way:

> *The presentation was what many of us would call a fairly egregious breach of professional protocol on its own. It really was that bad... comparisons and examples that were out-of-date, and a general feeling like it was a presentation developed five*

years ago for an audience that clearly had no clue what he would be talking about. But we get it, we're there, we understand the channels; in this sense, we were well ahead of the keynote.[2]

Don't let this happen to you.

BE VERY CLEAR ABOUT YOUR TAKE-HOME MESSAGE

Think about how your participants will describe your talk to their colleagues the next day, when they get back to the office. What three or four sentences would describe your central message? Better yet, can you summarize your take-home message in 140 characters (the length of a tweet)? It will be much easier to build your keynote if you have a solid idea of your take-home message.

CONNECT EMOTIONALLY

For a talk to deserve keynote status, it needs to strike an emotional chord with the audience. This means that no matter how well you know your material or how much knowledge you will impart, for your speech to be a keynote, it needs to touch people's hearts. You need to connect with people emotionally, by inspiring them and firing them up.

To achieve an emotional connection, you must also be sincere. You have to truly believe what you are saying. You also need genuine passion and enthusiasm for your subject. Because your customized talk taps into the audience's interests and needs, your conviction and sincere enthusiasm for the topic will easily be infectious. The next section explains how to express your enthusiasm and passion.

SHOW YOUR ENTHUSIASM AND PASSION

How do you show passion in a presentation? You do it on two levels: delivery and content. For the delivery, think amplified: you must project energy and dynamism. You do this with movement. Insist on a lapel mike so that you can move on the stage. If possible, step down and walk around the tables for a small part of the keynote. If you are normally soft-spoken, make an effort to speak louder. Smile often, and make eye contact with the entire room: back rows, front rows, sides, and middle. Don't leave anyone out. This is not about being theatrical and eroding your authenticity; it's simply about making an effort to project energy. If you have a preference for introversion, and find this somewhat difficult, do so within the confines of your comfort zone. We each have a boundary for our comfort zone—simply go to the edge of that boundary.

The other way to show passion in a presentation is by making your content compelling. Attendance at conferences and large industry gatherings is expensive, and the keynotes are a draw. People come with great expectations, one of which is to learn something new and useful. Abandon tired facts that everyone knows; share novel material and amazing statistics. Be extra generous with solid tools and advice.

Show people that you live and breathe the topic. Tell them how you became interested in it, how long you have been studying or practicing in your field, and the intriguing things you have accomplished. Convey why you are passionate about the subject and how the audience will benefit from listening to you.

DON'T READ YOUR KEYNOTE

Know your material so well that you can move around, making eye contact with the audience rather than with your notes. Here is what one audience member blogged about a bad keynote speaker:

> *His eyes are glued to his prepared speech, his stance as rigid as a statue, and his words as disembodied as whispers in the breeze. His paper is also his paperweight, and all you can hope for is that someone has the energy to lift up the vaudeville cane and yank him from the stage.*[3]

You can avoid this kind of review by not reading your material.

START POWERFULLY

Grab the audience's attention right from the start. This means dropping the formulaic opening of thanking everyone and saying how pleased you are to be there. If you must say thank you to anyone, keep it very brief. Formalities and platitudes rob your beginning of its dynamism.

Watch as many keynotes as you can to get comfortable with the idea of what starting strong means. For example, Bill Cosby opened his keynote at Carnegie Mellon University by taking off his university robe and unveiling the university's sports outfit underneath.[4] He removed his cap and sunglasses and started talking. The first words he uttered were, "Nerds. [pause] Why anybody would accept themselves [pause] as nerds [pause] bothers me." This brief introduction had all the elements of a strong start: surprise, humor, good timing, pacing, and a strong message honoring the audience—all in one sentence!

USE STORIES TO MAKE YOUR POINTS

Pertinent stories that drive the message home are an essential ingredient of a good keynote. Stories teach and entertain. They have that "lean in" quality. Nothing beats a good story to keep an audience engaged. One caveat: while self-help literature exhorts us to be the hero of our own life story, in a keynote, this would be treacherous. It could take us on an ego path, which distances the audience from us. Dickens says in *David Copperfield*, "Whether I shall turn out to be the hero of my own life, or whether that station will be held by anybody else, these pages must show." Let someone else tell a story in which you are the hero. In your own story, it is best to talk about lessons learned and challenges overcome rather than how great you are.

Tell stories that illustrate your passion and enthusiasm for whatever you are speaking about. Why this topic? Why you? What happened? What led you down this path? What fuels you? What keeps you committed to your purpose? People want to hear you speak from the heart. Watch an instructive interview between Lisa Nirell of EnergizeGrowth and Guy Kawasaki, in which he explains how to tell your story and sell your dream.[5] (See Chapter 21 for the characteristics of effective storytelling.)

USE POWERFUL LANGUAGE

Metaphors, analogies, and sound bites are elements that gain and maintain attention in a presentation. Good, solid content and an interesting delivery are a winning combination. Following are examples of figures of speech you might choose to include in a keynote presentation.

TRICOLON

A tricolon uses a series of three to emphasize a point. Here are two examples of tricolons from President Barack Obama's speeches:

> *I stand here today **humbled** by the task before us, **grateful** for the trust you have bestowed, **mindful** of the sacrifices borne by our ancestors.*

> *There are people all across this great nation who... **can't afford** another four years without healthcare; they **can't afford** another four years without good schools; they **can't afford** another four years without decent wages...*

ANAPHORA

This rhetorical device is the repetition of a word or phrase at the beginning of several successive sentences or paragraphs to reinforce an idea in the listener's mind. An example is the anaphoric word *more* in Ronald Reagan's speech following the Space Shuttle *Challenger* disaster: "We'll continue our quest in space. There will be **more** shuttle flights and **more** shuttle crews and, yes, **more** volunteers, **more** civilians, **more** teachers in space."

Here is another example from President Obama's speech. The anaphoric phrase is "We have a deficit":

> **We have a deficit** *when CEOs are making more in ten minutes than ordinary workers are making in an entire year; when families lose their homes so unscrupulous lenders can make a profit; when mothers can't afford a doctor when their children are stricken with illness.*

We have a deficit *in this country when we have Scooter Libby justice for some and Jena justice for others; when our children see hanging nooses from a schoolyard tree today, in the present, in the twenty-first century.*

We have a deficit *when homeless veterans sleep on the streets of our cities; when innocents are slaughtered in the deserts of Darfur; when young Americans serve tour after tour after tour after tour of duty in a war that should've never been authorized and should've never been waged.*

And we have a deficit *when it takes a breach in our levees to reveal a breach in our compassion; when it takes a terrible storm to reveal the hungry that God calls on us to feed, the sick that He calls on us to care for. The least of these He commands that we treat as our own.*

ANTITHESIS

Antithesis is a figure of speech in which contrasting ideas are juxtaposed in a parallel phrase or grammatical structure. For example, from Dickens: "It was the best of times, it was the worst of times..." A powerful example of antithesis appears in Martin Luther King Jr.'s famous "I have a dream" speech: "I have a dream that my four little children will one day live in a nation where they will not be judged by the color of their skin but by the content of their character."

For more ideas on rhetorical devices to enliven your keynote, check out these two websites:

- "A Handbook of Rhetorical Devices," by Robert A. Harris[6]

- "American Rhetoric: Rhetorical Figures in Sound," by Michael E. Eidenmuller, Ph.D.[7] This site contains a wealth of resources, including a rhetorical literacy section with dozens of important speeches in twenty-first-century America.

BE MINDFUL OF THE ENTERTAINMENT FACTOR

Audiences expect a keynote to be entertaining as well as informative. As Johnny Carson once said, "People will pay more to be entertained than educated." One of the best ways to entertain is with storytelling: brief, well-developed, relevant personal stories are gold threads that you can weave throughout your keynote.

Another way to entertain is through humor. Sir Ken Robinson started his "Schools Kill Creativity" speech at TED by referring to the powerful speeches the audience had already heard at the event: "I've been blown away by the whole thing. In fact, I'm leaving."[8] The audience laughed. Simple humor is the best.

Self-deprecating humor is one of the most effective speech tools, as it doesn't require comedic abilities. Marc A. Brackett commenced his TEDxTalk "Educating the Whole Child (and Adult) with Emotional Literacy" by remarking, "As you can tell, I am not from San Francisco. [pause] [smile] I look a little uptight."[9] He gestured to his formal blue suit. The audience chuckled. Again, humor doesn't have to be complicated.

Another example is John Maeda's "The Simple Life" presentation at TED.[10] He started by showing a cover of one of the books in the *For Dummies* series. He circled the image of the "Dummies" man and said, "My daughters point out that I am very similar looking." It elicited a great deal of laughter.

If you need help incorporating humor, consider using the services of humor consultants and coaches.

PLAN YOUR PAUSES

The sign of a seasoned speaker is a sense of timing and control. Practice using pauses in your keynote rehearsals. Record your rehearsal on video, and then listen with your eyes closed. Without the visual distraction, you will have a sense of the ebb and flow of your speech and where your audience would benefit from a pause.

Plan your pauses. For example, pause after saying your most humorous lines, to allow the audience to laugh. We have a tendency to continue to speak over the laughter, which prevents the audience from hearing our next statement. Pause, as well, after a particularly important insight or powerful quote.

MAKE IT INTERACTIVE

A keynote is not a lecture. You must find ways to add interactivity throughout your talk. Ask questions as you go. Even rhetorical questions or questions that ask for just a show of hands are useful. A popular keynote speaker uses this effective phrase for speaking to large audiences: "Clap if you know what I'm talking about."

If you can, give your audience something to do. Ask them to stand up. Ask for a volunteer to come up on the stage with you. Or walk over to a group and start to interact with one person. Then move on to another group.

Another way to be interactive is to be provocative. John Chambers, CEO of Cisco, said to the audience during a keynote at UC Berkeley, "If you agree with everything I say here today, I failed. I want to challenge you in terms of what's possible. I want to make you think out of the box … kinda challenge you and hopefully make you a little bit uncomfortable."[11]

A master of interactivity in keynotes is motivational speaker Victor Antonio. Watch his keynote "Torpedo Your Dream" to get some inspiration.[12]

MAKE CONNECTIONS FOR THE AUDIENCE

Show your audience how your keynote has relevance for them. Put the information you give into context—whether it is the context of your listeners' industry, their economy, their country, or important events in their lives. Don't speak theoretically, from your own world and experiences, without connecting the dots to *their* world and its issues and concerns.

SPEAK FOR THE EAR

Read each sentence out loud to yourself and judge how it sounds. Is this the way you speak to your friends and colleagues? If not, you need to change it. If people "hear the written word," it disconnects you from them; the audience starts to experience you as a "presenter" who is reading or spouting memorized sentences.

Beware, in particular, of very long sentences with subordinate clauses. This is not the way we speak. Turn the sentence around by starting with the main thought. For example, instead of saying,

"After we have carefully examined the latest findings, we will make a decision," say, "We will make a decision after we have carefully examined the latest findings."

Aim for a colloquial style of speaking, what presenter Garr Reynolds terms a "human voice."[13]

CONNECT YOUR MESSAGE TO THE BIGGER PICTURE

Tie your comments and overall message to the bigger picture—to a larger cause or a global perspective. A famous, illustrative example comes from Churchill. When he spoke about winning World War II, he connected it to a larger cause (a free Europe) and to a grand ideal (liberty).

Consider that your keynote needs to touch and influence not only the immediate audience at the speaking event but others who are not physically there. It is quite likely that your presentation will be video-recorded and uploaded on YouTube to be seen by people around the world. At a minimum, it might be posted on the conference's website as a sample keynote for those contemplating signing up the following year. Thinking about this potential audience will help you generate ideas on how to amplify your message.

CREATE WHITE SPACE

This idea comes from professional speaker Mariah Burton Nelson, who derived her inspiration from Coco Chanel's famous quote, "I always take off at least one piece of jewelry before I leave the house...to ensure that I am not overdoing it." Nelson uses the technique with keynotes by removing one precious element she had planned to include in the speech: a fact, quote, or story. "Figuring out what to remove helps me decide what's essential. It also creates room—for dramatic pauses, for repetition, for digressions, and for spontaneous interactions with the audience. It helps me not feel rushed."[14] Creating space in your keynote buys you precious time to be in the moment on the day of the event and to capture opportunities to spontaneously connect with the audience.

ALWAYS BE MINDFUL OF THE WOW FACTOR
After you have completed writing your speech, go over it, section by section. After each section, ask yourself, "Where is the wow factor? Is this fascinating, interesting, different, important, new? What emotion will it stir up in the audience? Will they be interested, intrigued, surprised, inspired, riveted, shocked, happy, amused?"

HOPE: DON'T LEAVE HOME WITHOUT IT
No matter how dire your topic, always give your audience hope. Outline the problem but give a solution. Talk about the failure but end with the lesson learned. Explain the setbacks but give a recommendation. No matter how dark the situation is, open a window of light. This is a keynote, so think baptism rather than requiem.

USE "WE" NOT "YOU"
Don't set yourself apart from the audience: always imply that the challenges they are experiencing in their lives are ones you share. Phrase the setbacks, failures, or problems as well as the recommendations for overcoming them with "we" rather than "you."

CHOOSE A DESCENDING ORDER

Start with your most inspiring, most important, or most salient points and work downward. This is important, not only to grab the audience's attention but also as a safety measure in case you run out of time, for whatever reason: a late start, a technical snafu, miscommunication about timing, questions and other interactions, or one of a host of unpredictable situations that may prevent you from speaking for the total allotted time.

USE THE TITLE TO ATTRACT ATTENTION

Choose a title that is catchy, piques people's interest, and creates an expectation. If your title is dull and uninspiring, it will suggest that you are dull and uninspiring; so you are off to a negative start. Jeremy Gutsche's presentation "Unlocking Cool: The Power of Customer Focused Innovation" is an example of a keynote with an intriguing title, one that is buzz worthy.[15]

How do you choose the right title? You can learn a lot from bloggers, who describe how to create enticing headlines for articles. The same principles apply to keynote (and presentation) titles. In his report "Why Do Most Headlines Fail?," Sean D'Souza provides excellent advice, such as using psychological triggers.[16] For example, use a question-based headline ("Do You Know Where You Fail in Your Marketing Strategy?") instead of a statement-based one ("Fix Your Marketing Strategy"). Use a problem-based headline ("Struggling to Get Ahead in Your Small Business?") instead of a solution-based one ("Ten Steps for Getting Ahead in Your Small Business").

Consider, as well, how you can weave the title into the keynote. The perfect example of this technique is Mario Cuomo's keynote at the 1984 Democratic National Convention.[17] It is perhaps one of the greatest keynotes ever given. In the speech, titled "A Tale of Two Cities," Cuomo referred to Ronald Reagan's metaphor of "a shining city on a hill" to showcase that there were two groups: the haves (those who lived in the "shining city") and the have-nots (the rest of the country).

CONNECT TO THE SPEAKING VENUE OR CITY

Take inspiration from Guy Kawasaki, who always includes a photo or two of the city where he is speaking: "My best efforts happen when I speak in a foreign city. I usually get there a day early and tour the city to expand my horizons and to take pictures of what enchants me about it."[18] He then utilizes these local pictures as part of his opening pitch.

Find a way to weave a few comments about the venue or the city into your talk. Connect with the audience by saying something gracious, topical, or interesting about the host city. You can view an effective example of this in a keynote given by Victor Antonio, a motivational speaker mentioned earlier, in North Carolina.[19] Before entering into the main content of his keynote, he mentioned beautiful downtown Raleigh and the war memorial there: "That's one of the most gorgeous memorials I've ever seen ... so let me just say God Bless America for those who defended it and those who are still defending it." There was a lot of applause from the audience members, who appreciated the speaker's honoring of their city.

HONOR SOMEONE IN THE AUDIENCE

Tom Peters tells the story of arriving at a hotel at the same time as Doris Drucker, who was attending the talk he was to give in honor of her husband, Peter Drucker. Tom told the audience that he arrived at the hotel's front desk the night before, jet-lagged and wanting to go to sleep. He found out from the hotel clerk that Doris Drucker, on the other hand, arrived at the hotel and immediately went to play tennis. Honoring someone with a little self-deprecating humor worked well.[20]

AVOID COMPLAINING

A well-known author and giant in his field once opened his keynote in a low-energy manner and mentioned that he was suffering from jet lag. This was disappointing to the listeners, who had come with high expectations. They didn't pay to hear excuses. The same goes for admissions that you are anxious or unwell.

EDUCATE BUT DON'T PONTIFICATE

Don't use an oratory style. Watch that you don't point a finger as you speak, or use a dogmatic tone. All of these behaviors alienate the audience.

BRING EXAMPLES FROM OTHER COMPANIES

If applicable, inspire your audience with powerful examples from other companies. These can be items in the media or events that you have personally witnessed. A beautiful example of this is provided by Steve Farber, who talks about the energy that employees of companies such as Gillette, The Container Store, and Huggies bring to their work every day. He ends his keynote with, "If you can generate energy around that, don't tell me there's nothing to get excited and energetic about in the kind of work that you folks do."[21]

LEARN FROM OTHERS

Watch as many keynotes as you can and observe what works and what doesn't. Your gut will tell you what is effective and what is not. Take notes. Here are some recommended materials:

- Watch or read President Obama's address at Ebenezer Baptist Church in 2008. Check, in particular, his speech's past/present/future structure and his skillful use of a variety of rhetorical techniques.[22]

- Check out the Six Minutes blog, where you can view a number of famous keynotes and read a thorough review of each.[23]

- In his article "So Who Are They Trying to Kid? Some Lessons You Won't Learn About Presenting from This Dufus Competition," Les Posen, a clinical psychologist, provides a step-by-step explanation of how he created a keynote for an annual general meeting of psychologists. The article is well worth reading.[24]

- The Resources section of this book provides a compendium of keynotes that you can view for inspiration.

CHAPTER 9

TEACHING OR TORTURE: YOUR WORKSHOP

"Anyone who tries to make a distinction between education and entertainment doesn't know the first thing about either."
—**Marshall McLuhan**

Delivering a seminar or workshop in your area of expertise is a great opportunity to boost your credibility in your professional network or your organization.

Someone once defined a lecture as something that can make you feel "numb on one end and dumb on the other." Most of us have been through the ordeal of listening for long hours to dreary lectures delivered by professors or teachers who had quit long ago but still showed up for the job. Many adult participants arrive at training sessions with memories of this experience.

If you run workshops or seminars, remind yourself that it is a privilege to have a group of adults sign up to listen to you. With that privilege comes a large responsibility: to deliver on their expectations. This seems like stating the obvious, but how often do we read an enticing description of a learning event, and the description ends up bearing only a slight resemblance to what is actually experienced?

The cardinal rule of teaching adults is to be practical. Adults ask themselves questions like these when signing up for a workshop:

- "How is this going to help me do my job better?"
- "How is this going to help me improve my XYZ skill?"
- "How is this going to make me more competitive?"
- "How is this going to improve my personal life?"

They will not ask themselves, "How is this going to expand my theoretical knowledge of this topic?" With this in mind, design every part of your teaching to satisfy your participants' need for practical application. For every lecture item you add, ask yourself, "How relevant is this to my participants' everyday world?" If it is irrelevant, omit it.

This chapter will provide you with practical tips to help you deliver a dynamic learning experience every time.

TEACH SOMETHING WITHIN THE FIRST FIVE MINUTES

I have attended countless seminars where, by 10:00 a.m., an entire hour has passed and I haven't learned anything useful. The time was spent engaged in a long icebreaker, introducing the participants, covering the agenda, and going over housekeeping rules—all done at a slow pace. Stand out from the crowd by reversing this trend. Plan to teach something useful and important within the first five or ten minutes. Watch what happens to the state of alertness in the room. And see how good you feel when you see participants taking notes that early in your presentation. Then proceed with whatever else you need to cover, e.g., icebreaker, agenda, housekeeping rules.

HANDLE ICEBREAKERS WITH CARE

Icebreakers must be planned with care and empathy for the participants. This means that you need to carefully tailor them to your audience so that no one is embarrassed or bored. If you have a room full of engineers, for example, don't ask them to participate in a silly icebreaker; for instance, having them all drop one of their shoes in a pile and then pick up a shoe randomly, go find its owner, and interview them.[1] Use an icebreaker that is intellectually stimulating. What works for one group does not necessarily work for another.

An icebreaker should not exceed ten to fifteen minutes, if it is the opening activity. Don't waste people's time with a forty-five-minute icebreaker unless it is clearly teaching something of importance to your topic (and your workshop is three days long).

Consider including a quick, energizing icebreaker after returning from lunch or when you reassemble the room into groups of participants who don't know each other. The key to success with icebreakers is a fast pace and brevity.

ASSIGN AN IMPORTANT ACTIVITY BEFORE THE COFFEE BREAK

Plan an activity that requires a small group discussion, such as a relevant quiz or a debatable question, before the morning coffee break. Give participants ten to fifteen minutes, maximum, to work together. Then debrief them, explaining how the exercise ties in with what will be covered. The key concept here is to get participants immediately engaged in a useful activity that requires interaction with others.

POSTPONE INTRODUCTIONS
UNTIL AFTER THE COFFEE BREAK

As part of your orientation, announce that there will be participant introductions but not until after the coffee break. This is counterintuitive, and it works. A few introverted participants are sometimes uncomfortable having to introduce themselves to an entire group of strangers, even after they have participated in an icebreaker. Following the coffee break and icebreaker, they will have had a chance to connect socially with a few people and will, therefore, be more relaxed.

BE COMPLETELY READY
WHEN THE FIRST PARTICIPANT ARRIVES

Consider that the workshop starts the minute the first participant arrives. This means that your PowerPoint is up and running, background music is playing, and all other preparations are complete. This will free you up to be totally present with participants as they arrive, welcoming them and making small talk. We can't underestimate the value of some small talk with participants before a workshop begins.

USE AN OPENING SUMMARY

For complex topics, present major points and conclusions at the beginning of the lecture, to help participants organize their thoughts as they listen to subsequent material. This structure maximizes understanding and retention.[2]

LIMIT LECTURES TO
TWENTY- TO THIRTY-MINUTE MODULES

In *What's the Use of Lectures?*, Donald A. Bligh suggests that "lectures should not be longer than twenty to thirty minutes—at least without techniques to vary stimulation."[3] More recently, David Rock, founder of the NeuroLeadership Institute, echoed this advice: "A session can't have more than 30 minutes of formal, preplanned delivery."[4]

Break up the lecture with interactivity tools. After about twenty minutes, introduce a change to recapture your audience's waning attention. Following are some ways to sustain interest. Choose whichever is appropriate for your topic but make sure that there is variation so that you are not always choosing the same activity after each twenty-minute lecture.

THE DEAQ MODEL[5]

This is a classic model for maintaining attention and ensuring that the information from the lecture is absorbed. It involves using one of these four components:

- **Digestion.** Ask participants to discuss the ideas amongst themselves. This will help them assimilate the information before you move on to new information.

- **Exercise.** Ask participants to complete an activity on their own or with each other in order to experience what they have just learned.

- **Application.** Ask participants to discuss the applications or implications of an idea. Have them appoint their own facilitator.

- **Questions.** Conduct a standard Q&A session before moving on to new information.

QUIZ OR SELF-ASSESSMENT

Find or create a quiz that helps participants determine their existing knowledge of the topic or their level of capability in whatever you are teaching. If you are conducting a workshop on how to start a business, for example, include a quiz to help participants measure their entrepreneurial potential.

REFLECTION ACTIVITY

After a lecture on a variety of tools or solutions, give participants a few minutes to note one way that they might use the idea in their personal or work life. Ask two or three people to share their ideas with the room.

ONE-MINUTE SUMMARY

After a particularly complex module, give participants a few minutes to write down the answer to the following question: "What do you want to remember from this module?"

WRITE, PAIR, SHARE—SQUARED

This is a variation of the classic think, pair, share strategy. It works well for more complex issues. Here is how it works:

1. Craft an open-ended question that expands on your lecture or serves as an introduction to your next lecture.

2. Give participants about two minutes to write down their answer to the question. Tell them that their note will be shared with someone else in the room later. This forces those who might otherwise use the time to do a quick check of emails to be engaged in the process.

3. Ask participants to pass their note to a person at another table.

4. Instruct participants to pair up with another person in the room (not the one who received their note). Give them five minutes to share the answers/ideas from the notes. They can elect to disagree with what was written and give their own opinion instead.

You can stop here with the exercise, or you can ask each pair to pair up with another pair. Now give this group of four a follow-up question that expands on what they have just discussed.

REAL PLAY

Avoid role play, as most people, especially technical and senior people, dislike it. Research shows that out of thirty-two learning tools, role play is the least favorite.[6]

The technique I use is a variation of role play, which I call "real play." Setting up a fake scenario and inviting people to play roles creates discomfort for most people and ends up being a waste of time. Instead, I ask participants to select a real situation from their work life—a past, present, or expected one. For example, if you are training participants to handle a difficult conversation, ask them to select such a conversation that they need to have with someone and practice it with a partner. The partner does not role-play the other party in the conversation but rather acts as a coach/advisor or sounding board, reflecting back what they heard, how the speaker came across, what worked, and what didn't work. The partner also helps the speaker analyze the problem from different perspectives. The key to success in this type of exercise is to make it about real situations, clearly drawing a link between the activity and each participant's real life.

Here are some tips for conducting real play in a workshop:

- Connect the real-play exercise to the theoretical concepts you taught in the lecture.
- Try to match a more junior person with a highly skilled or senior co-worker to maximize the chances of full engagement. If you pair together two veterans, they may not be seriously engaged in the process.
- Announce clearly that this is not role play but real play. Alternatively, you can consider calling it "skills practice" or "simulation," as some trainers do; this name will be better received, and it more accurately describes what the activity is about anyway.

SIMULATION GAMES

Find a good-quality simulation game that applies to what you are teaching. For example, for leadership training, consider a high-end package such as Leadout.[7] This simulation shares theories and skills developed by management experts. Big Fish is another company that provides high-quality games.[8] For free training games, check out Thiagi.[9] Check out, as well, the Six Seconds site for team-building games, such as Sneetch Marbles.[10]

Make sure that any games you use totally support the lecture's content; otherwise, they will be perceived as a waste of time.

GET THEM MOVING

It is estimated that about 10 to 30 percent of learners are kinesthetic. Therefore, plan to add physical movement to your workshop experience. This approach is appreciated even by non-kinesthetic learners. Here are some ideas for including physical movement:

- **Switch partners.** Have participants change partners for each new activity.

- **Change the mix.** Alter the mix of participants in each group. A good time to do this is after lunch, and again in the morning on the second day of a multiple-day workshop.

- **Divide the class.** Divide the class in half and ask participants to stand in two lines, facing each other. Conduct a brief activity, such as sharing some thoughts on a topic for ninety seconds and receiving thirty seconds of advice. Once one round is completed, have the first person from one line move to the end of that line; ask everyone in that line to move ahead one spot. When everyone has moved, each person will be facing a different individual. Ask them to go through the exercise with their new partner. Repeat three times in total. This is a high-energy exercise that works well for afternoon sessions.

BE THE GUIDE ON THE SIDE

Writer Kate Halverson has said, "If you are all wrapped up in yourself, you are overdressed."[11] There is a seduction to being the one with all the knowledge. Being in charge feeds our ego and makes us feel good. But it is also a slippery slope. Audiences pick up subtle signals if we indulge ourselves in the role of workshop guru; this most certainly erodes our credibility. Josh Freedman, CEO of Six Seconds, put it best: "It's seductive to be the one with the answers ... I have to notice this seduction, stay out of that pattern, and continually re-choose to be who I mean to be as a teacher—a partner in a shared process of meaningful discovery."[12]

An average facilitator tells you what to do. A great facilitator shows you how to do it. A superb facilitator sets the stage for you to arrive at your own conclusion.

ENGAGE, ACTIVATE, REFLECT

Consider using a method such as the one provided by Six Seconds in their training. In this highly effective method, learning is designed to take advantage of the way the brain works, to create a state of highly activated brain engagement called "hot cognition." Hot cognition is defined as "a motivated reasoning phenomenon in which a person's responses ... are heightened. A learner who displays hot cognition is highly attentive and interactive with information. Basically, hot cognition is the masterful entwinement of both a person's emotions and their thoughts."[13]

With this process, learning is structured into three phases: engage, activate, and reflect.[14]

- **Engage.** Engaging is about creating both cognitive and emotional readiness for what you are teaching. This is a crucial first phase because if you've successfully engaged learners, then at the end of this phase, they will be more eager to accept the ideas and take them further.

- **Activate.** Activating is about bringing the concepts you are teaching to life. Using meaningful experiential exercises and real play (as discussed earlier) gives participants an opportunity to experience key ideas right in the workshop. Learning requires practice and application. At the end of this phase, participants have new knowledge, changed attitudes, and stronger skills.

- **Reflect.** Reflecting is the opportunity for participants to synthesize and apply the information they have learned. Using many of the methods discussed in this chapter, such as pair sharing and group sharing, learners pause to recognize what they've learned and to reflect on how they can apply that learning back at the workplace. Reflecting propels learners into action.

For more details on this method, visit http://www.6seconds.org/2012/01/27/structuring-transformational-learning/.

HONOR PEOPLE IN THE ROOM

Most of us are focused on how we feel when we deliver a presentation or training session. I challenge you to switch this around and consider how others feel about themselves when they are in your presence. Shift the focus away from you and find opportunities to recognize, encourage, and support your participants. Practice appreciative intelligence by seeing the potential in everyone in the room. Maya Angelou once said, "People will forget what you said; they will forget what you did; but they will never forget how you made them feel."

USE MUSIC STRATEGICALLY

Nothing enlivens a workshop experience like music. Here are some guidelines for utilizing music in a workshop:

- Play upbeat instrumental music softly in the background when participants arrive in the morning.
- Play similar music during the first coffee break.
- Play instrumental music softly in the background when participants do self-reflection exercises.
- After lunch, five minutes before starting the afternoon session, play an upbeat song.
- During the afternoon coffee break, play your most upbeat music.
- Play a mellow piece while the participants complete workshop evaluations.
- Always end a workshop with an upbeat piece.

HAND OUT PRIZES

Winning something, even if it is small, has an emotional impact on us. Hand out gifts for various activities. Good-quality chocolate bars wrapped in gold paper, small books pertinent to your topic, and coffeehouse gift certificates make good prizes.

TAKE FIVE

Schedule five-minute breaks every hour. This provides a quick, energizing respite. Play music and get the participants used to the fact that when the music stops, you resume the workshop whether everyone is in the room or not. Watch them all come back on time.

LIMIT THE TIME YOU SPEND ON THE BUSINESS CASE

A common error that trainers make is to spend a long time at the beginning of a workshop explaining the need for whatever it is they are teaching. While it's important to set the context, spending too much time on this is sure to erode your credibility as a dynamic, engaging facilitator. People know that the topic is important; that's why they signed up! Don't waste their time. Give them what they came for, which is the *how*, not the *why*.

ASK, DON'T TELL

Develop questions that encourage participants to analyze, synthesize, and evaluate the information presented. This is an effective way to engage the audience intellectually and emotionally.

A common error is not allowing participants enough time to think. Studies show that a pause of five to thirty seconds results in a more in-depth discussion.[15] Be comfortable with silence. For in-depth questions, you can say, "I am going to give you a minute or so to write down some of your thoughts and we will then open it up for discussion." Listen to several answers. This prompts everyone in the room to continue to think about the question. It can also deepen learning by adding dimensions that the first answer may have missed.[16]

Know how to ask questions that probe deeper and keep the discussion flowing. Types of questions you might ask include the following:

- **Clarification.** Example: "Can you give me an example of how this worked out for you?"
- **Hypothetical.** Example: "What would happen if...?"

- **Linking.** Example: "How does your observation fit in with what was discussed earlier regarding…?"

If you need help in this approach to teaching, consider reading *Discussion As a Way of Teaching*, by Stephen D. Brookfield.[17]

CREATE INTERACTIVE SLIDES OR HANDOUTS

To re-engage the brain, have participants write something. One way to do this is to leave out key words or phrases in your slides or handouts, forcing participants to write them in as you disclose them. One word of caution: don't overdo this. It is very annoying to get handouts with a large number of blank spots.

USE A VARIETY OF SUPPORTING MEDIA

Consider incorporating the following types of media into your workshop:

- **Cartoons.** A relevant cartoon, once in a while, when unexpected, re-engages attention and drives the message home through humor. The Resources section provides an extensive list of sources for buying cartoons.

- **Cool websites.** At strategic points, share websites that are pertinent to your topic. Most participants appreciate this. It's a way of expanding their knowledge beyond what is discussed in the room.

- **Videos.** Today, there is a wealth of online video clips on every imaginable subject. Find a video that adds value to your content. One of the best sources is the thought-provoking talks presented at TED.[18] Keep video clips to no longer than three to four minutes.

PRACTICE EMPATHY WITH EVALUATION FORMS

While workshop evaluations are essential, completing two- or three-page evaluations is an annoying chore for most participants. Here is an opportunity to practice empathy, by putting yourself in your participants' shoes and providing them with a brief, one-page evaluation. An evaluation of this length is more likely to be completed by a larger percentage of participants.

CLOSE WITH A BANG

Send everyone home inspired. Craft your parting words with care. Honor participants by thanking them and praising them for their contributions to the presentation. Reinforce what went well. Stress your belief in their ability to succeed in whatever they learned in the workshop. End with an upbeat tone and, if time permits, conclude with a celebratory activity.

END EARLIER THAN SCHEDULED

Ending fifteen minutes earlier than the announced time is always a bonus. Even five minutes earlier is appreciated. The worst thing you can do is end later than the announced wrap-up time.

BE COMFORTABLE WITH BEING WRONG

There is a proverb that says, "When one teaches, two learn." Participants don't arrive at a workshop with a blank slate, and you will encounter some who may challenge you, contradict you, and even correct you. I encourage you to move from seeing this as a possible personal attack to embracing it as a sign of engagement in the content. There is a noble feeling when you divert the spotlight in the room from you to an audience member.

If a workshop participant corrects you, relinquish your fear of being wrong and accept the correction. We become bigger and stronger when we can gracefully admit, "You're quite right. Thank you for making me aware of this." This approach keeps us on the path of authenticity. As public speaker Kathryn Schulz puts it in her insightful book *Being Wrong: Adventures in the Margin of Error*, we spend a great deal of effort trying to conceal wrongness.[19] But it is what makes us human: "The capacity to err…is inextricable from some of our most humane and honorable qualities: empathy, optimism, courage and conviction."

PRACTICE EMOTIONAL INTELLIGENCE

Nowhere is the practice of emotional intelligence more powerful than when we are in front of a room of people, in charge. Following are just a few of the emotional intelligence skills that we need to master:

- Awareness of our emotional reactions and those of others
- Effective management of our reactions
- Awareness of our brand (how we come across)
- Ability to sense the mood in the room
- Reading faces
- Practicing empathy
- Being cool under fire
- Helping others save face
- Validating others

In helping others learn, whether they are adults or children, these skills are as important as our knowledge of the topic. According to renowned psychologist Daniel Goleman:

> *The neural wiring between our thinking and emotional centers…means our feelings can either enhance or inhibit the brain's ability to learn. And now the new field of social neuroscience has shown that while two people interact, their emotional centers impact each other, for better or for worse.*[20]

There is much we can do as workshop facilitators if we are emotionally self-aware and socially intelligent. We can create a climate that will boost participants' ability to stay engaged and learn.

Above all, be human. Don't make your workshop just a cognitive learning experience. Train with heart. In Chinese, there is one character for heart, mind, and spirit; we can derive inspiration from this wisdom. Mark Walsh of Integration Training in the U.K. wrote a beautiful article on the topic. It is well worth reading. As he says, "In the future we may no more want our training to be heartless than mindless—both are integral parts of…being a person."[21]

The winning combination is expertise in the subject matter and a high EQ (emotional intelligence). It's the journey from good to great.

UPDATE YOUR MATERIAL

Update and renew your content on a regular basis. This will make your workshop a more engaging experience for your participants and will help you stay energized. It is said that knowledge doubles every fourteen months. Don't let yourself become stagnant.

If your passion and enthusiasm are dampened from continuing to teach the same material, get out of the business. "A good teacher," someone once said, "is like a candle—it consumes itself to light the way for others." Be that type of teacher.

BE EMOTIONALLY ENGAGED

"The emotional labor of engaging with the work and increasing the energy in the room," Seth Godin has said, "is precisely what you sell. So sell it."[22] Emotional labor is the work you do with your feelings. It is of paramount importance when you present, and especially when you teach. The concept of emotional labor originated with Arlie Hochschild, author of *The Managed Heart: Commercialization of Human Feeling.* Hochschild writes about managing our emotions, which can be done in two ways: surface acting and deep acting.

Surface acting refers to when we display an emotion that we don't experience. The emotion is deliberately created rather than natural or spontaneous. Surface acting is akin to wearing a mask. It's artificial, and it doesn't work. Most audience members have a built-in radar that detects such pretense.

Deep acting is when we show emotions that are real: "Here, display is a natural result of working on feeling … a real feeling that has been self-induced."[23] We do this by recalling personal experiences in which the feeling was actually present. It's "acting" from the heart. This is the only credible way of displaying our emotions, of showing others how emotionally engaged we are with our material.

A wonderful example of deep acting occurred in Sam Harris's TED presentation, "Science Can Answer Moral Questions."[24] At the point in the presentation when Harris talked about honor he paused, and you could see that he was emotional. In his blog, he describes the experience:

> *I almost burst into tears when describing the practice of "honor killing." I knew that I was going to talk about fathers who murder their daughters for the crime of being raped, and I knew exactly what I was going to say about them. But I hadn't known that my own daughter would take her first steps the morning of my lecture.*[25]

This is a brilliant example of a speaker's emotional engagement.

When we present, we must ask ourselves what emotions or feelings we want to telegraph to the audience. Here is a partial list to consider:

- Joy at the opportunity to speak about things that matter
- Love of our topic and our audience
- Hope that we can inspire
- Optimism that we can make a difference
- Anxiety that our participants miss the point or that we waste their time
- Trust in others and in the human process
- Empathy in understanding our participants' hopes, aspirations, and needs
- Humility to honor the audience's intelligence
- Courage to be ourselves
- Gratitude for the privilege to have others listen to us

CHAPTER 10

POWERPOINT IS NOT EVIL: BOZO USERS ARE

"If you start reading your material because you don't know your material, the audience is very quickly going to figure out that you are a bozo. They are going to say to themselves: 'This bozo is reading his slides. I can read faster than this bozo can speak. I will just read ahead.'"[1]
—**Guy Kawasaki**

No matter how well you know your material, if you are inept in your use of PowerPoint slides, it can tarnish your credibility as a presenter. It is important to remind yourself of a few universal principles for effective PowerPoint usage.

Edward Tufte, a Yale University professor, is a staunch critic of PowerPoint. He wrote his famous essay "PowerPoint Is Evil" in 2003.[2] We have made some strides since then. Today, a small band of astute presenters not only avoids the evils that Tufte talks about, they use PowerPoint to great advantage.

Unfortunately, they are a small group. Notwithstanding the plethora of books and articles on how to avoid the evils of PowerPoint usage, there is still a large group of presenters in whose hands PowerPoint becomes a mangled mess. They are like novices at the potter's wheel. The majority of presenters create mind-numbing slides, which erode their credibility as speakers and inflict pain on the audience.

This chapter provides fourteen pointers to help you avoid using PowerPoint in a way that detracts from your credibility.

SHOW ONLY ONE IDEA PER SLIDE

Don't cram several points on one slide. This reflects a non-digital mentality, i.e., approaching the slide with the attitude of saving "paper." By crowding six points on one slide, you force the audience to continue to stare at all six while you navigate through each of the points. Simply create six slides, one for each point. Use a very large point size for the type and add a supporting visual—and now you have a powerful slide!

USE THE ASSERTION-EVIDENCE SLIDE DESIGN

The assertion-evidence technique for designing slides is particularly effective for technical information and for long presentations. This method replaces presenting information in bullet form. Instead, as the slide title, use a concise, complete headline sentence, no longer than two lines, to state your main idea for that slide. In the body of the slide, add a visual (an image, chart, graph, equation, etc.) to support the assertion. This method is described fully at Penn State College of Engineering's website.[3] You can watch a fun video from James Madison University for another great illustration of this method.[4]

Figure 6 shows an example of an assertion-evidence slide.

Oxygenated blood begins its journey through the body in the lungs

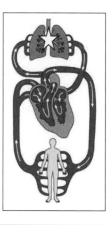

Figure 6
Source: Lauren Sawarynski, Bioengineering, Pennsylvania State University. Cited in Michael Alley, "Rethinking the Design of Presentation Slides: The Assertion-evidence Structure", http://www.writing.engr.psu.edu/slides.html.

USE GOOD-QUALITY PHOTOS

Avoid all clipart, which almost always looks cheap and chintzy. Also stay away from stock photos that come with PowerPoint, if you want your presentation to be unique. Invest in some good-quality photos instead. Here are some sites that provide creative photos at a very low cost. (These and other sites are included in the Resources section.)

- **Fotolia.** High-quality, royalty-free images and vector illustrations, starting at a very nominal fee. (www.fotolia.com)

- **iStockphoto.** High-quality, royalty-free images and vector illustrations, starting at a very nominal fee. (www.istockphoto.com)

- **Sprixi.** This site requires a small monthly membership fee, for up to 2,000 searches per month. It has images with liberal licenses such as Creative Commons. (www.sprixi.com)

- **Flickr.** Search within Creative Commons–licensed content for stunning free photos. Read Seth Godin's advice on using this site.[5] (http://www.flickr.com/)

- **Stockvault.** On this site, photographers and designers share their free photos for non-commercial usage. (www.stockvault.net)

- **Stock.XCHNG.** This free stock site offers browsing and sharing. (www.sxc.hu)

Mason Hipp wrote a good article on a five-step process for finding the perfect image.[6] One of the steps entails turning the abstract idea for your photo into concrete search terms that you can use to find your image; this speeds up the search and gets better results. For example, the concept of "freedom" can be represented by sitting on the beach; "difficulty" can be symbolized by hurdles, a narrow staircase, or a rock climber; "inviting" can be an open door, outstretched arms, or an embrace. Brainstorm as many concrete terms as you can.

In *Brain Rules: 12 Principles for Surviving and Thriving at Work, Home, and School,* John Medina states, "Vision trumps all other senses... We learn and remember best through pictures, not through written or spoken words."[7] Wherever possible, substitute a relevant image for text. Don't just add the image for background decoration. The image needs to help the audience understand and identify with your point.

Choose novel images that engage the audience's attention. For example, if you are looking for an image to illustrate "giving a helping hand," you might choose one of the two photos in Figure 7: either a traditional photo, such as Image 1, or an edgier photo, such as Image 2. It takes a little more time to source a more unique image, but the results are worth the effort.

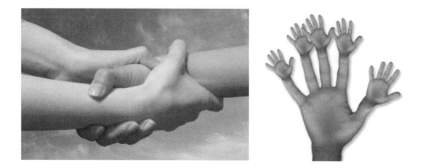

Image 1   Image 2

Figure 7
Source: iStockphoto.

USE THE "HOME PAGE" HYPERLINK TECHNIQUE

Create a "home page" slide at the start of the presentation that links to slides within the same deck, so you can skip from slide to slide in response to questions without leaving the slide show view. This gives you a way to present in a non-sequential manner, if necessary, to respond to the audience's questions. This technique dramatically enhances audience interaction and releases you from the tyranny of a sequential PowerPoint presentation. You can watch a brilliant video from James Madison University, which takes you through an entire hyperlinked presentation.[8]

ADD INFOGRAPHICS

Infographics (information graphics) are representations of complex data in simplified, easy-to-understand visuals. They make information instantly clear. You can see examples of infographics at the website Cool Infographics.[9] You might also find the article "10 Awesome Free Tools to Make Infographics" helpful.[10]

CREATE POWERFUL GRAPHS

Consider purchasing business graphic software to produce flow charts, graphs, and charts of high visual quality. You might consider Three D Graphics[11] and SmartDraw.[12]

AVOID STANDARD POWERPOINT TEMPLATES

Everyone is by now accustomed to all of the templates that come preinstalled with PowerPoint. Using these templates signals a lack of distinction. If you don't have a corporate template, consider buying a professional one.

Check out various template vendors and choose the most distinguished template you can find—one that is uncluttered, without distracting backgrounds and extraneous design objects. Here are some sources to consider:

- **SlideRocket.** This company helps you create beautiful presentations online. (http://www.sliderocket.com/resources/)

- **SlideShop.** This company offers inexpensive, professional slides for graphs, maps, shapes, and diagrams. (http://www.slideshop.com)

- **Template Monster.** Check out the template identified "Marketing Plan" as a sample of a professional, uncluttered PowerPoint template. (http://www.templatemonster.com/powerpoint-templates/31318.html)

CHOOSE COLORS WITH CARE

Spend some time learning which color is best suited for your audience. For example, dark blue is a good corporate color, as it signals trust and reliability. The same color for healthcare professionals indicates death! Red is great for a healthcare presentation, as it symbolizes energy and good health, but for a financial presentation, it evokes unprofitability.[13]

Avoid red and green text, as these colors bleed and are harder to read. Also, statistics show that 10 percent of males or approximately one person in twenty suffers from red-green color blindness.[14]

CREATE CONTRAST BETWEEN THE TEXT AND BACKGROUND

A recommended color scheme is a dark blue background with white letters; or a white (or warm beige) background with black, dark blue, or other dark text.

Here is what Garr Reynolds has to say about color:

> *If you will be presenting in a dark room (such as a large hall), then a dark background (dark blue, grey, etc.) with white or light text will work fine. But if you plan to keep most of the lights on (which is highly advisable) then a white background with black or dark text works much better. In rooms with a good deal of ambient light, a screen image with a dark background and light text tends to wash out, but dark text on a light background will maintain its visual intensity a bit better.*[15]

Your biggest struggle will be with branding or marketing professionals in your organization. Their mission is to maintain brand identity by coordinating the colors used in corporate presentations with the colors in the company's logo and other design elements. This sometimes results in poorly legible text-and-background combinations for slide projection. A recent example from a client involved light turquoise text on a white background. If you find yourself in this situation, you have no choice but to follow company rules; however, you can exercise some small measure of intelligent disobedience by using the darkest shade of the required text color.

PRACTICE JUDICIOUS USE OF FONTS

Research by the Stanford Persuasive Technology Lab showed that fonts impact the perception of credibility.[16] Avoid script fonts such as Comic Sans, which scored high as youthful and casual. "Use the same font set throughout your entire slide presentation," advises Garr Reynolds, "and use no more than two complementary fonts (e.g., Arial and Arial Bold)."[17]

Two of the safest fonts to use are Arial and Tahoma, because they are sans serif and project well even on low-resolution projectors.

If you are preparing the presentation on one computer and using another computer to deliver the presentation, you run the risk that the fancy font you selected is not installed on the second computer. In this case, PowerPoint will use the next best font, and this does not always work well: the text may look jagged and will not display well. If you are given a PowerPoint presentation with a font that is not installed on your computer, and you want to avoid manually changing the font throughout the entire presentation, there are sites that will help you identify the font. Check out Identifont[18] and What Font is.[19]

The larger the type size you use on a slide, the better. The *minimum* type size you should use is 28 points. This forces you to display less text on a slide. Remember that a lot of text on a slide is the quickest way to be labeled a poor presenter.

As part of his video discussion of his 10-20-30 rule, Guy Kawasaki advises that the smallest type you should have on a presentation slide is 30 points.[20] The larger the type, the better. As he says, this forces you to know your material.

He also advises using no more than 10 slides and talking no longer than 20 minutes. While this is good advice for presenting to venture capitalists who have to listen to many presentations in a limited time frame, it doesn't necessarily apply to all situations. Not all presentations need to be limited to just 10 slides and only 20 minutes.

Some technical and educational presentations, for example, may need to be delivered over several hours. In this case, you can have a lot more slides—provided they are not mind-numbing, all-text slides with 12-point type!

ELIMINATE THE WORD CONTINUED

Adding the word *continued* in the header or footer is fine for a Word document. It is not okay for a slide. Your PowerPoint slide is not a document; it is part of a live show that supports what you say.

AVOID LOGO OVERLOAD

Your company logo should appear on the first and last slides only. The same applies to the company tag line and other items, such as confidentiality and copyright information. Don't subject your audience to continuously viewing these items, which add nothing to the content. People are not there to be bombarded by your brand; they are there to learn or gain something from you. (You can keep the logo and confidentiality and copyright information on each page of the handout.)

ADD A BEAUTIFUL TITLE SLIDE

Spend some time creating an attractive title slide for your presentation. This is the "first impression" slide that people see as they enter the presentation room, and it is likely to be displayed for some time until the presentation starts. Add an attractive and powerful visual, in addition to the title of the presentation, your company name and logo, and your name.

DON'T EVER READ YOUR SLIDES

Reading your slides is a credibility killer. Avoid this by creating slides that contain key words and images, not entire sentences. If a slide contains some information that the audience needs to read (e.g., a quotation), read silently along with them. Only read the slide out loud if it is not clearly visible to everyone.

As Yogi Berra said, "You can see a lot by observing." Nowhere is this more helpful than when we set out to learn how to create powerful, professional slides. For inspiration, view professional slides at the following sources:

- "World's Best Presentation Contest Winners" for 2007[21] and "Winners of World's Best Presentation Contest" for 2009[22]
- "A Collection of Some of the Best SlideRocket Presentations"[23]

The Resources section lists other sites where you can view professional slides as well as the best books on PowerPoint design by some of the giants in the field. Familiarize yourself with the concepts in these books. Buy one or two copies and make them available to any personnel who craft your slides. Consider hiring a coach to help you, or get a professional to design your slides. It is worth the investment if you want to boost your credibility as a presenter.

With the proliferation of books, articles, and blogs on how to create effective PowerPoint presentations, as well as SlideShare,[24] there is no excuse today for bad slides. Audiences are becoming more discerning and, if you show up with mind-numbing, crowded, all-text slides, you can be sure that this will erode your credibility as a presenter, sooner or later. Invest your time in acquiring this skill now.

CHAPTER 11

A LONG-DISTANCE AFFAIR: VIRTUAL PRESENTATIONS

"You're hosting the event,
but it's a cocktail party, not a lecture."[1]
—**Guy Kawasaki**

Chances are that if you haven't already delivered an online presentation, you will be required to do so someday very soon, as virtual presentations are becoming increasingly common. Don't be caught off-guard. Start developing your competence in this essential skill now, so that you can pull it off with composure and credibility when the time comes.

First, let's briefly look at some audience reactions to online presentations. The percentage of individuals who sign up for a webinar and then leave it before completion is high. What are the reasons for this? MarketingSherpa produced a useful survey, which is summarized in Figure 8.[2]

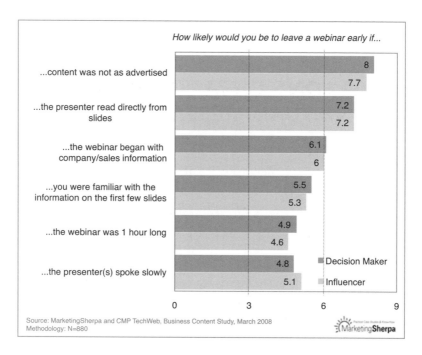

How likely would you be to leave a webinar early if...

...content was not as advertised — Decision Maker 8, Influencer 7.7

...the presenter read directly from slides — Decision Maker 7.2, Influencer 7.2

...the webinar began with company/sales information — Decision Maker 6.1, Influencer 6

...you were familiar with the information on the first few slides — Decision Maker 5.5, Influencer 5.3

...the webinar was 1 hour long — Decision Maker 4.9, Influencer 4.6

...the presenter(s) spoke slowly — Decision Maker 4.8, Influencer 5.1

Source: MarketingSherpa and CMP TechWeb, Business Content Study, March 2008
Methodology: N=880

Figure 8
Source: MarketingSherpa, "Attendees Share Webinar Turnoffs: Find Out Which Ones Top the List," July 15, 2008.

Most audiences today are used to fast-paced, multimedia presentations. They schedule attendance at a webinar in the midst of a busy day, charged with a multitude of other commitments. This means that they are very prone to become distracted by other priorities, and they will very quickly relegate your voice to the background if your webinar is not intellectually stimulating, interesting, educational, and fast-paced.

If they are forced to attend because the web conference is mandatory (e.g., for a corporate sales, support, or service initiative), they will stay for the duration. But in the safety of their unseen presence, they will tune you out frequently and start to multitask.

To present online with credibility, you need to show care and empathy for your audience. Put yourself in their shoes and ask yourself these questions:

- How is your information coming across? Is it clear?
- Can they see what you see?
- Are your instructions easy to follow?
- Is your voice distinct and audible?
- Are you projecting enthusiasm?
- Are you providing them with what they need?

Here are some tips for practicing virtual empathy.

BE BRIEF

A cardinal rule is that your content needs to be to the point. Say only what is essential, and be ruthless in pruning out extraneous material. Ken Molay, President of Webinar Success, has this to say about the optimal webinar length:

In most cases, marketing and general informational webinars should have a maximum length of 60 minutes. Training and educational webinars can go as long as 90 minutes. After this, attendees have a hard time maintaining concentration and remaining sedentary in front of their computers. Sessions of 90 minutes or more should include a break for people to get up, stretch, and take care of critical needs.[3]

SCHEDULE WEBINARS AT THE OPTIMAL TIME

Research shows that it is best not to schedule webinars on Mondays or Fridays. In North America, a time that works for a wide variety of time zones is 10:00 a.m. PST (11:00 a.m. MST, 12:00 p.m. CST, and 1:00 p.m. EST).[4] Of course, if your webinar will have participants outside of North America, you must take their convenience into consideration.

PLAN FOR INTERACTIVITY

Plan to deliver information in short segments (ideally, no longer than seven to ten minutes) before you add interactivity. Web conferences used to be mostly one-way: from the speaker to the audience, with limited audience interaction. This setup was much like a Webcast, which transmits information in one direction, as when you watch a concert online. The format is changing, however; now, a successful virtual presentation needs to contain some audience interactivity or it will fall flat.

One of the most effective tools for adding interactivity to your virtual presentations is the polling feature. Learn how to use it. Once you conduct a poll, remember to share the results with the audience, either immediately after the poll is completed or at some point later in the presentation. I prefer the latter, if it works from a logical point of view, as it adds another opportunity to break the flow of "lecturing" and interact with the audience.

It is important that your polling questions add value; in other words, they need to tap into issues of concern to the audience. If the polling questions are clearly there to stimulate some gratuitous interactivity, you will not get a good response—and, even worse, you will waste the audience's time.

FACILITATE CLEAR COMMUNICATION

There are some basic logistical items to keep in mind when planning and conducting a webinar. Having co-presenters can be very effective: one presenter speaks and accepts questions orally, while the other presenter focuses on the chat functionality and other written interaction.

On a technical note, if possible, it is helpful to have a third person overseeing practical issues—muting noisy lines, giving microphone rights to callers, and the like. This division of labor allows the presenters to focus on the substance of the session.

MENTION PEOPLE'S NAMES

If it's a small group and you know the participants' names, address them by name as you respond to their questions. This practice helps you bond with the participants and creates a sense of closeness. Using people's names can also help you manage traffic. Participants in a webinar often can't see each other, so a lot of cross talk occurs. Calling on people controls the flow of communication. Also, participants pay more attention if they think they might be addressed specifically.

MAKE SURE YOU ARE IN A QUIET ROOM

I attended a webinar once where the speaker's dog was heard barking in the background. Other times, participants could hear honking horns or a lawn mower. Don't shuffle papers, as microphones amplify this noise, and it's irritating to listeners.

Put your cell phone and other devices on silent, and disconnect any other phones in the room. Don't forget to close your office door and place a sign on it to let others know that you are on a web conference. If you are conducting a webinar from a home office, place a sign on your front door to prevent any interruptions or noise in the house. Use a headset to eliminate echo and feedback; be sure to test this equipment before the event.

PUT OUT A WELCOME MAT

Just as a well-planned workshop starts the minute the first participant enters the room, a well-planned webinar starts the minute the first person accesses the virtual room. Approximately fifteen minutes before the official start of the presentation, have some soft music playing. Show a welcoming, introductory slide that provides the following information:

- Name of the online presentation
- Date of the event
- Start and end times
- Company name and logo
- Name(s) and photo(s) of presenter(s)
- Any other general information, such as programs participants may need to access during the presentation (e.g., Excel)

This virtual welcome mat accomplishes three important objectives: it creates an immediate, positive first impression; it helps audience members test and adjust for sound; and it puts participants' minds at rest that they have successfully accessed the right conference or webinar. It is not unheard of that someone accesses the wrong one. It happens!

START AT THE SCHEDULED TIME

Starting right on time is a common courtesy for audience members who have already signed in and are ready to go. It's annoying to have to wait online and be forced to listen to idle chitchat about the weather or other inanities from a well-meaning moderator or other participants trying to fill the air until the show can start.

START WITH A BANG

Immediately catch your listeners' attention with a startling visual, question, rhetorical question, outrageous statistic, cartoon, video clip, photograph, quick anecdote—anything that is relevant to your topic and is engaging. It is a signal that the time they will spend listening to you will be well spent.

Minimize opening platitudes such as, "I am delighted to be here. We have a large number of people on this webinar. This will be a great presentation ..."

DISPLAY AN AGENDA SLIDE

Include a slide that clearly outlines your road map for the presentation. It should answer these questions: What are your objectives? What are you planning to cover? What benefits will your audience take away? Be specific, and make promises that you will fulfill.

MENTION HOUSEKEEPING ITEMS

Remind people to mute their phones. Be clear on how you plan to handle questions; explain the "raise hand" and "chat" features. It is best to allow questions as you go along. Often, a presenter runs out of time and the question period is omitted. This leaves the listener with a negative impression. Depending on your presentation, you can announce that you will take questions at the end.

If you find that you are about to run out of time, it is much better to deliberately shorten the presentation and be candid about it. Simply say that you will stop here in order to allow for questions. If you find that there are fewer questions than you anticipated, you can always end by briefly covering the points you left out.

Another strategy is to promise to email participants the part that was not covered. While this can be more cumbersome and add work, it is the mark of a professional. Consider any promise you make an unpaid debt.

BE SUCCINCT WITH INTRODUCTIONS

Keep introductions of yourself and your company to a minimum. I have attended webinars where the presenter and the host spoke for ten minutes about themselves, their company, and all of their achievements. This is an outrageous waste of the audience's time. Participants will hang on if they need the information that you are going to provide, but you will have encouraged them to think, "This is going to be painful to listen to. I'll check some email or read the budgetary report while they are speaking. I will keep an ear open for anything important that they say."

TEACH SOMETHING RIGHT OUT OF THE GATE

Consider delaying introducing yourself and your company until after you have provided one or two pieces of information that are useful to the audience. Engage the participants right away with powerful, practical information that they need—before you force them to listen to your spiel. Patricia Fripp expressed it best: "You'll need to say something the listeners care about before they will care about who you are."[5]

KEEP YOUR PROMISES

Be scrupulously honest when you conduct an educational webinar. Even if it is free and not fee-based, stick to your promise to deliver value—and don't use it as an opportunity to insert a sales pitch. Today's audiences are very astute at spotting disguised sales pitches. If you are delivering value, your webinar will be a natural sales tool without your having to peddle your wares. It is a question of integrity.

Duping the audience into signing up with the expectation that they will receive useful information and then hitting them with infomercials is a quick way to lose credibility. I recently attended an online paid educational web conference, which featured five speakers. One of the speakers spent about 40 percent of the time inserting comments and hints about the number of assessments his company sold a year, the happy clients they have, and the fact that they were the first to come up with the concept of the topic they were discussing. This didn't add any value to me or the other listeners. We signed up to understand the topic, not the economic success and achievement of the presenter's company. I cannot stress enough that subtle advertising destroys credibility.

MAINTAIN A BRISK PACE

Think lively! A monotonous voice is a detriment any time you present in person and even more so when you present online. Remember to add enthusiasm to your voice. People can hear a smile. Speak faster when covering routine items, and slow down when covering more complex aspects. Remember to pause after an elaborate or significant point to allow the message to sink in. Occasionally, pause to ask questions like the following:

- "Is everyone with me?"
- "Are there any questions?"
- "Is it all clear so far?"

Pause before a new section, to help listeners keep the pace.

SPEAK LOUDER THAN NORMAL

Not infrequently, I attend a webinar where, for the first few slides, I have to strain to hear what is being said. Then a moderator takes me out of my misery by signaling to the presenter that their voice is not clearly audible. Ask if the audience can hear you once you begin your talk. Don't use the speakerphone. The audience will hear you better if you speak directly into the phone.

In a webinar, speaking louder and projecting your voice add energy and presence—which are particularly important, as participants experience you only through your voice. Often, people speak with more power and volume when they are standing. If you must sit, avoid slouching, which compresses your voice and reduces your energy.

CATER TO DIFFERENT LEARNING STYLES

While auditory learners can follow your voice easily, visual learners need additional pointers. For example, use the animation feature to introduce bullets one at a time, as you address each point. If you have several bullets on a slide and you spend several minutes on each, clarify how what you are saying connects to the slide. For example, you might say, "The second bullet on the slide refers to our pricing..." As an added help, use a pointer to help the visual learner follow you without effort.

USE TWO COMPUTERS

If you can, work with two computers. Use one to conduct the presentation and the other to log into the webinar as a participant. This gives you an opportunity to see, in real time, what the participants see. It will increase your confidence and give you the power to make any adjustments needed. For example, if you move to the next slide but the participants don't see the slide right away, you will know to slow down so that they can catch up.

GIVE THE AUDIENCE SOMETHING TO LOOK AT

Use a large number of slides in a webinar so that the audience has something to look at while you speak. Move quickly through your slides. Experts recommend that a slide remain on for no longer than ninety seconds. It goes without saying that you should not read your slides—but this guideline is too important *not* to mention. For an online presentation, it is doubly important to craft slides that are visually appealing.

FREQUENT WEBINAR CIRCLES

To learn from professional speakers, sign up for as many webinars as you can. Listen critically; note what you like, what worked, and what didn't work. I like this recommendation from meeting facilitator Julia Young: listen to the Peabody Award–winning *Fresh Air* with Terry Gross, on NPR.[6]

DISTRIBUTE QUALITY HANDOUTS AHEAD OF TIME

Providing a handout is the ultimate sign of empathy for your online listeners. Visit Ken Molay's *The Webinar Blog* and read, in particular, his article "Using PowerPoint Notes to Create a Handout."[7] Generally, it is best not to provide all of the handouts in advance, as participants will read ahead. Instead, supply a partial set of handouts before the presentation and follow up with the balance of the handouts afterward. (Let participants know at the start of the presentation how they can obtain the balance of the handouts after the event.)

END AT THE PROMISED TIME

Concluding the webinar punctually is a sign of professionalism and respect for your listeners' time.

PART TWO

AUTHENTICITY

CHAPTER 12

MAKING IT REAL: YOUR AUTHENTICITY

*"Just be what you are and speak from your
guts and heart—it's all a man has."*
—Hubert Humphrey

Authenticity is the watermark for trust—the crown jewel of credibility. It's the audience's perception of our integrity, the clarity of our message, and our genuine care and attention. It's the total absence of artifice.

We live corporate lives that call for conformity and adherence to convention as a prerequisite for belonging, getting along, and getting ahead. As a consequence, in the majority of jobs, there are few channels of true self-expression. Over time, we take on a corporate persona that becomes entangled with our self-identity. When we present, all eyes are upon us, watching us closely—and that persona becomes magnified. It's as though we now "act the part" onstage. Presenting becomes, subtly, a thespian activity where the presenter is almost portraying a person giving a speech rather than being a person giving a speech. People who are normally comfortable in their own skin suddenly go into "presenter mode" and start to lose their genuineness and spontaneity.

Guard against unwittingly turning your presentation into a staged performance. Focus on delivering your content sincerely, with genuine enthusiasm. In his autobiography, James Earl Jones said it well: "Make sure the words are yours. Push them from the very bottom of your soul. The performance will take care of itself."[1]

Here are some pointers to boost your authenticity in presenting. The next chapter will delve further into the topic.

WATCH VIDEOS OF AUTHENTIC SPEAKERS

Someone once said, "A good example has twice the value of good advice." Just as some animals can detect the earth's magnetic field and use it as a compass for migration, so the audience who listens to a presentation is able to detect when a person is being himself or herself and when they are "on." Audiences are very adept at spotting counterfeit attitudes; they are distanced by what they perceive to be fake, and they respond positively to genuineness.

Take inspiration from the sincere demeanors of speakers such as Sir Ken Robinson, Seth Godin, and the late Randy Pausch, to name a few. These individuals speak in an uncontrived and unpretentious way that oozes authenticity. When you watch them speak, you have an overwhelming sense that what you see is what you get. They might as well be sitting across from you, having a conversation with you over coffee. There is no mask to keep in place—a total absence of artifice. They are simply immersed in the conversation with the audience, sharing their message. They have taken their insecurities and ego out of the equation. The Resources section provides links for videos of some of the best presenters today.

Watching great speakers is not about imitating them. As Emerson said, "Imitation is suicide." Trying to imitate another speaker becomes another form of acting, of playing a part; therefore, it is a further erosion of authenticity. Instead of imitating authentic speakers, be inspired by the naturalness of their delivery and of the words they use. They show us the power of being genuinely oneself. This is a most attractive place to be.

DON'T USE INFLATED LANGUAGE

We often unwittingly erode our authenticity with the language we choose to use. As John Reh aptly put it, "If you want your service department to handle more calls per day, tell them that. Don't tell them they need to 'reduce the time interval between customer-interface opportunities.'"[2] The corporate lexicon is littered with such inflated language. Why do we say "eating establishments" when we mean "restaurants," or "instructional delivery skills" when we talk about "teaching"? We believe that inflated language sounds more professional, when in fact, it rings hollow and comes off as artificial. Audiences know that this is not the way the presenter normally speaks.

One of the formulaic expressions of the corporate vocabulary is the ubiquitous word *solution*. Here is an example: a company claims to have "a suite of integrated, innovative, and cost-effective solutions that deliver targeted results." This doesn't tell us very much about what they do until the following statement, which explains in plain language that they provide a system for making airline reservations online.

And what exactly do the following expressions mean?

- "Accelerating value realization"
- "Value-added enterprise"
- "Value-added service"
- "Leveraging our expertise to provide a seamless platform"

Table 1 provides a brief list of commonly used expressions that weigh down our communication and detract from authentic talk. They are only a small representation of the repertoire of inflated language—words or expressions that have lost their energy and power from overuse. They lack freshness and are the equivalent of a factory-prepared meal.

A window of opportunity	Arguably	At the end of the day
Bandwidth	Best of breed	Blamestorming
Bleeding edge	Blue sky thinking	Business entity
Client-centric	Competitive landscape	Cutting edge
Deliverables	Drill down	End-to-end
Enterprise	Granularity	Guesstimate
Holistic	Iconic	Impactful
Incent	Initiatives	Interface
It's in the company DNA	It's not rocket science	Knowledge transfer
Leading/industry-leading	Mission critical	No brainer
Open architecture	Organic growth	Out-of-the-box
Paradigm shift	Radar screen	Robust
Scalable	Seamless integration	Secret sauce
Solution provider	Synergy	Ten-thousand-foot view
Toxic asset	Value proposition	Win-win
Wake-up call	Well positioned	World class

Table 1

I recommend three resources to help you eliminate inflated language. The first is Brian Fugere's book *Why Business People Speak Like Idiots: A Bullfighter's Guide*.[3] The author's website, *Fight the Bull*, is also worth visiting.[4] Download Bullfighter 1.2. This free application includes a jargon database and what the authors call a "Bull Composite Index Calculator," which allows you to see how much jargon is in your PowerPoint or Word document.

The second resource is David Meerman Scott, who has analyzed hundreds of websites and press releases looking for meaningless "gobbledygook" words. Have a look at his Gobbledygook Manifesto[5] and his Gobbledygook Grader,[6] which evaluates your written content for jargon, clichés, and hyperinflated words. While the program deals with language used in press releases, it also applies to presentations.

The third resource is Lake Superior State University, which has been compiling "The Complete List of Banished Words" since 1998.[7]

ELIMINATE FILLER WORDS

In ancient Rome, anyone looking for a fine-quality marble statue would seek shops or stalls that bore the sign "Sine Cera" (Latin for "Without Wax"). *Sine cera* is the root of our word *sincere*. Some artisans used melted beeswax to fill the cracks and imperfections in lesser-quality marble statues. Ethical artisans, however, didn't hide the flaws; they hung the sign "Sine Cera" on their statues. Today, we use *sine cera* as a metaphor or symbol of authenticity.[8] We can use the same metaphor for "fillers" that are added to pad sentences—meaningless words that act as verbal caulking. These have been referred to as "wax words." Table 2 gives a small selection of wax words that illustrate the point.[9]

Wax Words	Sine Cera (Without Wax) Words
Until such time as	Until
In the final analysis	Finally
Due to the fact that	Because
In spite of the fact that	Although
In the event that	If
Each and every one	Everyone

Table 2

Every word you use in a presentation requires more work from your listeners to process, so lighten their listening burden by removing unnecessary words. English poet Robert Southey put it beautifully: "It is with words as with sunbeams. The more they are condensed, the deeper they burn."

BE CONVERSATIONAL

Seth Godin advises to speak "in English. Like the person you are, not the flat, stressed, boring person you become when you have a PowerPoint under your control."[10] Approach your presentation as a conversation. One of Bill Clinton's strengths as a speaker is the absence of linguistic gyrations; he speaks in plain, everyday language that connects him to his audience. He doesn't speak as though he is reading.

How can we achieve this? It's very simple. Speak for the ear. Presenters often fall into the trap of speaking the written word. They derive their information from written sources and then use the information "as is"; that is, they take the written words and speak them, or more accurately, recite them.

The listener can hear that the speaker is repeating written passages, which always sounds stilted. This is particularly important to remember for those who learned English as a second language. Foreign speakers typically learn formal, written English in the education system, without extensive exposure to colloquial English.

Carefully review your presentation and replace everything that sounds like written language with colloquial expressions. Table 3 provides some examples to illustrate the point.

Corporate Non-speak	Human Speak
expeditious	fast
afford an opportunity	let, allow
adjacent to	next to
ascertain	find out
adversely impact	hurt, set back

Table 3

One of the most useful sites for avoiding stilted language is *Plain Language: Improving Communication from the Federal Government to the Public*. It offers a wealth of resources, including a table of simple words that can be used to replace stilted ones.[11]

In an effort to sound erudite, we also end up using sentences that are convoluted and grammatically incorrect. It seems to be a business convention, for example, that the word *I* or *me* is replaced by the word *myself*. We hear phrases such as "an email from myself." You need to overcome your misguided fear of using the word *I* or *me* when it is grammatically correct.

Tell stories in your own words. One of the most illustrative examples of before (stifled) and after (uncluttered, conversational) storytelling comes from Ira Glass, host and producer of Chicago Public Radio's *This American Life*. As he has said, "Everything is more compelling when you speak like a human being." Watch his video on how *not* to tell a story.[12]

MAKE SURE THE WORDS ARE YOURS

When you are given a corporate script that you didn't write, for a presentation that you have to deliver, take the time to make some of the words your own. You can still respect the core of the message that the company wants you to deliver while rewording some of the material so that your delivery doesn't sound mechanical. It's the difference between a rigid presentation and a fluid one. Even if the audience doesn't know you, they will sense if the words are not yours.

DON'T BE AN ARTFUL DODGER

It's a sad commentary on our times that people who dodge questions *artfully* are more trusted than those who answer questions truthfully but with less polish. This is the conclusion from the research of Michael I. Norton at Harvard Business School.[13] One of the ways artful dodgers do this is by using transition devices:

> *The first 10 words of an answer are key to creating an artful dodge. You'll hear phrases such as "That's a good question" or "I'm glad you asked that." But what follows is the answer to another question. We humans have finite attention. The more words there are in a transition, the harder it is to make the cognitive link between the question and the answer.*

After hearing an artful dodge, subjects in the study had lower recall of the question asked.

Don't dodge questions. Practice truthful answers so that you can respond with integrity and polish. Style and substance are key.

AIM TO BE GENUINELY LIKABLE

There is a growing body of research on the link between likability and authenticity and trustworthiness. Even expert witnesses, providing court testimony, are viewed as more credible if—in addition to appearing trustworthy, knowledgeable, and confident—they are also likable.[14]

During presentations, we often unwittingly behave in ways that make us unlikable. We may subtly manifest our annoyance if someone asks us a controversial question, use veiled sarcasm with an audience member we may not like, inadvertently ridicule someone who makes what we consider to be a stupid point, or not mask our impatience and irritation if something goes wrong while presenting.

This brings us to a second important point about likability. While it is important to work on being likable as a presenter, it is also important that you genuinely like the audience. People can tell when we like them. Robert Cialdini, author of *Influence: Science and Practice*, states, "Everything changes in the hands of somebody who likes me. Maybe I believe an insurance agent or a stockbroker is a real expert. Well, expertise may not be enough. I want an expert who likes me and then I've got both sides covered."[15] We are more likely to protect the interests of those we like, which boosts our trustworthiness and credibility.

As a presenter, being likable is as important as being knowledge-able about your topic. Keep in mind the 15/85 percent rule of presentations: 15 percent of your presentation's success is based on your formal education, background, and knowledge. The other 85 percent is based on who you are rather than what you know. As Keld Widinberg Jensen (nominated best speaker in Scandinavia) put it, "The main reason you will be successful is whether people will trust you and believe in you ... whether they will find you cred-ible and likable."[16]

What is likability behaviorally? Here are some pointers:

- Show friendliness to the audience. The most mundane way to do this is to smile and to use people's names.
- Use "we" or "us" when referring to groups.[17]
- Disclose some personal information. This makes you approachable and more familiar and natural to the audience.
- Be confident without being arrogant. A little humility is attractive and makes us likable. Even if you don't agree with an audience member, don't use defiant contradiction.
- Be authentic. If you don't know something, admit it. Acknowledge a potential error or an uncertainty.
- Be respectful. Don't arrive late or go over the time allotted for the presentation.
- Respect the listeners' intelligence by not lecturing to them.
- Dress for the occasion.

- Don't forget to thank an audience member for asking a question or making an observation.
- Use a conversational tone and less technical jargon.
- Use direct eye contact.

In the words of Roger Ailes, president of Fox News Channel, "If you could master one element of personal communications that is more powerful than anything…it is the quality of being likable… If your audience likes you, they'll forgive just about everything else you do wrong."[18]

CHAPTER 13

THE CROWN JEWEL OF CREDIBILITY: YOUR TRUSTWORTHINESS

"The truth is that trust rules."[1]
—James Kouzes and Barry Posner

Trustworthiness is a critical dimension of credibility as a speaker. While your expertise and competence are quantifiable, trustworthiness is an abstract notion. It is about the audience's perception of your character—who you appear to be.

BE WORTHY OF OTHERS' TRUST

To ensure that the audience sees you as trustworthy, keep in mind the following fourteen questions. If you can answer *yes* to all of them, then you will be seen as trustworthy. If not, ask yourself what you can do to be worthy of the audience's trust before you start speaking.

1. Are you providing your audience with all of the information they need, or are you choosing to withhold important facts?

2. Are you making honest and true statements, or are you sugarcoating your words?

3. Are you sincere? That is, do you mean everything that you say?

4. Are you being fair by presenting both sides of an argument or all the pros and cons of an issue?

5. Are you unbiased in your assertion? Are you presenting an objective point of view?

6. Do you have the audience's best interest at heart—or, at least, are you not impeding their best interest?

7. Are you showing the audience that you have taken their needs into account?

8. Do you have a hidden agenda? Is your motive for speaking clear to the audience?

9. Are you avoiding the use of business speak to "spin" negative situations as positive?

10. Can the audience rely on what you are saying? Are you going to do what you say you will?

11. Can the audience rest assured that the information you are providing is up-to-date?

12. Are you using data from reliable sources? Is the audience aware of where the data is coming from?

13. Are you giving due credit to other people's ideas?

14. Are you well prepared to deliver the presentation in a competent manner?

If you cannot give a categorical *yes* to all of these questions, you can be sure that some audience members will sense it. Certain telltale gestures and facial expressions will signal a lack of trustworthiness.

SHOW GOODWILL TOWARD YOUR AUDIENCE

Goodwill is an essential component of credibility as a speaker. It's more important than your degrees and titles. As D. Joel Whalen humorously put it, "We prefer a skilled doctor who shows tenderness and a good heart over a world-class bastard."[2] Goodwill is the audience's perception of your concern for their interests or needs, also referred to as perceived caring. Communication research has shown that there are three elements that comprise perceived caring:

- **Understanding.** This element of perceived caring refers to exhibiting behavior that tells the audience that you grasp their concerns.

- **Empathy.** This element refers to exhibiting behavior that tells the audience that you not only understand their concerns but that you accept them as valid—even if you don't agree with them.

- **Responsiveness.** This element refers to how attentive you are to others, how well you listen, and how quickly you acknowledge a person's attempts to communicate with you.[3]

Remember these three dimensions and make them part of your toolkit. Use them throughout your presentation, and especially during the question-and-answer period. Empathy, in particular, is the most fundamental element of goodwill toward others. "If there is any one secret of success," Henry Ford said, "it lies in the ability to get the other person's point of view and see things from his angle as well as your own." This is empathy.

ALIGN YOUR ACTIONS WITH YOUR ESPOUSED VALUES

Consider that your reputation often precedes you. When you speak about values, do you live these values on a daily basis, in good times and bad? The quickest way to erode your credibility is to profess what you don't consistently practice.

How often have we heard an executive speak of employees as "our most important asset"—yet that person rarely ventures out from behind their desk to truly connect with the people who actually do the work? Or do you speak about the importance of quality, but when there is a tight deadline, you tell people to take shortcuts in order to get the job done? When you do this, people start to tune you out and stop believing in you. They end up just paying lip service the next time you speak.

Credibility requires alignment between actions and values. First, you have to truly know what you stand for. As Jim Kouzes and Barry Posner state in *The Leadership Challenge*, spend some time exploring your "inner territory."[4] Do this by finding your voice and clarifying your values: "You *must* know what you care about. Why? Because you can only be authentic when leading others according to the principles that matter most to you. Otherwise you're just putting on an act."[5]

To align your actions with your values requires self-awareness and self-management, two foundational aspects of emotional intelligence. If you need guidance in this area, study one of the numerous frameworks for emotional intelligence that are available. One example is the Six Seconds Model of EQ (emotional intelligence), which helps to develop skills in three areas:

- **Know Yourself.** What are your emotions, values, goals, reactions, wants, needs, etc.? In other words, what drives your behavior?

- **Choose Yourself.** In the moment, how do you want to present yourself? How do you step out of your habitual reactions, patterns, fears, and assumptions so that you can live up to your values and show up authentically?

- **Give Yourself.** Stay focused on what is important in the long run, on what makes a difference. Remind yourself that your actions should serve your larger goal. Concentrating on your long-term goal makes presenting less about being "onstage" and more about connecting to your higher self and staying focused on your deeper purpose, on what matters. This is liberating and empowering.[6]

You can find information about this model and other emotional intelligence models in the Resources section.

ADMIT MISTAKES EARLY

Mistakes can be credibility killers—or boosters. A mistake is less important than how you deal with it. As Tom Peters puts it, "Foul up. Fess up. Fast. Fastidiously."[7] In other words, tell the whole truth; don't sugarcoat what happened. Call a meeting quickly and deliver your message about what happened and why. If it is your mistake, own up to it. Watch your credibility soar. We trust those who risk being vulnerable in order to maintain integrity.

I strongly encourage you to take a few minutes right now to watch Tom Peters's video "Leadership: The Problem Isn't the Problem."[8] In it, Peters delivers a compelling message about establishing and maintaining credibility when things go wrong.

PART THREE

PERSONAL PRESENCE

CHAPTER 14

WHEN YOU ENTER A ROOM: YOUR PERSONAL PRESENCE

*"'Tis very certain that each man carries in his eye
the exact indication of his rank in the immense scale of men,
and we are always learning to read it. A complete man
should need no auxiliaries to his personal presence."*
—**Ralph Waldo Emerson**

An important component of credibility as a speaker is presence. Presence is a calmness in your bearing and appearance. It's the first thing people notice about you when you enter a room.

Nalini Ambady, a psychology professor at Tufts University, conducted extensive research on first impressions, based on observing someone's behavior for a very brief time. She named these brief exposures "thin slices" of experience; they were as short as six seconds. The experiments asked volunteer students to watch silent, six-second video clips of teachers they didn't know delivering a lecture and then to rate the quality of their performance. Surprisingly, they were able to accurately predict the successful teachers from these thin slices of exposure.[1] Other studies have shown that snap judgments of other people can occur in even as little as thirty-nine milliseconds![2] Often, that initial impression changes very little after longer exposure to the person.

Recently, neuroscientists at New York University and Harvard University discovered the ancient neural circuitry—comprising the amygdala and posterior cingulated cortex—that is responsible for these first impressions. They scanned the brains of volunteers forming opinions of people they newly met and found that activity surged in the brain areas that help us make very quick assessments of people. This age-old circuitry is designed to keep us safe by allowing us to make a rapid-fire assessment of our environment; this circuitry is now used for social situations. "Humans have always been engaged in making decisions on what's important and what's not, and social decision making is taking advantage of these primary systems in the brain," according to Daniela Schiller, the scientist at the forefront of this study. "When you meet a person, they might say something, or look a certain way, or behave a certain way…you have very little information on which to form an opinion, but it is almost instantaneous and you can't withhold from doing it."[3]

These rapid, automatic assessments by the audience can affect our credibility before we even speak. It is important, therefore, to develop presence and intelligently manage those first impressions rather than leave them to chance. Even if you are nervous, you can control some of the elements of presence. By practicing the tips in this chapter, you can adopt a poised, composed demeanor.

A speaker who has presence exhibits these six features:

1. Proper posture
2. Sustained eye contact
3. Effective pausing

4. Appropriate dress

5. Adaptability

6. Composure

This chapter deals with the outward manifestations of presence: posture, eye contact, pausing, and clothes. The next three chapters deal with the internal manifestations of presence: adaptability and composure.

POSTURE: YOUR MOTHER WAS RIGHT

One of the most immediately visible—and mundane—aspects of presence is your posture. You have heard this before, and it bears repeating: catch yourself if your shoulders are drooping and your head is tilting forward. The combination of slumped shoulders and downward gaze creates a dint in your self-assuredness. Guy Kawasaki put it succinctly: "Relaxed sternum = loser; high sternum = winner."[4]

A January 2011 article in *Scientific American* reported that changing our body posture, by literally standing tall, not only makes us look more powerful but actually makes us *feel* more powerful. Most interestingly, standing tall with an expansive posture (widespread limbs, spread-out body) as compared to a constricted posture (limbs touching torso, collapsed-in body) correlated with higher levels of testosterone and a lowering of cortisol.[5] Higher testosterone makes us feel more powerful, in charge, and willing to take risks. Higher cortisol produces negative effects (such as impaired cognitive performance), which lead to feeling less powerful. This gives new meaning to our mother's exhortations to stand tall.

I am not advocating postural rigidity. In Japan and South Korea, for example, postural rigidity is a sign of credibility—it signals someone who is higher up on the hierarchy. In North America, however, it is quite the contrary. It detracts from perceived credibility and is associated with lower social influence. Here, a relaxed stance that conveys grace and "being comfortable in one's skin" telegraphs credibility.

How do you know if you are maintaining the right posture? Try this little trick from Pat Hough: "Imagine someone grabs your hair at the crown and pulls you skywards. Your neck straightens and your shoulders move back to their proper rest position."[6] This also helps you avoid looking at the audience with your chin up, which can be misinterpreted for arrogance.

Dance experts know the importance of posture for conveying confidence and fluidity. They advise their students to keep a good base or balance. For a speaker, this means standing with feet hip-width apart. Feet need to be parallel, toes pointing forward—not in Charlie Chaplin or duck position. Weight needs to be evenly distributed on both feet. Feeling the weight in the inside edges of the feet adds good posture. It will make you feel rooted and balanced.

Contrast this with the "John Wayne" stance: slumping to one side by resting on one leg. This posture may feel comfortable, but it detracts from your presence. Avoid, as well, the "Miss Goodie Two Shoes" stance: feet so close together that you look like a thin reed, easily shaken by the wind. There is no expanse in such a stance, no stability—and consequently, no presence, no power.

Another stance that telegraphs a lack of confidence is standing with legs wide apart in an overly exaggerated open stance. You've seen it before. Sometimes it is accompanied by closed arms. It is the equivalent of a peacock spreading its plumage to make an impression. People notice the exaggeration, and all it signals is a lack of self-assurance.

Being mindful of posture is not about being unnatural and overly concerned about stance in order to "make an impression." It's simply about raising awareness of how we carry ourselves. Adopting a balanced stance not only conveys confidence and comfort but, more importantly, makes us *feel* more genuinely confident and comfortable on our own two feet. To put it simply, the correct body posture leads to genuine feelings of confidence and power.

An excellent showcase of presence through posture is Mark Walsh's video demonstration "Evocative Leadership: Length, Width and Depth."[7] Watch how Walsh takes the audience through an exercise to center themselves and adopt a posture of confidence and substance.

EYE CONTACT: ARE YOU LOOKING AT ME?

Empirical studies have proven that eye contact is a nonverbal determinant of credibility as a speaker.[8] Generally in North America, we know that not looking someone in the eye carries negative connotations: the person can be viewed as insecure, aloof, cold, arrogant, uninterested, bored, afraid, anxious, shifty, untrustworthy, or even lacking in intelligence or understanding. This perception is a hefty price to pay for avoiding eye contact.

Eye contact plays a pivotal role in developing presence and in connecting with others. It is not possible to connect with furtive eye contact! A study at the University of Alaska proved the crucial importance of gaze direction.[9] The researchers measured the function of the brain's frontal lobes and found that during the observation of a direct gaze, the left frontal lobe of the person being tested was more active than the right frontal lobe. However, when the person observed an averted gaze, the right frontal lobe was more active. The left-dominated reaction is linked to approach, while the right-dominated one is linked to avoidance.

Eye contact, then, whether it is direct or averted, affects the functioning of the neural mechanism that regulates approach or avoidance behavior: "Another person's direct gaze prepares for an approach, an averted gaze for avoidance," discovered Professor Jari Hietanen, head of a research project at the University of Tampere in Finland.[10] In the context of a presentation, direct eye contact invites the audience to "approach" you (mentally come nearer to you); averted eye contact causes the audience to "avoid" you (mentally stay away from you). Obviously, you will connect more effectively with an audience that approaches you rather than avoids you.

Eye contact narrows the distance between you and the audience. It is impossible to have presence without mastering eye contact. In some cultures, especially those that are hierarchal, looking someone directly in the eye is to be avoided, as it is seen as a sign of disrespect. However, if you are presenting in North America, you need to get out of your comfort zone to master direct eye contact. It will pay dividends.

Here are some tips to help you with eye contact.

MAINTAIN SUSTAINED EYE CONTACT

One of the worst habits is continuously pivoting your head from side to side to address the audience, without stopping to look at anyone in particular. For eye contact to be effective, it has to be sustained: you need to look at one person until you complete a thought or make a point, then move on and look at another person. Even seasoned presenters often forget to do this.

Don't break eye contact with someone in the middle of a thought. When you maintain eye contact with an audience member until you complete one thought, you are essentially having a small conversation with that person for the duration of that thought. Otherwise, you end up flitting from one person to the next, scanning the room and never connecting with anyone. Skilled speakers give the impression that they are having a small conversation with each member of the audience. And indeed they are.

Once you are comfortable with maintaining eye contact for one complete thought, consider extending it and maintaining eye contact with the same person for two or three thoughts. Then do the same thing with another audience member. The audience will have the experience that you are holding a conversation with many members and, by extension, with all of them—even those who don't feel looked at get the feeling that you are speaking with the entire audience. Give this technique a try. Even if you are already a seasoned presenter, incorporating sustained eye contact into your style will take your presentation skills to the next level and power your communication. This is my promise to you.

SPOT THE FRIENDLY FACES IN THE ROOM

If you are very anxious, start by looking at a few friendly individuals and having a personal conversation with them until you feel comfortable; slowly increase your sphere and look at more people until you are able to connect with everyone. In extreme cases, if you are very nervous at the beginning of your presentation, you can gaze at the audience but rest your eyes between two people. You can also look at their eyebrows instead of directly into their eyes. This gives the impression that you are looking at them. This is a strategy for the first few minutes only, until your initial nervousness subsides.

PAUSES: SAY LESS, SLOWLY

"Sometimes when a room is silent," author and speaker Scott Berkun has said, "people pay more attention than when you are speaking."[11] Pauses make you look composed and thoughtful. They tacitly tell the audience, "I don't have to rush through what I say because I belong up here." Well-timed pauses telegraph self-assuredness and are the secret of powerful presenters such as President Barack Obama, who speaks variously at a rate between 90 and 110 words per minute. Martin Luther King's famous "I have a dream" speech was spoken at 90 words per minute. Contrast this with a speech by Hillary Clinton where she spoke 188 words per minute.[12]

My workshop participants often ask me what the right rate of speech is. The right speed is your normal way of speaking. Anything else will be contrived. Speak at your normal, conversational rate and just remember to slow down somewhat when you deliver your main thesis and important points. If you naturally speak too fast, just remember to add pauses. Don't speak as though you are rushed but as though you have adequate time to deliver the presentation.

While speaking very fast is normally the mark of a nervous presenter, there is another group, the highly creative, high-ability "everyday genius," who is referred to as the highly gifted/talented type in Mary-Elaine Jacobsen's book *The Gifted Adult: A Revolutionary Guide for Liberating Everyday Genius.* One of the common criticisms that this type hears is, "Can't you just slow down?" This group has a need to move quickly from idea to idea. Here is how one of them describes his perception of others:

> *It's like the rest of the world is moving along at twenty-four frames per second, normal film speed, but to me that's slow motion. Even when somebody's talking during a meeting, I swear I look at their mouths and it's like I'm advancing the tape frame by frame on my VCR … it's more like the world's a blender on stir and I'm on liquefy.*[13]

While slowing down and adding deliberate pauses are no doubt frustrating for this type, these measures are particularly important given the nature of the topics that they normally present. If you are in this group, remember that pauses give your audience a chance to see the concept you are outlining—to mentally view the image you are painting. Skillful pausing is not about oversimplifying content, it's about being an astute communicator.

A question I am sometimes asked is, "How long should I pause?" There is no specific rule. It would be unnatural and almost impossible to try to time a pause. All we need to remember is that there are short and long pauses. Here are some tips for mastering pauses.

SHORT PAUSES (ABOUT ONE TO TWO SECONDS)

A short pause is the equivalent of a comma in a sentence or the period at the end of a sentence. It is the way we pause when we speak naturally, in a conversation.

- **Pause frequently, especially at the beginning of your presentation.** This will help you to slow down. Take inspiration from Bob Kerrey, President Emeritus of The New School and former Nebraska governor and senator: "You'll get the audience's attention by pausing. Without that, you can actually insult the audience. They'll know you're in a hurry and you want to get your speech over with."[14]

- **Pause between points.** This will allow your audience to absorb what you've just said.

- **Pause after you have displayed a slide with a complex visual, such as a diagram or chart.** If you don't take this time, the audience will tune out your first words while they are examining the entire slide. They cannot focus fully on both at the same time.

- **Pause after saying something humorous.** Comedians know to do this; they have a sense of impeccable timing. Speakers often forget to allow for this, and their subsequent statement is lost in the din of laughter. A polished presenter is fully present in the moment and responds to the audience's feedback instead of being on autopilot and continuing with their delivery.

- **Pause to allow people to take notes.** Even if people are not writing down notes, they are making mental notes.

Give people time to assimilate an important point you make before moving on to the next.

* **Pause slightly after asking a rhetorical question.** The rhetorical question does not elicit an answer but rather makes a point. The slight pause allows the audience to hear that unsaid point.

LONG PAUSES (ABOUT THREE SECONDS OR LONGER)

A longer pause forces the audience to pay attention to what you just said. It emphasizes the importance of your statement.

For inspiration, watch Bill Clinton's speech at Harvard's 2007 Class Day. Clinton is a master of long and short pauses.[15] Below is a sample of his speech:

> *And when I think that I might be 99.9 percent the same as him, I can't* **[SHORT PAUSE]** *even fathom it.* **[LONG PAUSE]** *So, I say that to you.* **[SHORT PAUSE]** *Do we have all these other problems, these Darfur atrocities? Do I wish America would adopt sensible climate change regulation, do I hate the fact that ideologues in the government doctored scientific reports, do I disagree with the thousand things that are going on? Absolutely.* **[SHORT PAUSE]** *But it all flows* **[SHORT PAUSE]** *from the idea that we can violate elemental standards of learning and knowledge and reason and even the humanity of our fellow human beings because our differences matter more.* **[SHORT PAUSE]** *That's what makes you worship power over purpose. Our differences matter more.* **[LONG PAUSE]**

What do you notice?

- There is a short pause just before and a long pause just after he talks about feelings: "... even fathom it."

- There is a long pause before he delivers an important message: "So, I say that to you ..."

- He speaks fairly fast when he is enumerating a list of items that he knows the audience knows: "Darfur ... climate change ... doctored scientific reports."

- There is another short pause after "it all flows," to announce the next message.

- He adds a short pause for emphasis after delivering a key message: "our differences matter more." He then repeats the key message and adds a long pause.

A study reported in *ScienceDaily* found that individuals who engaged in frequent pauses were more successful in persuading others than those who were perfectly fluent![16] "When people are speaking, they naturally pause about 4 or 5 times a minute," said Jose Benki, a research investigator at the University of Michigan Institute for Social Research. "These pauses might be silent, or filled, but that rate seems to sound the most natural ... If interviewers made no pauses at all, they had the lowest success rates getting people to agree to do the survey. We think that's because they sound too scripted." In the study, even people who paused too often and were seen as disfluent had higher success rates in persuading others than those who were perfectly fluent.

CLOTHING: DO YOU LOOK THE PART?

Whether we like it or not, the ghostly communication of clothing is real and, on a subconscious level, it can impact our credibility. Yoon-Hee Kwon at Northern Illinois University conducted a study to explore the role that being properly dressed or not properly dressed plays in enhancing ten occupational attributes.[17] The results showed that males generally believed proper clothing can enhance the occupational attributes of intelligence, competence, knowledge, honesty, and reliability.

A study by Gwendolyn S. O'Neal and Mary Lapitsky at Ohio State University, "Effects of Clothing As Nonverbal Communication on Credibility of the Message Source," showed that when individuals being rated were appropriately dressed, they were assigned significantly higher credibility and intent-to-purchase ratings.[18]

Gordon Allport, one of the pioneers in developing ideas of human personality, said, "With briefest visual perception, a complex mental process is aroused, resulting within a very short time in judgments of... profession and social caste of the stranger, together with some estimate of his temperament,... friendliness, neatness, and even his trustworthiness and integrity."[19] Clothing is a part of that visual perception.

Think of your clothes as packaging. If packaging was not important, we would not be spending billions of dollars on the packaging of products. Consumers, including you, judge a product by its packaging before buying. The same goes for our digital habits. The Stanford University Persuasive Technology Lab conducted an interesting study, "How Do People Evaluate a Web Site's Credibility?"

Nearly half of all consumers in the study assessed the credibility of sites based in part on the appeal of the overall visual design.[20]

If you are in the camp that considers style and substance to be mutually exclusive, I encourage you to shed that notion. We are a visual society and there is vast empirical evidence supporting the importance of the visual in influencing people's opinions, particularly the opinions of those who don't know us well. Your clothes can have an impact on your presence as a speaker, whether you buy into the notion or not.

Even if you work in an extremely casual environment, for the day of the presentation, you need to dress *slightly* better than you normally would. This sends a tacit signal that you care enough about the presentation to have made an effort. A person with a professional mindset uses situational awareness and adjusts accordingly. As Guy Kawasaki states in *Enchantment: The Art of Changing Hearts, Minds, and Actions,* "Underdressing says, 'I don't respect you. I'll dress any way that I please.'"[21] Respect pays dividends.

Dress sense is really common sense. Most people will not pay undue attention to what you wear except in two circumstances: if you are overdressed or underdressed for the occasion. The best impression you can make is no impression at all when it comes to clothing. Aim for an understated simplicity to match your composure and calm demeanor.

With that in mind, here is Clothing 101—what to do to enhance your credibility as a speaker or, more importantly, to prevent your clothes from detracting from your credibility:

- **Observe your executives.** For guidance on appropriate business casual, take an inspiration from the executives or middle managers in your organization.

- **Ask for advice.** If you are presenting before an unfamiliar audience or in a foreign country, seek advice regarding appropriate attire.

- **Remove distractions.** Avoid elaborate jewelry and shiny watches. They catch the light and are distracting.

- **Choose appropriate shoes.** For men, avoid athletic shoes. For women, avoid open-toed shoes or sandals. Mid-high heels are more appropriate for presenting.

- **Avoid what hides your face.** Avoid tinted glasses, so that people can see your eyes. Forget the ill-advised hairstyle of having bangs so long that they cover one of your eyes.

- **Cover any tattoos.** While tattoos have now entered the mainstream and are no longer an emblem of the sailor, there is no doubt in my mind that visible tattoos will detract from your credibility. Burleson Consulting has this to say about tattoos: "Today, a prejudice still exists within corporate America about tattoos, especially since there is a clear and direct correlation between income, education and the percentage of those populations who have tattoos."[22]

- **Don't wear wrinkled clothing.** While this is common sense, today, it's no longer common practice. A recent survey, "Do Clothes Make the Manager? Employers Weigh In," reported that wearing wrinkled clothing is among the top four personal attributes employers say would make them less likely to extend a promotion. The same negative impression extends when you are delivering a presentation.[23]

Don't forget the basics that you know about dress. As speaker Gini Dietrich put it, "…everyone complains that we still don't have a seat at the boardroom table, yet we think it's okay to wear jeans as our professional dress. If you want to sit at the table in the greater business conversation, you have to look like you belong there."[24] Nowhere is this truer than with presentations in the corporate world.

For more tips on appropriate dress, check out the CareerBuilder site, which contains extensive information on the topic.[25]

Lastly, dressing well when you present boosts your authority. As Robert Cialdini said, "People are more willing to follow the directions or recommendations of a communicator to whom they attribute relevant authority or expertise." A study showed that three times as many pedestrians were willing to follow someone crossing against a red light if the person was wearing a business suit and looked like an authority.[26] Clothes are powerful. Don't leave them to chance.

CHAPTER 15

STEP OUT OF YOUR COMFORT ZONE: ADAPTABILITY

*"To effectively communicate, we must realize that we are
all different in the way we perceive the world and use this
understanding as a guide to our communication with others."*
—Anthony Robbins

There is a Chinese proverb that says that the wise adapt themselves to circumstances, as water molds itself to a pitcher. Adaptability is the willingness to step out of one's comfort zone and learn to adapt to different circumstances. It marks a key difference between successful and unsuccessful individuals. It's a manifestation of personal presence and a powerful way to boost our credibility in the eyes of the audience.

Adaptability is also one of the key results of emotional intelligence. It is a particularly important quality when we are presenting to different audiences: it entails high self-awareness, awareness of others, and the willingness to manage our approach in order to reach our listeners and meet their needs and ours.

This chapter is about raising your self-awareness regarding your communication patterns. It will provide you with tips to help you get out of your comfort zone and mold your approach, so that you can connect with your audience and ensure that your message is received.

It is well known that our strengths, taken to the extreme, often become liabilities. Think about your strengths as a communicator. Are you very good at dealing with details but poor at dealing with the big picture? Is your natural preference to look at the bottom line rather than to be concerned with the people involved? Do you value a systematic and structured approach or do you tend to be more open and flexible? All of this will have an impact on how you present.

How can you use this information to become a more effective presenter and boost your credibility? Here are some tips, based on the type of presenter you are.

IF YOU ARE DETAIL ORIENTED

If you thrive on dealing with details, your presentation might be focused on what is tangible. You are likely to want to include a lot of verifiable, tested facts. You might value the safety of the known because you place trust in established procedures, customs, and norms. What might be lacking from your presentation is the big-picture perspective, the 30,000-foot view. Here are some guidelines to avoid these pitfalls:

- Start with an overview or executive summary of your topic.
- Be careful not to overwhelm your audience with too many details and facts.
- Move quickly over the routine items.
- Put more emphasis on process and application than on data and statistics.
- Control your impatience with questions that seem to go beyond your immediate concern.

- Listen attentively to what may appear to you to be overly idealistic ideas. Don't dismiss them off-hand but help your listeners make a connection to pertinent realities; in other words, be open to ideas while providing a reality check if needed.

- Flex outside your comfort zone by examining the future or longer-term implications of your proposal or ideas; you may not have to address this information in your presentation, but you should be prepared for questions and a discussion on it.

- Be flexible by temporarily setting aside your prepared slides if the audience wants to explore different ideas or solutions. Be prepared to abandon your sequential presentation to conduct a conversation on new ideas that might come up during the presentation.

IF YOU ARE A BIG-PICTURE THINKER

If you are a big-picture thinker, you are very comfortable dealing with abstractions. Your strengths lie in looking for patterns of association or interconnections. You thrive on looking for innovative and unique ways to approach your topic. Perched in your metaphorical helicopter, you might lose your audience as you neglect the practical implications of your views. Here are some guidelines to avoid these pitfalls:

- Be specific and provide pertinent details to explain your vision.

- Make an effort to express your ideas in concrete, not just abstract or theoretical, terms.

- Follow a sequential method of presenting.

- Give specific examples to substantiate your ideas.
- Be ready to outline a complete plan rather than present an idea only.
- Avoid a tendency to use too many elaborate metaphors.
- Provide background documentation, handouts, and other take-aways.

IF YOU ARE A BOTTOM-LINE THINKER

If you are a bottom-line thinker, you value logical principles and equitable solutions above all else. This means that you might place less importance on how your proposal or views will affect others personally. Being comfortable with controversy, you might appear to be more callous and less concerned with how people are affected. Here are some guidelines to avoid these pitfalls:

- Do your homework prior to the presentation to know as much as you can about any personnel issues that might be impacted by your views.
- Start your presentation with a rapport builder; for example, share a personal perspective or experience related to your topic.
- Don't just focus on the bottom line; talk about the human impact of your proposal.
- Show genuine concern about any issues related to people.
- If you cannot avoid challenging an audience member's logic in the discussion or question-and-answer part of the presentation, do it with great care.
- Work on developing a more friendly, approachable style when you speak: smile, use some humor, and be less intense.

- Take a moment to acknowledge anyone who needs to be acknowledged.

- Honor people in the room by thanking them or praising that which deserves praise. Look for what is right.

IF YOU ARE A "PEOPLE PERSON"

If you are the type of individual who values consensus and likes to avoid controversy, you will place a great deal of importance on how your proposal or talk affects others. You value harmony, which may lead you to lose some of your objectivity in presenting issues or topics. You may have difficulty delivering bad news. Here are some guidelines to avoid these pitfalls:

- Bolster your points with well-thought-out reasoning and proof of facts.

- Put particular emphasis on being organized, clear, concise, and to the point.

- Show objectivity and impartiality in how you arrived at your conclusions.

- Prove your competence; for example, structure your presentation to follow a pattern of cause and effect or pros and cons.

- Use diagrams, charts, graphs, and other visual mapping tools to show the logic behind your ideas.

- Provide data and documentation.

- Don't get overly excited if a debate ensues; manage your emotions and remain focused.

- Decide in advance that you will stay calm if you encounter pushback and criticism. Don't take it personally if some of your listeners are direct and blunt; they may not place as much emphasis on tact as you do.

- Be prepared for questions that are aimed at gaining clarity and problem solving.

BE SELF-AWARE

It is a good practice to raise your self-awareness and become intimate with your communication patterns. Use a balanced approach in preparing and delivering your presentation; that is, use your strengths and mitigate your weaknesses.

Be prepared. Push the envelope. Get out of your comfort zone, and continue to adapt. As Warren Bennis says in *On Becoming a Leader*, "It's like snakes. What do snakes do? They molt, they shed their outside skins... It's a matter of continuing to grow and transform."[1] Growing and transforming in your presentations will pay dividends and make you more credible as a speaker.

If you need some help raising your self-awareness as a speaker, consider taking the Myers-Briggs Type Indicator® (MBTI®). Knowing your Myers-Briggs type is a valuable tool in your public-speaking toolkit. You can learn more about the MBTI from the Myers & Briggs Foundation.[2] To assess your emotional intelligence, which plays a powerful role in presenting, there are a number of assessments available.

For an overview of some of the best known assessments, see the Resources section.

CHAPTER 16

PERFORMANCE ANXIETY: YOUR SURVIVAL TOOLKIT

"Anxiety is a thin stream of fear trickling through the mind.
If encouraged, it cuts a channel into which all other thoughts are drained."
—**Arthur Somers Roche**

Composure is an important component of personal presence and credibility as a speaker. Unmanaged fear about public speaking can have a negative impact on your composure—it is, therefore, imperative to acquire a few tools to help you master any anxiety you might feel about presenting.

If your anxiety is mild—a natural response that most individuals experience when presenting—just follow the common-sense advice of knowing your material, adapting the presentation to your audience's needs, and preparing well. The initial anxiety will dissipate as you get into your presentation.

If your anxiety is more pronounced, this chapter presents some strategies that you can adopt to reduce your stress so that you perform well, despite your fear. This enhances your leadership presence.

One of the best definitions of leadership presence comes from leadership speaker John Baldoni, who has called it "earned authority."[1]

You gain it through three salient attributes that apply equally when you present:

- **Control.** This attribute refers to maintaining control of whatever situation you are in. While you cannot control what might go wrong, you can control your response.

- **Composure.** This attribute refers to not losing your composure when under pressure. Composure is about speaking calmly and coherently.

- **Confidence.** This attribute refers to projecting a sense of confidence about yourself—acting as if you know what you are doing.

As Baldoni has articulated, "When leaders act in control, remain composed and exude confidence, they demonstrate…credibility." Manage your anxiety and watch your credibility soar.

Here is your toolkit for managing your fear.

UNDERSTAND HOW THE FEAR RESPONSE WORKS

Our prehistoric ancestors lived in constant danger of being attacked by wild predators. Their survival depended totally on how well they read signs of threat and how quickly they reacted to imminent danger. This is our hardwired "fight or flight" response. When we are afraid, adrenaline and cortisol are released into the bloodstream. There is less blood going to the cortex, because it flows to the large muscles instead—getting us ready to flee. The result is cortical inhibition: racing thoughts and the inability to think rationally. While all of this is helpful to keep us out of harm's way, these physical reactions also occur in situations that are not actually dangerous but that we have interpreted as dangerous—such as speaking in front of a group.

Why does the brain perceive public speaking as dangerous? Scott Berkun, in *Confessions of a Public Speaker*, put it best: "The design of the brain's wiring—given its long operational history, which is hundreds of thousands of years older than the history of public speaking…makes it impossible to stop fearing what it knows is the worst tactical situation for a person to be in."[2] The worse tactical situation is being up front, on your own, and not part of the group—with a large group of people staring at you. This is unnatural, because we are a social animal, and we feel safer as part of the herd. Being out on your own, separated from the group, signals to your brain that you are in danger of being attacked by a predator.

To manage the fear of public speaking, you need to start right here: understand that the brain cannot tell the difference between a real, physical threat (a hyena about to attack you) and an imagined threat (a group of people watching you speak). The imagined threat is the "false alarm" that occurs in the absence of real danger.

So how does this awareness help you? It helps you if you consciously remind yourself, on the spot, to change the catastrophic interpretations of the physical cues you get when you are nervous in front of an audience. When you stop to reframe what is happening, you engage your cortex to reinterpret the situation so that the bodily reactions—such as a racing heart—don't trigger a prolonged or intensified fear response.

Even though initially you may not be able to prevent the automatic fear response, you can quiet the reaction more quickly by allowing your rational brain to correctly reinterpret the situation as nonthreatening—as a misfiring of the caveman "fight or flight" response.

This takes practice. The more often you interrupt the fear response with a rational thought (i.e., "This is a false alarm, not a true alarm"), the quicker you will be able to prevent the fear response from being your default response any time you speak in front of a group.

REHEARSE FIVE TIMES

Even the most confident person will experience anxiety if they don't know their material well. A rule of thumb is to rehearse out loud no fewer than five times.[3] Use spaced repetition to encode the material into your long-term memory. This is particularly important if you suffer from stage fright.

Video-record each rehearsal and watch the recording several times. Use the recording to practice adding smooth transitions from one slide to another. The Resources section includes a list of transitions. Practice anticipating the next slide without having to look at the screen to know what comes next. All of this increases your confidence in the material. Again, the exercise of rehearsing is not about memorizing a script but about knowing your key points and the flow of your presentation.

REHEARSE TIMINGS

One of the common fears about presenting is that we will run out of time and fail to cover all of the material or that we have too little material and end earlier than announced. Here are three pointers for preventing these situations:

- **Use the "Rehearse Timings" feature in PowerPoint.** This will help you to accurately gauge how long it takes to deliver your material and which parts you need to shorten or lengthen. If you don't know how to use this feature, see the link in the Resources section.

- **Plan for the actual presentation to take longer.** So if your rehearsal for a particular point takes ten minutes, plan for fifteen to twenty minutes.

- **Have back-up material.** Prepare additional material (or activities, if you are a trainer) that you can elect to present if you finish earlier than anticipated.

- **Know what to cut.** In advance, identify a few slides or discussion points that you can skip if you fall behind. That way, you won't have to make adjustments on the fly and risk leaving out something crucial.

DILIGENTLY PREPARE ANSWERS TO POTENTIAL QUESTIONS

One reason we experience anxiety before a presentation is our fear that we will be asked questions that we can't answer. Chapter 6 provides you with best practices for preparing for questions.

VISUALIZE YOUR PRESENTATION

Those who fear public speaking spend time before the presentation visualizing what will go wrong: "I will forget what I have to say; the audience will be bored, critical, or even hostile; someone will make me look bad…" Since you are spending time visualizing anyway, why not focus on a positive outcome? Concentrate on all the positives of your presentation and visualize the entire day, in detail, from the moment you wake up to the time you complete the presentation.

Why does visualization work? The human brain is plastic. This means that new neurons are constantly being produced. The brain reaches out to various cerebral parts to learn new skills, creating new neural pathways. Repeating a skill strengthens the neural networks representing that action. The same thing happens in the brain whether you perform the action or visualize it. From that point of view, your brain cannot tell the difference between an action you perform and an action you visualize.

In a Harvard University study, two groups of volunteers were presented with a piece of unfamiliar piano music. One group was given a keyboard and told to practice. The other group was instructed to just read the music and *imagine* playing it. When their brain activity was examined, both groups showed expansion in the motor cortex, even though the second group had never touched a keyboard.[4] Why not take advantage of what we know about brain plasticity and visualize yourself delivering a successful presentation instead of visualizing everything that can go wrong? Worrying is visualizing failure.

Visualization is mental rehearsal. It is one of the tools peak sports performers use regularly. American water-skier Camille Duvall has said the following about visualization:

I train myself mentally with visualization. The morning of a tournament, before I put my feet on the floor, I visualize myself making perfect runs with emphasis on technique, all the way through to what my personal best is in practice... The more you work with this type of visualization, especially when you do it on a day-to-day basis, you'll actually begin to feel your muscles contracting at the appropriate times.[5]

Tiger Woods practiced visualization even as a child. His book, *How I Play Golf*, documents how he prepares mentally and thinks through the shots.[6] "Preparation—both physical and mental—is so important in anything you do, and it can give you an edge."[7]

Einstein, who is credited with saying that "imagination is more important than knowledge," used visualization throughout his entire life.

Use visualization as part of your preparation for a presentation. Visualization will boost your confidence in your ability to manage your anxiety. As Clifford N. Lazarus, licensed psychologist and Clinical Director of The Lazarus Institute states: "Visualization activates the non-dominant or 'right brain' in most people thus exercising important neural structures that further enhance optimism, confidence, and personal effectiveness."[8]

Finally, consider that there is one major difference between those who love to present in front of a group and those who dislike it. The former have no fear because they feel that the audience will enjoy listening to them. They are typically well prepared and know their topic well. Conversely, those who are afraid visualize that the audience will dislike them and judge them harshly. Think about this and make a mental shift. Visualize the opposite!

GET ENOUGH SLEEP

John Medina's Brain Rule #7 is, "Sleep well, think well."[9] According to Medina, "Loss of sleep hurts attention, executive function, working memory, mood, quantitative skills, logical reasoning, and even motor dexterity." Get adequate sleep, not only the night before but two or three nights before a major presentation. Not getting sufficient sleep before a stressful event magnifies the effect of the stress by increasing the level of cortisol in your body, affecting not only your mood but also your memory. As E. Joseph Cossman said, "The best bridge between despair and hope is a good night's sleep." Strengthen that bridge with two or three nights' adequate sleep.

CALM YOUR BODY

Practice these common-sense prescriptions for quieting your body.

DRINK GREEN TEA

If you are very nervous when you speak, replace coffee with warm water or green tea. It's a simple strategy that calms the nerves. A study of over 40,000 people, published in the *American Journal of Clinical Nutrition,* found that stress was lowered by 20 percent in those who drank at least five cups of green tea per day.[10] As well, avoid cold drinks before you are scheduled to present.

EAT LIGHTLY BEFORE A PRESENTATION

Consider eating a banana or drinking a nourishing banana smoothie prior to your presentation. Bananas are natural beta blockers, which help with performance anxiety by blocking adrenaline. For a list of similar foods, read the eHow article "What Foods Are Natural Beta Blockers?"[11]

TAKE DEEP BREATHS
Just before speaking, go outside the presentation room and take a few deep breaths. To relax deeply and quickly, close your eyes, breathe in through your nose for a count of three and exhale through your mouth for a count of six. Do this three times. For inspiration, watch the short video "Breathe" from The Energy Project.[12]

PAUSE FREQUENTLY
When you are nervous, pause more frequently than normal. In *The King's Speech*, a movie about the true story of King George VI, one of the strategies the speech therapist utilizes to help the king overcome his speech impediment is the use of pauses. Pausing helps the king regain his composure whenever he feels acute anxiety in delivering a speech. The same strategy can help you.

PRACTICE THE "RELAXATION RESPONSE" REGULARLY
The "relaxation response" is the brainchild of Dr. Herbert Benson, M.D., at Harvard Medical School.[13] Benson is a pioneer in mind/body medicine. We have within us a response opposite to the "fight or flight" response: the relaxation response. It is our body's innate ability to lower blood pressure, reduce heart rate, and slow down breathing. The relaxation response is a simple technique to be practiced ten to twenty minutes, once or twice a day. Once learned, it becomes a powerful tool for relieving tension. You can learn the steps of this technique at Dr. Benson's website.[14] The Resources

section also includes a video interview with Dr. Benson, who describes the method.

LOWER STRESS WITH BIOFEEDBACK

Consider HeartMath's emWave2®. This is a scientifically validated, handheld device with a convenient interface that shows you, in real time, the effect of your thoughts and emotions on your heart rhythm—and therefore your performance. It's an innovative, award-winning biofeedback tool that helps you train your heart and brain to release stress so that you can improve your ability to focus and perform. The device was tested and is used in organizations such as Stanford Business School, Mayo Clinic, NASA, and the U.S. Armed Forces, among many others. You can read about the science behind the device online.[15]

A low-tech biofeedback device is Biodots® or stress dots. These tiny dots act as thermometers that monitor skin temperature and change color accordingly. This signal helps you know when you need to take some quick steps to calm yourself down, such as taking a few deep breaths.[16]

The Resources section provides some links where you can purchase the emWave2® and Biodots®.

FOCUS ON A SINGLE ATTRIBUTE

This idea comes from Sims Wyeth's article on mastering the body language of leadership: "Research in...Scientific American suggests that focusing on one word is the most effective way to learn a new behavior."[17] Focus on one attribute such as calmness or composure, and practice this throughout your entire day, from the moment you wake up. While this strategy may seem artificial in the beginning, it is very effective.

DRESS WELL AND APPROPRIATELY

While dressing well won't replace knowing your material and being well prepared, it does help in managing your public speaking anxiety. Sharp attire acts as symbolic armor. Wear the most appropriate, top-quality clothes that you can afford, and opt for simplicity. See what happens. Quality and simplicity are key. Take this popular adage as your guide when you choose clothes for a major presentation: "Spend twice as much, buy half as much."

HAVE A CHECKLIST

Plan for even the smallest detail and create a checklist for everything you need to do and take with you. Have a backup for your slides, have a plan B if the equipment fails, take along a hard copy of your slides, check that imbedded video clips work, check the sound coming out of your laptop, and confirm important names you will need to remember. Be meticulous. A considerable amount of stress is caused by overlooking small details.

ARRIVE EARLY

If it is feasible, try to be in the room before others arrive so that you can greet them and schmooze a little before the presentation. It helps to calm you down if you can hear your voice in the room on a social level first. This makes you feel like part of the group rather than the isolated "presenter" up front.

LISTEN TO UPBEAT MUSIC

On your way to the presentation, listen to upbeat music. Research shows that upbeat music decreases the level of cortisol in the body.[18] Create a library of such tunes. Music tastes are individual, but here are some songs to get you started:

- "I Feel Good" (http://www.youtube.com/watch?v=SzlpTRNIAvc)
- Music from the training scene in the movie *Rocky* (http://www.youtube.com/watch?v=WoLVWvqEwzs)
- "Celebration" (http://www.youtube.com/watch?v=3GwjfUFyY6M&ob=av2n)
- The overture from the opera *Carmen* (http://www.youtube.com/watch?v=PQI5LtRtrb0)
- The *William Tell Overture* (http://www.youtube.com/watch?v=xoHECVnQC7A)
- Top 10 oldies songs (http://www.youtube.com/watch?v=zkKz_fgrfHw)

DON'T AIM TO BE PERFECT

Even veteran speakers make mistakes; case in point, President Obama at a particular town hall event.[19] Several times, on that occasion, he fumbled and repeated his words, without completing his statement. What was his reaction to this? He reacted the same way every great speaker does in a similar situation. He moved on. Consider the lesson in this. Use all of the mental and emotional energy you expend worrying about having a flawless presentation and, instead, put that energy into knowing your material well and planning the presentation so that you have a clear focus and don't ramble.

Don't become obsessed with being perfect. There is a beautiful concept in Japanese culture called *wabi-sabi*, which refers to the quintessential aesthetic that centers on accepting the imperfection and transience of things—for example, the asymmetry in a ceramic bowl, which reflects the handmade craftsmanship, as opposed to the perfect but soulless machine-made alternative. Focusing on perfection is a form of self-sabotage, which can make a speaker look slick and inauthentic. When an error occurs in your presentation, don't let it destroy your composure. Focus on everything else that is going well. Take inspiration from design philosopher Leonard Koren's beautiful words:

> *Forget your perfect offering*
> *There's a crack in everything*
> *That's how the light gets in.*[20]

Practice self-acceptance. One way we do this is by telling ourselves "I am enough"—and meaning it. This concept originated with Carl Rogers, the influential American psychologist, who was asked how he did what he did so successfully. He said, "Before a session with a client, I let myself know that 'I am enough.' Not perfect, because perfect wouldn't be enough. But I am human and there is nothing that this client can say or do or feel that I cannot feel in myself. I can be with them. I am enough."[21] We can derive a great deal of inspiration from this.

Above all, remind yourself that the audience doesn't want you to fail. If you fail, it means they are wasting their time. Your fear of public speaking will be magnified or diminished in direct proportion to your courage. Courage means you can stand in front of an audience and perform well, even when something goes wrong. Courage is an emotional muscle—the more you practice it, the stronger it becomes, so take every opportunity to speak.

INCREASE YOUR SELF-EFFICACY

Self-efficacy is defined as our belief in our ability to succeed in reaching a specific goal. It's trusting that we have what it takes to cope with whatever situation we are facing—it's having a "can do" attitude. We can increase our self-efficacy in four ways:

- **Mastery experiences.** We achieve successes through repeated effort.

- **Vicarious experiences.** We watch other people, similar to us, succeed through perseverance; this experience leads us to believe that we, too, can improve our performance in comparable activities.

- **Verbal persuasion.** Others convince us that we have what it takes to successfully master given activities.

- **Physiological and emotional states.** We lower stress and tension, and manage our emotional states, which can influence how we view ourselves.[22]

As presenters, we foster self-efficacy by taking every opportunity to speak and build on our successes; watching accomplished speakers present and learning from them; and adopting some of the best practices for managing stress. Above all, we must be vigilant about whom we spend time with before a major presentation. Here are some tips:

- **Listen to the whispers of those who encourage you.** Spend more time with people who support you. They are gifts in your life. A study at the University of Exeter showed that emotional support and encouragement improve our performance in areas such as sports. The same applies for presentations.[23]

- **Avoid those who undermine you.** It's easier for others to lower our self-efficacy with their criticism than it is for them to raise it with their encouragement. Therefore, be particularly vigilant of people in whose presence you may feel diminished or dispirited. Stay clear of them if you can—especially before an important event such as a major presentation.

- **Create a list of individuals who inspire you.** Look for social models of people similar to you who accomplished great things, despite adversities and setbacks. Actively observe these people and derive inspiration from their ability to persevere through tough times. These people inject us with hope about our ability to succeed at whatever we undertake.

For more tips on self-efficacy, please see my article "Self-Efficacy: The First Requisite for Success."[24]

PLACE A MORATORIUM ON ASKING FOR ADVICE

There is a fine line between seeking others' input once in a while and being hooked on their advice. We can become addicted to seeking advice, which dilutes our own insights. Worse still, this addictive habit can insidiously erode our self-confidence. Trust yourself!

If you ask too many colleagues for feedback on your presentation's content, take care that their input doesn't end up weakening your authentic voice. Accept the comments with grace but use your intuition to determine what feels right for you. Always preserve your voice—it's your intellectual integrity. In the article "How to Teach Yourself to Trust Yourself," Peter Bregman puts it beautifully: "As we shape ourselves to the desires, preferences, and expectations of others, we risk losing ourselves... Instead, take the time, and the quiet, to decide what you think. That is how we find the part of ourselves we gave up. That is how we become powerful, clever, creative, and insightful."[25] This is how we speak authentically.

PRACTICE SELF-COMPASSION

As executive coach Marshall Goldsmith has said, "If we tell ourselves we can't sell or are bad at public speaking or don't listen well, we will usually find a way to fulfill our prophecy. We doom ourselves to failure."[26] By far the most frightening and judgmental audience we will ever encounter is what T. S. Eliot calls the "silent observer, severe and speechless critic, who can terrorize us." This is our own internal critic. A habit of self-criticism breaks your spirit and prevents you from showing up as your most secure self—whether it is for a presentation, a meeting, or a social event.

Break this habit by practicing self-compassion. We all know the value of showing compassion to others but paradoxically place little value on turning compassion inward. Self-criticism is rarely constructive.

One way to take control of self-criticism is to analyze the pattern that is at its root. It will be different for each person. Acknowledging frequently recurring reactions and behaviors is a powerful component of self-awareness as a speaker.[27] Part of knowing your patterns is understanding the unique triggers for your feelings of stress. Are they remnants from your past? If so, what can you do to let them go? Are they brought about by something in your current life? For example, does the anxiety of presenting manifest particularly when a certain colleague is in the audience? Gathering this intelligence about yourself is the first step in overcoming the habit of self-criticism.

If self-compassion is new to you, consider that habits become hardwired: they create neural pathways, which show up as an actual thickening of brain circuitry. This becomes the brain's default mode, or as Shaquille O'Neal put it, "You are what you repeatedly do." The only way to master self-compassion is by continuing to repeat this new behavior. By persisting, the old habit of self-judgment becomes weaker—that is, the circuitry for it grows thinner and finally withers. Meanwhile, the circuitry for the new habit of self-compassion becomes stronger. "That means the circuitry has become so connected and thick," says Daniel Goleman in *The Brain and Emotional Intelligence: New Insights*, "that it is the brain's new default option."[28] How long does it take for you to achieve this? Forget the twenty-one days you were told. "It usually takes three to six months of using all naturally occurring practice opportunities before the new habit comes more naturally than the old."

For more information on breaking new habits, read my article "The Chains of Habit."[29] If you think that practicing self-compassion is a New Age concept, I encourage you to reconsider. Adding self-compassion to your toolbox for managing anxiety is smart.

ASK YOURSELF QUESTIONS THAT WILL MAKE YOU FEEL TERRIFIC

Replace negative questions, such as "What will happen if I forget my material?" and "What if I mess up?," with questions that bring about positive answers and make you feel good. Speaker Seymour Segnit, who specializes in helping individuals get rid of their fear of public speaking, recommends that you ask yourself these two questions:

- "What will happen if I knock it out of the park?"
- "How can I give my gifts to the audience?"[30]

Both of these questions take the focus away from you and shift it either outside yourself or to a more positive frame of mind. Watch *all* of Seymour Segnit's video blogs on public-speaking fear to move to a more empowering place.[31]

GET PSYCHED BEFORE THE PRESENTATION

This tip comes from Harvard Business School professor Amy Cuddy, who has been studying body language: Before you start your presentation, find a space where you can have some privacy, such as your office, and prepare yourself psychologically by adopting expansive poses, which are associated with power. Make yourself as big as you can. Stretch your arms out, spread your legs out, adopt the "CEO pose" of resting your legs over a desk and crossing your ankles. "When you do that, you increase your testosterone which is the dominance hormone, and you are decreasing your cortisol which would make you endure stressful situations better." Cuddy's research has illustrated that practicing expansive poses versus contractive poses for just two minutes leads to these positive hormonal changes.[32]

FOCUS ON THE MESSAGE

A study from the University of Southampton shows that being overly self-absorbed increases negative thoughts and feelings, can interfere with performance, and prevents us from seeing that our fears are ungrounded.[33] If you are self-absorbed, you become insulated and mentally separated from the audience. Your anxiety will cause a sort of attention disorder, so stay focused on the message!

SHIFT YOUR FOCUS AWAY FROM MALCONTENTS

Seth Godin once said, "It's a mistake to focus on the frowning guy in the back of the room."[34] No matter how great you are, there will always be a small percentage of audience members who are critical of you. Resolve to worry only about doing remarkable work. Go the extra mile to ensure that you deliver a quality presentation, from start to finish. Worrying about the one or two people who appear not to like you is an emotional and intellectual drain. Be too big to worry about this.

OTHER PRACTICES

Consider these additional ways to conquer performance anxiety as a speaker:

- **Join Toastmasters.** It's one of the most powerful initiatives for overcoming public-speaking fear. It will pay dividends for your career. (http://www.toastmasters.org/)

- **Attend several improv classes.** This is the best way to learn how to get out of your comfort zone. It will build your courage and make you impervious to embarrassment. This is a guaranteed confidence booster.

Finally, take heart at the thought that being a little nervous means that you really care about what you have to say. Audience members see this as a signal that you are solicitous of their esteem—there is a graceful humility in this—and that you care enough to want to do a great job. Caring for your audience almost always has a boomerang effect.

CHAPTER 17

WHEN THINGS GO WRONG: DON'T GO WITH THEM

"Things get worse under pressure."
—Murphy's Law of Thermodynamics

No matter how much you prepare, anything can happen, and something usually does. How you handle these calamities says a lot about your composure as a presenter. When things go wrong, rather than let the audience see your consternation, decide in the moment to use the situation to showcase your leadership skills. Calmly and professionally dealing with the adversity will be a major boost to your credibility. People notice how we behave when things go wrong.

This chapter will provide you with practical tips to help you when the unexpected occurs.

KNOW HOW TO RECOVER A CORRUPT POWERPOINT FILE

At times, you might be unable to open up your PowerPoint file just before your presentation. This can happen easily with large, complex files. There are a number of things you can do to recover your file. These are very well explained in an article by Echo Swinford,

Microsoft MVP, which is well worth reading.[1] Print it and keep it with your presentation materials, as you never know when you might need it.

There are also third-party recovery tools that are available as a last resort, should you be unsuccessful in recovering a corrupt PowerPoint file. Here are seven choices:

- Kernel PowerPoint Repair Software (http://www. nucleustechnologies.com/Powerpoint-Presentation-Repair-Software.php)
- OfficeRecovery, Recovery for PowerPoint (http://www. officerecovery.com/powerpoint/)
- OpenOffice (http://www.nucleustechnologies.com/ Powerpoint-Presentation-Repair-Software.php)
- Stellar Phoenix PowerPoint Recovery (http://www. stellarinfo.com/powerpoint-recovery.htm)
- StarOffice (http://www.echosvoice.com/recovering.htm)
- Unistal Quick Recovery for PowerPoint (http://www. unistal.com/powerpoint-file-recovery.html)

PACK A POWERPOINT VIEWER

If you are not using your own laptop for the presentation, make sure that the PowerPoint version used to create the presentation is supported by the PowerPoint version installed on the presentation laptop. To avoid any nasty surprises, simply download the free PowerPoint Viewer, and copy it onto a flash drive to take with you.[2]

The viewer will allow you to view full-featured presentations created in PowerPoint 97 and later versions.

DON'T MAKE LAST-MINUTE CHANGES TO YOUR PRESENTATION

While renowned author and speaker Tom Peters recommends that you continue to refine your slides until a few minutes before you are to present, this works for a super-seasoned presenter like Tom; for most people, however, this is a dangerous practice. If you find an error or omission of substance, then by all means, fix it. But avoid unnecessary, last-minute tinkering with the slides—as you will likely find yourself surprised by a "new" slide or some new information that was not part of your rehearsed version. It will interrupt your flow, disconcert you, and end up making you look unprepared (as the audience will likely notice). It's not a risk worth taking.

TAKE CHARGE WHEN YOU HAVE A LOW TURNOUT

If you find yourself speaking to an unexpectedly small audience in a large hall, immediately acknowledge the issue before you start the presentation, and ask audience members to move to the front so that you are addressing a more intimate group.

DON'T SAY, "THIS HAS NEVER HAPPENED BEFORE"

When you are dealing with a technology glitch, fix it, if it can be fixed quickly. Don't provide explanations such as, "This has never happened before." The audience doesn't care that it has never happened before—they only care that it is happening now.

If you can't fix it quickly, simply acknowledge it and move on. For example, while I was showing a video during a keynote address at a leadership forum, a small black box appeared in the middle of the clip. As I couldn't quickly remove it, I let the video run because it was a speech and the most important part was the audio, not the image of the speaker. I calmly paused the video and said to the audience, "Fortunately, we are able to hear the speaker's message, which is my main reason for showing you the clip. I will let it play and will fix the issue during the break for the next clip." Then I resumed playing the video.

Once the clip finished playing, I never referred to the black box and simply proceeded with the talk. I maximized my time with the audience. They were there to learn about speech making, not to listen to an explanation about why a black box had suddenly appeared onscreen.

On other occasions, during presentations, I have had to deal with loud noises from outside the room: road drilling, loud music from an adjacent room, and once even a drumming exercise for a team-building session. When these things happen, resolve them quickly; if you can't, work around them but don't apologize and don't make a big fuss. Irritation and annoyance are communicable—don't spread them to the members of your audience, and they will admire you for it. Do your best to continue with your presentation, regardless of the mishaps that occur. Such composure and perseverance are the signs of a professional.

DON'T OVER-APOLOGIZE

Generally, the more you apologize, the more the audience perceives that something is wrong. If you are the only one who knows you made a mistake, let it go! If you have a technical disaster, treat it as a minor issue, and so will the audience.

IMPROVISE

Melissa Harris-Lacewell of Tulane University delivered a keynote at Bates College called "The Relevance of King in the Age of Obama."[3] The planned presentation was to include a photograph of a meeting between Martin Luther King Jr. and President Lyndon Johnson; the photo was an integral part of her message. Due to a technology glitch, however, she was unable to project the image. With aplomb, she decided to improvise. She announced to the audience that she was going to describe the image instead and, making light of the mishap, added, "After all, every important African American art form—jazz, rap, hip hop—is based on improvisation."

Audience members admire this type of composure. Take inspiration from seasoned newscasters who react with equanimity when an announced photo or video does not materialize or when sound is lost.

TURN TRAGEDY INTO COMEDY

When something goes wrong, be prepared with a humorous one-liner that you can use to lighten the mood and maintain your composure. As it is often difficult to think of something witty on the spot, pick up some of the valuable resources available for this purpose.

One resource I suggest is *What to Say When...You're Dying on the Platform: A Complete Resource for Speakers, Trainers, and Executives,* by Lilly Waters.[4] Another good source of one-liners is "Humor for Speakers," at the website HaLife.[5] Here are examples from the page:

- If the room is hot: "I haven't sweated this much since my tax audit."
- If the crowd is small: "I forgot to bring something with me—my audience."

Another source of one-liners is *Presentations for Dummies,* by Malcolm L. Kushner.[6] Here are some examples from this source:

- If your microphone emits a loud squeal: "It must have been something I ate."
- If a police, fire, or ambulance siren disrupts your presentation: "I told them not to pick me up for another hour."

Get inspiration from these one-liners and develop your own.

BE PARANOID ABOUT BACKING UP YOUR PRESENTATION

Take extra precautions to protect your content:

- **Use two flash drives.** Back up your PowerPoint presentation on two flash drives, as these devices are not infallible. Never put your back-up flash drive in your checked luggage. Preferably, store it separate from your computer, in case your computer bag is lost.

- **Email the presentation to yourself.** As an additional back-up measure, email your presentation to yourself so that you can access it via email, if needed.

- **Use a free online service for large files.** If your PowerPoint file is too large to email, use YouSendIt to send it to yourself the day before the presentation.[7] If disaster strikes during the presentation, you can download the file in minutes. Dropbox is a similar service.[8]

- **Save a shortcut to your presentation folder on your desktop for quick access.** Make sure you don't have too many files on your desktop: an uncluttered desktop is a great help when you find yourself on edge, coping with the unexpected, with the audience watching.

- **Pack a hard copy.** Bring a hard copy of your presentation with you; in case of equipment failure, you can photocopy the handout on location.

TAKE ADDITIONAL PRECAUTIONS

Here are some more tips for avoiding potential mishaps and annoyances when presenting:

- Bring extra batteries for your remote.

- If you are presenting abroad, know the electrical voltage and outlets used in the country you are visiting, so that you can come prepared with the right adapter or plug. Electrical Outlet.org provides a helpful list of electrical outlets used worldwide.[9]

- Ensure that you have packed your speaking notes. Never put them in your checked luggage.

- Deactivate your screen saver, energy saver, and any pop-ups (such as appointment reminders and instant messages).

- Carry with you the name and cell phone number of the coordinator or person in charge.

- Not all venues have a wall clock, and it is unprofessional to look at your wristwatch during your presentation. Pack a small, unobtrusive clock and place it in a spot that is visible to you when you speak.

KNOW HOW TO CONNECT YOUR LAPTOP TO YOUR PROJECTOR

It's surprising how many people don't know how to connect their laptop to the projector, as they rely on technical support in their organizations. You may not always have a technician present, so you should learn how to do this yourself.

Here are some videos that take you through all of the steps in connecting an LCD projector to a laptop:

- http://www.youtube.com/watch?v=fD6oCyP15Es
- http://www.youtube.com/watch?v=6nkXPxX7EMs
- http://www.youtube.com/watch?v=qxo7Z9-deZY
- http://www.youtube.com/watch?v=7w1H_olhLe4

As a tip, learn which function key to press to signal to your laptop that you are using a projector as a secondary video output device.

This is usually one of the F (function) keys. To find out which key works for your laptop, consult the manual, ask your technician, or simply look at the F keys on your keyboard and you will likely see one that has an icon of a monitor and a laptop (or the characters "CRT/LCD.") If you are using a Mac computer, the function key to use is F7.[10]

Here is another tip: choose the maximum screen resolution that your projector supports. A safe choice is 1024×768.

TEST THE SOUND FOR EACH FILE BEFORE THE PRESENTATION

Video and audio files don't all play equally, and you might have to be prepared to manually adjust upward or downward for a specific video during the presentation. Plan this so that you are not caught off-guard once the show is on.

BE PREPARED TO PRESENT WITHOUT VISUAL AIDS

Make sure that you are always prepared to deliver your presentation without technology, in case disaster strikes. Know your material so well that you can stand at the front of the room and speak about your topic without the aid of slides, if need be. Bring a handout that outlines the key points of your presentation. That way, you have an alternative to your slide show.

CHAPTER 18

DIFFICULT AUDIENCES: DON'T LET THEM PULL YOUR STRINGS

"He who angers you conquers you."
—Elizabeth Kenny

For some people, a stressful aspect of presenting is the perceived threat of speaking in front of a difficult audience. A difficult audience, in the normal course of business presentations, is best described as one that vigorously opposes your views. They may express their disagreement bluntly, raise their voices a notch or two, or in extreme cases, disagree with your views or proposal by saying something uncomplimentary. While this situation is difficult, it is hardly life threatening.

More often than not, what we refer to as a difficult audience is simply a bored audience or one whose needs have not been met. Less frequently, we encounter the chronically malcontent—individuals who show up everywhere carrying grudges and a bad disposition.

Sometimes the audience is difficult and aggressively vocal because of the nature of the topic. You may be presenting on a controversial topic in a town hall meeting of citizens who are deeply affected by the position you take on matters of importance to them. Or you may represent an unpopular company; the audience views you as the face of the company and may react to you as the messenger of unpopular or bad news.

A difficult audience can also contain a few people who have hidden agendas or with whom you have had disagreements and office feuds in the past. Of all the types of difficult audience members, these individuals may require the most effort to deal with, because their opposing behavior is insidious and camouflaged.

These situations can threaten your credibility—and be an opportunity to strengthen your credibility. How you respond makes a difference. To handle difficult speaking situations with professionalism and composure takes mental preparation, a few strategic tips, and practice. Above all, it takes resolve not to let anyone pull your strings and tarnish your image at the front of the room.

This chapter will provide you with tips for handling difficult situations with poise.

PREPARE FOR AUDIENCE MEMBERS WITH STRONG OPINIONS

Expert negotiators and influencers remind us that objections are a gift: they are an insight into the other party's thought process that we can use to provide a counterargument. It is far better that they object on the spot instead of after we have left the room.

Prepare in advance for anticipated objections and have fully drafted responses. Each situation is different and will elicit different types of objections. You know best which ones are most likely to come up based on your topic. In general, the most common objections are about costs, perceived benefits, feasibility, and extra resources (such as personnel, time, or equipment). Other objections might be your company's expertise and/or your own. Create a list of all the possible objections regarding your topic, craft responses, and rehearse your responses so that you don't miss a beat when you are confronted during your presentation.

Enlist help from experts in your organization, going straight to the source. For example, if the anticipated objection has to do with engineering issues, get the engineers involved in crafting the best response; if it is a logistics issue, get your operations experts involved. Some companies have an intranet database of appropriate answers to commonly raised objections, for easy access by anyone making a presentation to a client or a group. If this resource is not available in your company, propose it as a new initiative.

The process for answering objections is simple: listen deeply, ask follow-up questions, acknowledge, and respond. I will cover these components in more detail.

LISTEN DEEPLY
If we accept the premise that an objection gives us a peek into someone's thinking, then it is imperative to listen deeply to the objection without interrupting so that you can fully understand the other person's line of reasoning and any related emotions. The initial silence works in your favor; make full use of it.

ASK FOLLOW-UP QUESTIONS

Before you rush to respond, it is advantageous to ask the person a follow-up question. Consider questions like the following:

* "Mary, can you explain exactly what you mean by…?"
* "Rob, could you give me an example of…?"
* "What led you to this conclusion, Jack?"

Ask this question in a nonthreatening manner, from the spirit of wanting to truly understand the person's position before you answer. This helps you and the other audience members to know more, but more importantly, it signals to the person that you are not reacting emotionally to their objection. They will feel "heard," which is always a good thing.

REMOVE THE "STING"

Acknowledge and respond. This is an important step: let the other person know that you respect their choice to object, even if you totally disagree with the objection. This is the oil that makes relationships run smoother; it is maturity and executive finesse. Convey respect with your demeanor: kind eyes, relaxed facial muscles, and a posture that is neutral or slightly leaning forward. (Contrast this with a cold stare, tight lips, sideways glance, and rigid stance.) Accompany the nonverbal language with a statement such as "I hear you" or "I see what you are saying." You don't have to agree.

You can then share your own view, which might be diametrically opposed. Here is how this may sound:

* "I see what you are saying, Bob. Let me explain how I view it."

- "I understand your position, Janet. This has not been my experience. Let me take you through what we have done to prevent XYZ from happening on this project."

If the person objecting did so in a caustic manner, then you need to respond in an emotionally-intelligent manner. A person delivering a critical remark causes negative reverberations in the room. Everyone present feels uncomfortable. A useful tip for handling this situation comes from Peter and Cheryl Reimold in *The Short Road to Great Presentations: How to Reach Any Audience Through Focused Preparation, Inspired Delivery, and Smart Use of Technology*: "A caustic question leaves a bad echo in the room…To erase that echo, you can insert a simple positive phrase such as "Right," "Yes, of course," or "OK" before you answer."[1]

Think about this: a person comes close to insulting you (saying, for example, "I don't know where you come up with these ideas. This makes absolutely no sense. There is no way in hell this is going to work."). Instead of having a negative reaction, which everyone in the room expects, the following happens:

1. You maintain a calm demeanor and simply say "OK" or "Thanks."

2. You acknowledge the objection and address it: "Bob, I hear your concern. Let me outline the measures we have taken to ensure that this plan works."

You may be infuriated or incensed on the inside, but outwardly you are in control. This response not only starts to calm you down but calms the air in the room, maintains a tone of civility for the meeting or presentation, and strengthens your leadership presence. It makes you look confident, and it earns you credibility. Anyone can react angrily. It takes a big person to manage others' outbursts.

Variations of the Reimolds' simple, positive acknowledgment phrases include "Thank you" and "All right." Replying this way does not mean that you agree with the objection—the positive phrase is used simply to take the "sting" out of the objection. The more you get used to doing this, the easier it will be to handle any caustic remarks that might come your way.

BE AWARE OF BAD NEWS AFFECTING YOUR AUDIENCE

Your audience may have received some bad news—about impending layoffs, a merger, restructuring, relocation, drastic budget cuts, cancellation of important programs, failure of a major project, some other organizational change, or controversy in the media. The bad news might be the death of someone in the company or the firing of a well-liked, key member of the team.

As you start your presentation, you notice that the audience is listless, anxious, and distracted; people are clearly not totally focused on your message. You sense the mood in the room but, not knowing the cause, you become anxious yourself and your performance goes downhill from there. It is wise, before your presentation, to diligently check for any news that might affect your audience.

After doing a Google search related to your audience, you can select from various time parameters; for example, "Past hour," "Past 24 hours," and "Past week." (See Figure 9.)

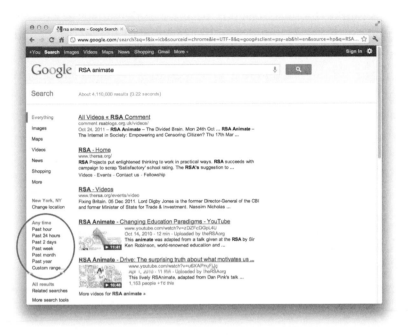

Figure 9

You can also call the meeting organizer, your sponsor, or the key executive who invited you to speak to find out if there is anything you should know. Generally, if the issue is major, they will give you a hint. Once you know, you can plan accordingly. At the minimum, you will be prepared to accept that there might be some anxiety in the room that has nothing to do with you.

I called the organizer of a technology company where I was scheduled to deliver a full-day session, and when I asked her if there was anything I should be aware of, she mentioned that the CEO had called a brief meeting of his vice presidents at 9:00 a.m. and that the staff was anxiously awaiting an announcement about a merger. Armed with this knowledge, at the opening of the session, I mentioned that I was aware of the important announcement that everyone was waiting for and that I planned to schedule a coffee break earlier than usual, to allow everyone to get an immediate update on the announcement. I could sense relief in the audience members, who now viewed me as part of the team—rather than an outsider who was not aware of their world. This set the tone for the rest of the day. Practicing social awareness is a key behavior of a presenter who is emotionally intelligent.

On the rare occasion where someone in the firm has died, you can make a thoughtful remark at the start of the meeting: "I heard about the very sad news concerning Bob Farley. I am very sorry for your loss. I know that he has been a valued colleague and friend for over twenty-five years. Please accept my sincere condolences."

This gesture of empathy signals that you understand their world. If done genuinely, such gestures go a long way toward improving a situation that could be difficult for you as a speaker.

AVOID MAKING CONTROVERSIAL OR INAPPROPRIATE REMARKS

Anyone who speaks frequently may, sooner or later, inadvertently make a remark that offends an audience member. More often than not, the offensive remark is the result of an impromptu attempt at humor that ends up sounding politically incorrect. Not everyone in the audience may be offended, but if the statement is embarrassing to one person or group, it ends up making everyone else uncomfortable. The atmosphere in the room goes cold, and the audience may appear unreceptive to anything that follows.

What can you do in this situation? If the transgression was minor, quickly apologize and use some self-deprecating humor to make light of the issue. This is one of the rare times that one apologizes during a presentation. For example, you could say, "Every time I make an attempt at humor, I need to remind myself not to quit my day job." And then quickly move on. If your faux pas was major, then apologize instantly, without joking, and move on with the program.

If you present to multicultural audiences, or deliver presentations abroad, do some research on cultural sensitivities and nuances. Every culture has a different sense of humor, and what might work in North America may offend an audience in another country. As speaker Tom Antion has said, "Much of our humor is based on making fun of someone else. This type of humor is not understood in most areas of the world and is considered disrespectful."[2]

Consider reading Roger E. Axtell's *Gestures: The Do's and Taboos of Body Language Around the World*.[3]

CONTROL YOUR ATTITUDE

I once said to my coach, "I have not had any audience members be unpleasant with me during any of my presentations." She responded, "That's because your attitude does not provoke it." The concept of "emotional leakage" refers to emotional information that we pass on to others through our body language. This information might be conveyed unintentionally in a threatening gaze, a haughty stare, or a cold or aloof demeanor. These micro-expressions may be fleeting, but people are able to detect them. "Leakage" refers to the fact that the emotion may not be what we want to signal, but it leaks through in small ways.

If you approach a speaking engagement from the point of view that you know everything and the audience knows very little (and this may very well be true in some cases), arrogance will leak through—and arrogance never serves us well. When people sense it, they generally want to bring us down a peg, because arrogance is an attempt to lift ourselves at the expense of lowering another—and no one likes to be diminished.

Or you might have interpersonal issues with someone who is attending your presentation. If you don't prepare yourself emotionally before the presentation, defensiveness might leak through. For example, the person might ask a legitimate, neutral question, but because of your predisposition toward this person, you might react with visible distrust; the person gets the message and might respond negatively. To avoid this situation, think about the person in advance of the presentation and decide how you will show up. Resolve that you will not show any hint of negativity toward this person, that you will be particularly careful to answer in a positive manner.

In general, any hint of impatience, arrogance, annoyance, or superiority will almost certainly be the impetus that turns some members of the audience into "difficult" participants. Raise your self-awareness and manage your emotions so that you prevent this from happening.

PART FOUR

DYNAMISM

CHAPTER 19

ARE YOU A VENTRILOQUIST TO THE SLIDES?: YOUR DYNAMISM

"If you want to catch the right mental attitude, go where that attitude exists. Start by going to the people who have the right mental attitude. If the right people aren't always available, then go to the right book, or to the right recording of a dynamic speaker."
—**Zig Ziglar**

In his classic book *Presenting to Win: The Art of Telling Your Story*, Jerry Weissman cautions against being a presenter who is subordinate to the slide show, "serving, at best, as a voice-over narrator and, at worst, as a ventriloquist."[1] You can have expertise in your topic and speaker "presence" (a confident, natural posture; effective eye contact; paced speech; and appropriate dress), but if you lack energy when you present, it will lessen your credibility.

Dynamism is an expansionist quality. It gives you an enlarged presence at the front of the room, from which you can increase your influence—the influence to maintain the audience's attention so that you can get your message across. Dynamism is moving toward the audience like a plant looking for light. Dynamism powers your communication. Lack of dynamism is the opposite: it's a contraction of the self. It's receding from the audience and diminishing your impact.

In a seminal study on source credibility, researchers Berlo, Lemert, and Mertz proposed that speaker credibility comprises three factors: competence, trustworthiness, and dynamism.[2] Since that time, this concept has been applied to teacher credibility as well as leadership credibility.[3]

What exactly is dynamism for a presenter? Above all, it's the energy that we bring to a presentation. This energy is two-fold: outer and inner. Outwardly, dynamism entails four components:

1. Your facial expressions
2. Your movement
3. Your vocal variety
4. Your gestures

These behaviors need to be natural byproducts of a speaker's enthusiasm for the topic—not mechanical affectations. Seasoned presenters, those with the most speaker credibility, have mastered these essential features of dynamism. They use all four naturally, in a harmonious combination that is received by the audience as a polished, smooth, and fluid presentation. Their delivery is natural and totally devoid of affectation; they exhibit personal mastery. The opposite of a dynamic presenter is one who stays glued in one spot, forgets that they have moving parts, is poker faced, and has a monotonous voice.

The internal manifestation of dynamism is your emotional engagement with your topic and with your audience. It's being interested and interesting. It's believing in your message and being genuinely passionate about your subject. It is also how you express yourself: your use of metaphors, symbols, analogies, and storytelling.

Let's look at the outer components of dynamism first.

YOUR FACIAL EXPRESSIONS: WHAT IS YOUR FACE SAYING?

It has been said that the most important thing you wear is the expression on your face. "Poker-faced" and "dynamic" are two descriptions that customarily cannot be applied to the same person. If your trademark is the former, you need to raise your awareness of how you come across. We like to see a person who is cool under fire but not dead cold for the duration of a speech. Know the difference.

Facial expressions keep the audience engaged and less likely to tune you out. There is a wealth of studies on the powerful effect that a facially expressive lecturer has on the engagement of listeners. Research published in the *International Journal of Human and Social Sciences* shows that a lecturer's facial expressions (such as smiling, opening the eyes wide, or raising the eyebrows) while asking questions or emphasizing something important increased the attention of listeners.[4] Your audience is directly affected by your facial expressions as a speaker. The more expressive you are, the more engaged they will be with you and the topic—and the more dynamic you will appear.

Self-awareness precedes self-management: if you are not aware of your habitual facial expressions when you speak, ask a trusted person to attend one of your presentations and give you feedback. If you can, video-record one of your speaking events and examine what you see. Do you need to make some adjustments? For example, do you have a habit of frowning? Nothing makes others more uncomfortable than this negative habit.

Adjustments may be simply to remind yourself once in a while during your presentation to relax your facial muscles. Go ahead and try it right now. Stop reading and focus on your facial muscles. Notice how they are contracted. Start by relaxing the small muscles around your mouth and your jaws, then relax your forehead and next the muscles around your eyes. Then relax the muscles in the back of your head that cause you to be stiff necked. Feel the difference. You can do this within seconds at any time in your presentation. This will give you a more relaxed expression, which has a positive effect on the audience.

Another adjustment you might need to make is to smile. Marianne LaFrance, an experimental psychologist at Yale University, stated, "A credible smile is a force to be reckoned with...It is the most instantly recognizable of all facial expressions...it is...a trustworthiness meter."[5] Some individuals are gifted with naturally smiling faces. The rest of us need to make a conscious effort to remind ourselves to do that.

Smile at the start of your talk, just as you would normally do when you first meet someone and shake hands. Starting your talk this way creates a positive impression; it makes you look confident, but more importantly, it actually relaxes you. Research on "facial feedback theory" has proven that, whether or not we are happy, the mere act of smiling triggers a decrease in heart rate—one of the body's natural responses to feeling relaxed. Even if your smile is mechanical, it generates a beneficial physiological reaction.[6]

Smile, as well, when you have concluded your presentation; again, just as you would normally do when you shake hands with a client at the end of a meeting.

For the rest of the time, remember to smile at natural points; for example, when you make a humorous comment, when an audience member says something funny, or when you announce positive news or any other positive turn of events.

Facial expressions divulge your inner feelings. I encourage you to show your emotions when you speak: Are you happy or excited about what you have just said? Why not show it with a smile? Reconnect with the passion you have for your product, your company, or your industry, and speak from the heart.

Are you disappointed? Show that, too, if it is a part of the message you want to convey. This is the only way we connect with people. Otherwise, you are going through the motions of presenting, and the audience is going through the motions of listening—and you have lost an opportunity to connect in order to bring your message home.

In *The Leader's Voice: How Your Communication Can Inspire Action and Get Results!*, Ron Crossland and Boyd Clarke discuss the four fatal assumptions we can make when we give a talk:

- We assume that the audience understands.
- We assume that the audience agrees.
- We assume that the audience cares.
- We assume that the audience will take some action as a result of our talk.[7]

When we don't connect with the audience, we fall prey to these four fatal assumptions. Take your speaking up a notch by increasing your dynamism with genuine facial expressions that show on the outside what is on the inside. This will increase your credibility as a speaker and strengthen your chances of connecting with the audience.

YOUR MOVEMENT: DON'T JUST STAND THERE

Benjamin Disraeli said, "Every product of genius must be the product of enthusiasm." Movement in the presentation space, provided it is not pacing or swaying, makes you look confident. It lowers your stress level, and it makes you look more relaxed and more in control. It signals to the audience that you own the space—and, for the duration of the presentation, you certainly do. Movement is the easiest aspect of dynamism to control.

Most importantly, every time you move, you reengage the audience's attention, as their eyes are forced to follow your movement. So if they have tuned you out, this is one way to bring them back. As Garr Reynolds has stated, "We humans—and virtually all other animals—are wired to notice movement above all else."[8]

Here are a few tips to help you incorporate movement into your style of presenting.

MOVE STRATEGICALLY

Start speaking from the center position. Then move to the left side, or to the right side, and continue speaking from that location. To do this effectively, you need to continue to speak and make eye contact with the audience while you walk to another spot.

Most importantly, once you are in the other spot, stay anchored for a while; don't move away immediately, or you will be pacing. This movement from center to left and to right, and vice versa, gives you an opportunity to "connect" with everyone in the room.

When do you move and how long do you stay in your new spot? There are no hard-and-fast rules. In fact, too many rules would end up making this look like a staged performance. The purpose here is simply to add energy, to be natural, and not to remain in one spot—which lacks dynamism.

If you are unaccustomed to doing this, think of staying in your new location until you complete one section of your presentation. When you move to another topic, it would be an opportune time to move to another location. Moving at this strategic point in your presentation signals to the audience that you are moving on with your agenda topics.

Once this movement becomes part of your high-energy style of presenting, you will do it naturally, without worrying exactly when to move. It doesn't matter when you move; what matters is *that* you move. You will feel good doing it. And the audience will be more alert and energized by your presence. The aim is to make this such a natural part of your style of presenting that you never have to think about it.

There are very few speakers who can break the rules and pace back and forth when they are presenting without doing any harm to their image. These are the giants in their fields, such as Gary Vaynerchuk and Tom Peters. They present at mega events on very large stages, with hundreds of people in the audience. When you deliver a business presentation in a boardroom or a workshop in a training room, pacing back and forth is distracting and very quickly becomes irritating.

For inspiration, watch John Chambers, CEO of Cisco Systems, presenting on the role of a CEO.[9] He walks comfortably on the stage, lingers, and then walks again. This movement adds energy without being distracting, as he doesn't pace back and forth.

Another speaker to watch is Guy Kawasaki, as he explains the art of innovation.[10] He walks comfortably on the stage, lingers, and then walks again. This movement adds energy to his presentation and makes him look natural and at ease.

DON'T WALK IN FRONT OF THE PROJECTOR

If you don't have a ceiling projector, set up the projector in a spot that allows you to walk behind the projector light, not in front of it. The shadow you throw every time you walk in front of the projector light is distracting and the mark of an unseasoned presenter.

If you have no room to maneuver and you cannot set up the projector behind you, change your movement pattern to work from one side of the room only. Stand on the left side of the screen, from the audience's perspective. By standing to the left of the slides, there is less effort required of the audience when their eyes move from you (standing on the left) to read the information on the slide. If you are standing on the opposite side (the audience's right), the audience has to sweep across the slide to the left in order to read the slide. (If you are presenting in Arabic, Hebrew, Urdu, or Farsi, stand to the right of the slides, as these languages read from right to left.)

For presentations in a small meeting, when sitting down, sit closest to the projection screen. Otherwise your audience will be forced to choose between looking at you and looking at the screen. If they look at the screen instead of at you, they can be totally tuned out to what you're saying.[11]

You should know your material so well that all you need to do is glance at the slide that appears; you should know its content without having to read it.

Better still, you should have rehearsed your presentation so well that you can anticipate exactly which slide is coming on before it is displayed, so that you can smoothly announce it. This is particularly useful when you have complex slides, with diagrams, charts, or graphs. Here is an example of something you might say: "The next slide we are going to see is our projections for the first quarter." Only the most polished presenters do this. Make it a part of your style. It takes a great deal of hard work to know your presentation so well that you can anticipate which slide is coming up next. But the payoff is immense. This is a credibility booster and it is well worth the effort.

Consider using Presenter View, a PowerPoint feature that allows you to view, on your laptop, your Speaker Notes while the audience only sees your presentation. Presenter View also allows you to view the slide thumbnails, so that you can see the upcoming slides.

If you are not familiar with this feature, the Resources section provides two videos that show you how to use it.

YOUR SPEAKING VOICE: THE MOST POWERFUL COMMUNICATION TECHNOLOGY

Another component of dynamism is the way you use your voice. Henry Wadsworth Longfellow said, "The human voice is the organ of the soul." The Gallup Poll conducted a study on the most annoying speech habits. One of these habits is speaking in a monotonous, boring voice; another is speaking with a heavy foreign accent or regional dialect.

(You can view the complete list in Lillian Glass's book, *Talk to Win: Six Steps to a Successful Vocal Image.*[12])

AVOID SPEAKING IN A MONOTONOUS VOICE

Speaking monotonously detracts from your dynamism. A few simple adjustments will help in this regard:

- Add strategic pauses at the end of a section to signal a transition to the next topic.
- Add a pause to emphasize important concepts.
- Speak faster on routine items.
- Slow down for important information.
- Where appropriate, emphasize certain words by speaking slightly louder.

These techniques add "light and shade" to your talk.

Enthusiasm is reflected in the voice. Let the audience know, through your voice, that you are happy to be there. The audience easily picks up on that.

MAKE YOUR ACCENT UNDERSTOOD

Goran Visnjic, a Croatian actor on the television series *ER*, said, "I don't want to lose my accent, I just want it to become smaller." Accents can make others find us more attractive and unique; they are the distinctive manner in which we speak. However, if your accent is so pronounced that the audience has difficulty understanding the message of your presentation, this can have a seriously negative impact on your credibility.

In the *Scientific American* article "Why the Brain Doubts a Foreign Accent," we learn that when a nonnative accent makes speech more difficult for native speakers to understand, listeners doubt the accuracy of what is being said.[13] People prefer stimuli that are easy to process over those that are difficult and that require effort. This preference influences the way we think, not just when we are listening to a presentation that is delivered in a hard-to-understand accent but even with regard to the purchase of stocks: shares in companies with names that are easy to pronounce are purchased at higher rates than shares in companies with names that are more challenging to pronounce!

If you have a difficult-to-understand accent, you need to take steps to remedy this, as a priority. Here are a few tips.

Add Key Points on Your Slides

While I normally discourage presenters from adding too much information to a slide, in this case, you would help the audience by accompanying your oral presentation with bullet points that outline key concepts.

Send a Handout in Advance

Send a handout prior to the presentation, outlining some key background facts that the audience will need to understand in order to follow your line of thinking.

Consult an Accent-reduction Specialist

Work with an accent-reduction specialist to determine the most common pronunciation traps. For example, create a list of minimal pairs (pairs of words that are often confused), and practice these out loud. Examples include ship/sheep, bit/beat, din/dean, feet/fit, hit/heat, live/leave, and shit/sheet.

Another pronunciation trap is the differing stresses on nouns and verbs that have identical spellings; for example, conflict (noun) and conflict (verb); record (noun) and record (verb); and progress (noun) and progress (verb).

Some speech therapists (or speech pathologists) are also accent-reduction specialists. In Canada, speech therapy is covered by extended health plans. Find out if the same benefit is available with your policy if you are in the U.S. If not, the expense is worth it.

The American Speech-Language-Hearing Association lists all speech pathologists in the United States.[14]

In Canada, contact the Canadian Association of Speech-Language Pathologists and Audiologists.[15] The association's website offers a database of professionals; choose one who specializes in accent reduction.

Watch English-language TV

Watch the news on English-language channels. Pay attention to how the announcers speak.

Study Accent-reduction Videos

Take time to view some of the video lessons that are available at the AccentMaster website.[16]

Rehearse Out Loud with a Coach

Practice an important presentation with a coach or a friend. Ask this person to point out any words that you mispronounce during the rehearsal. Practice these words out loud until you can say them without thinking.

Speak Slower

Pay particular attention to careful enunciation.

YOUR GESTURES: A WINDOW ON YOUR THOUGHTS

"To ignore gesture," psychologist Susan Goldin-Meadow observed, "is to ignore part of the conversation."[17] Gestures are an important part of dynamism. Research shows that natural gestures appear slightly *before* the words we speak. That's because emotions motivate and shape the gestures we make. It follows from this that the best gestures are those that occur naturally. They are spontaneous and reflect how you feel about what you are saying; they are not artificial or practiced.

Planned gestures occur *after* the words. This timing is a tell-tale sign that gestures are not genuine, as we learn from Aaron Brehove, fraud investigator and author of the book *Knack Body*

Language: Techniques on Interpreting Nonverbal Cues in the World and Workplace.[18] Nothing will detract from your credibility faster than planned gestures.

I was watching a video clip of a keynote speaker who had obviously been coached: every utterance was punctuated by a gesture. The effect was that of a maestro conducting an imaginary orchestra. It seemed as though the entire speech was mimed.

Much unfortunate advice has been written about gestures for public speaking. One example is to use gestures to mirror your words (such as raising your arm to signify "higher," or making a fist and gently bringing it into your other open palm to stress that you feel strongly about something). Following this advice will lead to a ruined presentation. You will not be able to pull it off, and you will look inauthentic. This is credibility anathema.

The reality is that practiced gestures work for professional speakers, politicians, performers who study stagecraft, media coaches, and public speaking instructors, but they generally don't work for a business person making a presentation to a client or to their board of directors. The gestures end up looking robotic, deliberate, and overly rehearsed. Business audiences, in particular, have a truth radar that instantly spots fakery. Their eyes quickly zoom in on the choreographed waves and karate chops. If you know your topic very well and are enthusiastic about it, your gestures will flow naturally. Gestures naturally reflect our mood as we speak. These are the best gestures, and the only ones you should use.

Having said this, it is important to be aware of seemingly natural gestures that detract from your image. For example, do not adopt the cowboy stance, where the thumbs are placed in belt loops or on the hips, with fingers pointing downward. While this may be a confident dating stance, it is immediately noticeable as a negative for a speaker seeking credibility. It is posed and lacks authenticity.

The most sensible advice I have encountered on hand gestures comes from Robert Lloyd, a great English actor: "Don't allow your hands to touch your body."[19] This simple statement summarizes all of the gestures that are not recommended when presenting: crossing your arms, wringing your hands in front of you, having both hands in your pockets, putting your hands behind your back, and clasping your hands in front in the fig-leaf position. It's okay if you find yourself using one of these gestures for a brief period. Simply decide to raise your awareness. When you catch yourself with your hands in any of these positions, just disengage.

I particularly like this advice from Richard Greene, who was Princess Diana's public speaking coach: he advises speakers to confine gestures to "the power zone" inside the shoulders. "Gesture outside the power zone will not be seen as authoritative."[20]

Gestures also include repetitive mannerisms, which can be distracting or even annoying to the audience. Here are six to avoid:

- **Pointing a finger and stabbing the air.** In Asian cultures, this gesture is considered downright offensive. Instead, use Obama's signature gesture: form a small circle with the tip of your index finger and thumb while the other fingers curve together below the circle. This allows you to emphasize a point without using the offending jabbing finger.

- **Repeatedly clicking your pen.** Once the pen or flipchart marker has completed its purpose, train yourself to lay it down.

- **Using air quotes.** Do not make virtual quotation marks in the air with your fingers while you speak.

- **Rising on your toes to emphasize points.** Keep your feet on the ground.

- **Repeatedly jerking or bobbing your head in agreement.** Doing this when an audience member makes a comment is a particularly annoying habit for your listener.

- **Frequently clearing your throat.** Keep a glass of water next to you and practice swallowing instead.

Let's now look at the inner manifestations of dynamism.

YOUR EMOTIONAL ENGAGEMENT

For a presentation to be credible, it needs to be the product of knowledge *and* feeling. It is more difficult to inspire our audience to action if we approach a presentation just as a cognitive exercise or a philosophical reflection.

When we are emotionally engaged, we strengthen our connection not only to our material but to everyone else in the room. As Norman Vincent Peale said, "If you have zest and enthusiasm you attract zest and enthusiasm. Life does give back in kind." Emotions are infectious—the audience responds to enthusiasm in equal measure. If we are sincere about our message, the audience will notice and pay more attention. As psychologist David Seabury put it, "Wholeheartedness is contagious. Give yourself, if you wish to get others."

Dynamism, then, is above all an inside-out job: It starts internally with genuine passion, enthusiasm, and deep conviction. It manifests outwardly as a high-energy delivery. What role does dynamism play, however, if you are an introverted speaker? Introverted speakers typically have an understated presence, a more "quiet" approach than extroverts.

Watch a video of "Zero Degrees of Empathy," a powerful speech by Professor Simon Baron Cohen.[21] We don't know if Professor Cohen is introverted, but his style of presenting is quiet and understated, and he doesn't display all of the usual outward components of dynamism, such as movement and vocal variety. Yet he oozes credibility. There is no question that he demonstrates expertise, competence, and authenticity. What else does Professor Cohen do to make himself credible?

- He believes in the importance of his topic. He has done extensive research in his area.
- He shows empathy for the audience (warning us that he will start with a rather depressing image).
- He speaks in a colloquial style, even though it is a scientific presentation.
- The words are flowing from his mind, unedited, without artifice.
- His slides are there to support the message and are not the main event.
- He uses understated, natural gestures.
- He makes consistent eye contact with the audience.

Could the presentation have been improved if he had added movement and vocal variety? No doubt about it, especially if the presentation had been longer. This is a fairly short presentation (about twenty-five minutes). But what he does, above all, that strengthens his credibility—despite his low-key delivery—is that he leaves us with the impression that he truly cares about this topic and his audience. This is the element of goodwill, which is a major component of source credibility. As D. Joel Whalen said in *The Professional Communications Toolkit*, "You can communicate dynamism through enthusiasm... All you have to do is care that they get it. That is all you have to do—care—and show that you care."[22]

To gain more insight on introverted speakers, I interviewed Susan Cain, author of *Quiet: The Power of Introverts in a World That Can't Stop Talking*. Here are her answers to three questions:

What are some unique strengths that characterize presenters who have a preference for introversion?

They prepare well; they tend to speak from the heart (since speaking for its own sake is usually not so interesting to them, while speaking from the heart helps a person transcend their normal inhibitions); and they tend to be thoughtful about their subjects, to give unique angles on things.

What is one piece of advice you would give to an introverted speaker who wanted to gain credibility as a presenter?

Look for role models of introverted speakers you admire. Don't try to act like a motivational speaker if that's not who you are. As a speaker, it's not about you; it's about serving your audience. Ask yourself what your audience needs to hear, and how you can share with them the knowledge they seek. Then you've done your job.

Can you please tell my readers how your book, published in January 2012, can help them be better speakers?

I do talk about public speaking in my book, but in addition to that I give introverts new ways to appreciate themselves and the role they play in society. This kind of self-awareness comes across the moment we step onstage.

Ultimately, every presenter can be dynamic by simply raising their self-awareness of how they show up and practicing some of the tips in this chapter. But we need to remind ourselves that it is not a point-and-click method. To be truly dynamic, it has to come from within. It is our vitality, our genuine passion and engagement in the material, that we are presenting. It's above all about connecting with the audience.

CHAPTER 20

THE ICING ON THE CAKE: METAPHORS AND ANALOGIES

"Syntax is the skeleton of a language. The lexicon adds flesh to the skeleton. But metaphors and idioms are those unique features of a language's skin that cause us to say, 'That's beautiful!'"[1]
—Wayne Leman

Metaphors are one of the most powerful weapons in your arsenal as a presenter. In today's fast-paced world of communication, a well-thought-out metaphor acts as a shortcut to meaning. You can say a thousand words with a metaphor. Get comfortable using apt metaphors and watch your presentations come alive. This chapter will help you develop the skills to craft powerful metaphors for your presentations.

METAPHORS

Business people often view metaphors as literary contrivances or adornments, inappropriate in a business presentation—yet our communication is littered with metaphors that we use unconsciously. In his book on metaphors, James Geary states that we use a metaphor approximately every ten to twenty-five words; that's about six metaphors a minute![2] Metaphors have become so ingrained in the way we speak that we no longer even notice them.

This chapter is about using metaphors intentionally. It's about crafting novel metaphors to deliver your message. Using fresh, powerful metaphors is a key tool in transforming your presentation from a mere recital of facts to a communication that is more likely to engage the audience.

Metaphors have the power to inspire and elicit strong emotions. Witness a metaphor that emerged in Egypt during the 2011 revolution: "If you are Pharaoh, we are all Moses." This metaphor alone takes the place of an essay: it tells as much as a thousand words.

Novel metaphors create vivid images for the listener—they bring information alive. Information that is imparted in the form of a metaphor is also more likely to be remembered long after it is heard. Consider famous metaphors such as Shakespeare's "the marriage of true minds," Churchill's "iron curtain," and Forrest Gump's mother's "Life is a box of chocolates."

Most importantly, replacing dull statements with powerful metaphors injects dynamism into your talk. Dynamism is the energy that we bring to a presentation not only physically, but also in the language we use. According to David Brooks:

> *Even the hardest of the sciences depend on a foundation of metaphors. To be aware of metaphors is to be humbled by the complexity of the world, to realize that deep in the undercurrents of thought there are thousands of lenses popping up between us and the world, and that we're surrounded at all times by what Steven Pinker of Harvard once called "pedestrian poetry."*[3]

What exactly is a metaphor? Simply put, a metaphor is a rhetorical figure of speech that suggests a resemblance between two seemingly dissimilar things that actually have something in common. The metaphor shows us this likeness—sometimes instantly—and allows our imagination to perceive a deeper meaning; therefore, a metaphor helps us say a lot with an economy of words. A well-honed metaphor is your shortcut to meaning. As novelist Orson Scott Card put it, "Metaphors have a way of holding the most truth in the least space."

Developing a facility with metaphors will take your presentation skills to the next level and boost your credibility. How can we learn to do this? This chapter will teach you how to hunt for metaphors and even how to create your own.

STUDY EXAMPLES OF POWERFUL METAPHORS

We can get a great deal of inspiration from paying attention to metaphors that successful speakers use. Here are some good examples.

Brick Walls

From Carnegie Mellon Professor Randy Pausch's last lecture, "Really Achieving Your Childhood Dreams":

> *But remember, the brick walls are there for a reason. The brick walls are not there to keep us out. The brick walls are there to give us a chance to show how badly we want something. Because the brick walls are there to stop the people who don't want it badly enough. They're there to stop the other people.*[4]

The Desert

Jeff Bezos, CEO of Amazon.com, in an interview with David LaGesse for *U.S. News & World Report*:

> *If you don't have a willingness to be misunderstood for a long period of time, then you can't have a long-term orientation... While we're crossing the desert, we may be thirsty, but we sincerely believe there's an oasis on the other side.*[5]

The Emergency Room

Warren Buffett, in an Op-Ed piece for the *New York Times*: "The United States economy is now out of the emergency room and appears to be on a slow path to recovery."[6]

A Garden

Jack Welch, former CEO of General Electric, in a lecture at Stanford Graduate School of Business:

> *The day you become a leader, it becomes about them... Your job is to walk around with a can of water in one hand and a can of fertilizer in the other hand. Think of your team as seeds, and try and build a garden... It's about building these people... Only you will know the team.*[7]

A Cat

Albert Einstein:

> *You see, wire telegraph is a kind of a very, very long cat. You pull his tail in New York and his head is meowing in Los Angeles. Do you understand this? And radio operates exactly the same*

way: you send signals here, they receive them there. The only difference is that there is no cat.

Bottled Water

Al Pittampalli, author of *Read This Before Our Next Meeting*: "Using a meeting to disseminate information is sort of like using bottled Evian water to wash your dishes. It works, but it's kind of expensive, and pretty ridiculous."[8]

DEVELOP METAPHORS
FOR DIFFERENT AREAS OF YOUR LIFE

Create metaphors and keep them in your arsenal as a speaker. Below is a list of areas where you would be well served to have some metaphors at your disposal. These metaphors will come in handy when you have a speaking engagement:

- Your personal values and beliefs
- Your organizational values
- Lessons learned (about life, leadership, business)
- How you deal with setbacks, disappointments, failures
- How you handle mistakes as a leader
- Your views on risk taking
- Your views on innovation
- The meaning of success for you
- Your product, service, or underlying technology
- The contributions made by you or your company to society
- Your relationship with your customers

- Your noble goals
- The legacy you want to leave behind

Think about other areas applicable to your presentation topics and add them to this list.

KNOW WHERE TO HUNT FOR METAPHORS

As you know now, metaphors abound in our lives. Some good ways to find them are described below. Consider incorporating appropriate metaphors into your presentations, to make them more dynamic.

Read Widely

Broaden your knowledge by reading abundantly in a wide array of fields that interest you. Don't limit your reading to what is within your industry. The *Book of Common Prayer* has this powerful quote: "Read, mark, learn and inwardly digest." Books and quality newspapers and magazines, such as the *Atlantic*, the *New Yorker*, and *Utne Reader*, are examples of excellent sources for inspiring metaphors.

Read the Scriptures

The Scriptures are rife with metaphors. President Obama recounted the Bible parable of two men, one who built his house on a pile of sand and the other who built his house upon a rock. Then he said the following:

> *We cannot rebuild this economy on the same pile of sand. We must build our house upon a rock. We must lay a new foundation for growth and prosperity—a foundation that will move us from an era of borrow and spend to one where we save and invest; where we consume less at home and send more exports abroad.*

Explore the Talmud

When the world was writing about Steve Jobs's recent passing, it occurred to me that the following Talmudic metaphor is descriptive of this legendary man: "There are stars whose light only reaches the earth long after they have fallen apart. There are people whose remembrance gives light in this world, long after they have passed away." The Talmud is rich with beautiful metaphors.

Search Online Speeches

Become a metaphor anthropologist by searching online for transcripts of speeches by business and political leaders. Visit sites that specialize in metaphors. (See the Resources section for a list of suggestions.)

Set Up a Metaphor Library

Develop a personal library of metaphor sources; for example, buy a dictionary of metaphors and some choice books that deal specifically with metaphors. (Some recommended sources are listed in the Resources section.)

Read Poetry

The poems of Rumi and Robert Frost are a good place to start.

Cull Metaphors from Movies

Many movies contain powerful metaphors. If you are inspired by a metaphor in a movie, don't lose that inspiration. Make a note of the metaphor in your speaker's journal or notebook, or email it to yourself. For example, in *Any Given Sunday*, Al Pacino delivers a powerful speech to his football team. The metaphor he uses is winning by inches: "The inches we need are everywhere around us ... we fight for that inch ... because we know, when we add up all those inches, that's going to make the ... difference between winning and losing."[9]

CREATE YOUR OWN METAPHORS

You don't have to rely on metaphors from other sources; you can invent your own, to suit the purposes of your presentation exactly. To do so, follow these steps:

1. **Choose the concept you want to amplify with a metaphor.** For example, your topic might be "change."

2. **Identify the important thing that you want to explain about your concept.** For example, you might want to say that change is important because without it, an organization doesn't progress.

3. **Think about an unrelated item that shares the same characteristics as your concept.** Something that doesn't move. What happens to it? It gets run over, it stays behind, it stagnates. These are some thoughts. Let's take "stagnate." What does "stagnate" make you think of? For example, you might come up with a body of water or a lake.

4. **Develop the metaphor.** For example, when water is confined and becomes motionless, there is an accumulation of debris, and the water becomes stagnant. But when there is wind and the water is allowed to move unrestricted, there is a flow and the water is fresh and rejuvenated. Therefore, a lack of change in an organization can be likened to a stagnant pool of water, littered with the debris of outdated modes and practices that hamper the flow of fresh ideas.

Let's do another example.

1. Let's say you want to speak about the importance of teamwork for the success of a project.

2. What are the important things you want to say about teamwork? It requires compatibility and cooperation, for example.

3. Think of an item unrelated to the project that shares the characteristics of compatibility and cooperation amongst individuals. You can consider any team sport, as they all depend on a team dynamic between members. But what would be one sport where the stakes are crucial, where incompatibility can have disastrous consequences? I think of mountain climbing.

4. Develop the metaphor. Successfully completing a mountain-climbing expedition requires more than just expertise in mountain climbing. It requires cooperation and trust amongst team members. This is a crucial element, as each member of the team relies on the others for their safety and their life. Now make the connection between mountain climbing and teamwork at the office: a project will only live and thrive if the team has the same dynamic of trust and collaboration as successful mountain climbers do.

Finally, you need to differentiate between fresh metaphors and banal ones—those that have been used so often that they have turned into clichés. For example, expressions like "trailblazing" and "leading edge" will go unnoticed. It pays to spend time to develop your own fresh metaphors. Doing so will electrify your talks and expand your mind as you practice looking for connections between disparate ideas. As Aristotle said, "The highest human capacity is the capacity for metaphor."

ANALOGIES

Attorney and politician Dudley Field Malone said, "One good analogy is worth three hours discussion." Participants in my workshops often ask me how to make a technical presentation more interesting. One of the most powerful tools at your disposal for achieving this is using analogies. An analogy compares two different things to highlight a similarity. Analogies are an essential communication tool for any presentation, but especially for technical presentations. Used well, they give you the power to explain complex bits of information with a minimum of verbiage. They help your audience, in particular nonspecialists, understand what you mean. They also inject an air of freshness and creativity into your presentation, especially if they are accompanied by a related, powerful visual.

Analogies help you explain the unfamiliar using the familiar, in order to help others understand new information. For example: "Angina is like the cramp in your side that you get when you are running." Angina is the complex/unfamiliar subject matter, and running is the straightforward/familiar basis for comparison.

Ask yourself these questions when you create an analogy:

1. Is the analogy simple? If you need an elaborate explanation for your analogy, then it's not effective.

2. Is the comparison used in your analogy related to something familiar? If the target comparison is also

unfamiliar, then you are essentially comparing one unfamiliar concept to another unfamiliar concept. Such a comparison would confuse your audience rather than help them.

A PROCESS FOR USING ANALOGIES IN YOUR PRESENTATIONS

Follow these steps for effectively incorporating an analogy into a presentation.

Step 1

Clearly state your point first.

Step 2

Introduce your analogy with words such as the following:

- "Imagine this as…"
- "Think of this as…"
- "It's like…"
- "You can picture this as…"
- "By analogy…"
- "This is similar to…"
- "Similarly…"
- "Another way to understand this is…"
- "An alternative way to view this is by comparing it to…"
- "This reminds me of…"

Step 3

If needed, *briefly* expand on your analogy to explain how the two concepts (the familiar and the unfamiliar) are related or similar.

Here is an example of how this works. Let's say you want to explain why defragmenting your hard disk is important.[10] The steps for creating an analogy might be as follows:

- **Step 1:** "If you don't periodically defrag your drive, your computer will slow down."

- **Step 2:** "Imagine you are making a cake. If you put each of the ingredients used to make the cake in a different room, it will take forever to get it done because you have to run around the house for each ingredient."

- **Step 3:** "Similarly, computers need all the pieces of a program together, so they can load the program faster. Defragmentation keeps all the pieces together."

CONSIDER YOUR AUDIENCE

Think of your audience when you choose an analogy. Will the analogy be understood or will it confuse the audience? Consider age, gender, culture, and industry when you choose your analogies.

The right analogy is like a wand that instantly creates a visualization of our thoughts. The more we help the audience to visualize what we are saying, the more effective we are—not only in aiding their understanding but in keeping them engaged. If people have temporarily tuned you out during your presentation, the mention of an effective analogy acts as an attention getter, much like metaphors and storytelling. Fresh analogies are attention magnets.

CHAPTER 21

GET THEM TO LEAN IN: STORYTELLING

"Tell me a fact and I'll learn. Tell me a truth and I'll believe.
But tell me a story and it will live in my heart forever."
—Indian Proverb

One of the earliest and most powerful forms of communication was storytelling. Whether in the form of myth, legend, fairy tale, parable, folktale, epic, odyssey, case study, novel, or situation comedy, storytelling is universal.

Cognitive psychologist Jerome Bruner states that our brains are hardwired for storytelling. He has observed how, from an early age, children tell stories—and their need to create stories precedes language. He even goes so far as to say that children are motivated to learn to speak because they have stories in them that they need to tell: "We are storytelling creatures, and as children we acquire language to tell those stories that we have inside us."[1]

Scientists believe that storytelling is hardwired through a gene called FOXP2, which was discovered in 2001. Dubbed the "storytelling gene," it makes language and narrative possible and helps us understand our linguistic heritage. As Richard Maxwell and Robert Dickman put it, "From a cellular level on up, we are all born storytellers."[2]

Stories are our primary method of relating to others. When something happens to us that we consider interesting or unusual or new, we craft a story about it to tell others. People love stories. There are innumerable books, articles, websites, workshops, and retreats on storytelling. Utilized for leadership, management, inspiration, or persuasion, storytelling is an industry in itself. This is because storytelling works!

A brief, well-crafted story that is relevant to your topic is one of the most potent ways to connect with your audience and add interest to your presentation. The keys here are "brief" and "relevant." If you ramble on, and provide minute, irrelevant details, your storytelling will actually backfire, as people start to lose interest—or worse, feel annoyed that you are wasting their time.

THE EIGHT CHARACTERISTICS OF AN EFFECTIVE STORY

Dale Carnegie had the following to say about storytelling:

> *Your purpose is to make your audience see what you saw, hear what you heard, feel what you felt. Relevant detail, couched in concrete, colorful language, is the best way to recreate the incident as it happened and to picture it for the audience.*

When you tell a story in a presentation, keep in mind the eight characteristics of an effective story.

A STORY MUST BE AUTHENTIC

Make sure your story is true and not manufactured. Invented stories erode your credibility as a speaker; invariably, something will leak through to make the story ring hollow.

A STORY MUST BE RELEVANT

Your story must be relevant to your topic. It needs to have a "message" or a lesson. Stories are told to help explain and reinforce your message, to provide support for your opinions and beliefs, to inspire change, or to persuade. In a business presentation, your story needs to make a point relevant to your main topic and not be told just to entertain. The entertainment factor is a bonus, not the main event.

A STORY MUST HAVE ONE THEME

Stories need to have just a single theme. Otherwise, they risk being convoluted and confusing.

A STORY MUST HAVE THE RIGHT AMOUNT OF DETAIL

Provide vivid detail to help the listener picture what you are saying but not too much extraneous detail. Brevity is key. Long stories are guaranteed killers.

A STORY MUST HAVE SUSPENSE

A story must elicit curiosity about what happens next. This is what gives the story its "lean in" quality. It's what engages our attention because we want to know how the story will unfold and how it will end. Ira Glass, host of the radio program *This American Life*, calls it the suspense that comes from relating a sequence of events or actions that makes even the most boring story compelling because we want to know what's next.[3]

A STORY MUST HAVE DIRECT DIALOGUE

Ron Crossland, in *The Leader's Voice: How Your Communication Can Inspire Action and Get Results!*, talks about the importance of including dialogue in your stories.[4] Say the exact words that the people in your story used: "The client said, 'I am extremely unhappy about the latest shipment.'" (This is an example of direct speech or quoted speech.) Don't talk in the third person: "The client said he was extremely unhappy about the latest shipment." (This is an example of indirect speech or reported speech.)

A STORY MUST BE CULTURALLY APPROPRIATE
Stories must be culturally appropriate; that is, they must resonate with your audience. Otherwise, the full message is lost.

A STORY MUST BE KIND
Benjamin Disraeli said, "Never tell unkind stories." Inconsiderate and insensitive stories do not bring grace to those who hear them and may actually leave people dispirited.

EXEMPLARY STORY
Below is an excerpt of a beautiful story, "We Are What We Choose," delivered by Jeff Bezos at the baccalaureate of Princeton's Class of 2010.[5] It incorporates all eight building blocks of great storytelling.

> *As a kid, I spent my summers with my grandparents on their ranch in Texas. I helped fix windmills, vaccinate cattle, and do other chores. We also watched soap operas every afternoon, especially* Days of our Lives. *My grandparents belonged to a Caravan Club, a group of Airstream trailer owners who travel together around the U.S. and Canada. And every few summers, we'd join the caravan. We'd hitch up the Airstream trailer to my grandfather's car, and off we'd go, in a line with 300 other*

Airstream adventurers. I loved and worshipped my grand-parents and I really looked forward to these trips. On one particular trip, I was about 10 years old. I was rolling around in the big bench seat in the back of the car. My grandfather was driving. And my grandmother had the passenger seat. She smoked throughout these trips, and I hated the smell.

At that age, I'd take any excuse to make estimates and do mi-nor arithmetic. I'd calculate our gas mileage—figure out useless statistics on things like grocery spending. I'd been hearing an ad campaign about smoking. I can't remember the details, but basically the ad said, every puff of a cigarette takes some num-ber of minutes off of your life: I think it might have been two minutes per puff. At any rate, I decided to do the math for my grandmother. I estimated the number of cigarettes per days, es-timated the number of puffs per cigarette and so on. When I was satisfied that I'd come up with a reasonable number, I poked my head into the front of the car, tapped my grandmother on the shoulder, and proudly proclaimed, "At two minutes per puff, you've taken nine years off your life!"

I have a vivid memory of what happened, and it was not what I expected. I expected to be applauded for my cleverness and arithmetic skills. "Jeff, you're so smart. You had to have made some tricky estimates, figure out the number of minutes in a year and do some division." That's not what happened. Instead, my grandmother burst into tears. I sat in the backseat and did not know what to do. While my grandmother sat crying, my grandfather, who had been driving in silence, pulled over onto the shoulder of the highway. He got out of the car and came around and opened my door and waited for me to follow. Was I in trouble? My grandfather was a highly intelligent, quiet man. He had never said a harsh word to me, and maybe this was to be the first time? Or maybe he would ask that I get back in the car and apologize to my grandmother. I had no experience in this realm with my grandparents and no way to gauge what the consequences might be. We stopped beside the trailer. My grandfather looked at me, and after a bit of silence, he gently and calmly said, "Jeff, one day you'll understand that it's harder to be kind than clever."

What I want to talk to you about today is the difference between gifts and choices. Cleverness is a gift, kindness is a choice. Gifts are easy—they're given after all. Choices can be hard. You can seduce yourself with your gifts if you're not careful, and if you do, it'll probably be to the detriment of your choices.

PART FIVE

OVER TO YOU

CHAPTER 22

YOUR FREQUENTLY ASKED QUESTIONS

"It is not the answer that enlightens, but the question."
—Eugene Ionesco

Our thought process is driven by questions, not lectures. I have been blessed with workshop participants and coaching clients who have asked me so many questions that these alone could constitute a book. Here are some of the questions that might be of help to readers of this book.

I always blush so badly—my whole face! It's really frustrating! Is there a way to keep this from happening?
Blushing is the involuntary and uncontrollable result of blood flowing to your facial veins. The veins become dilated so that more blood than usual can flow through them. This causes the reddened appearance that telegraphs our embarrassment to others. The best way to eliminate this problem is to work on the root causes of the stress. If you cannot eliminate the stress, here are a few tips to help you:

- Consider that, often, blushing is not nearly as visible to others as we think it is. People are focused on your message and on their own concerns. Not everyone is focused on observing changes in your skin coloration.

- When you feel the sensation of the blush coming on, such as your face heating up, put all your energies toward concentrating on your topic. Keep moving with your presentation. In most cases, blushing disappears after a minute or two. Chances are it will pass unobserved by the majority of the audience.

- Wear Merle Norman Cover Up in green and then apply MAC Studio Fix foundation (or other preferred foundation) to minimize the appearance of the redness when it occurs. Some people report that the redness becomes virtually unnoticeable.[1]

- Avoid lower-cut blouses and consider wearing turtlenecks. Wear a red blouse or shirt; it minimizes the appearance of red on your face.

- Don't wear warm clothes. If you can control the thermostat in the room where you are presenting, set it to a lower than normal position.

- Don't drink coffee before or during the presentation, as it may cause flushing.

- Avoid foods with monosodium glutamate (MSG), an additive often used in Chinese cuisine to enhance flavor. It causes flushing in some people.

- If you are taking niacin supplements, speak to your physician. Some report that niacin can cause flushing.

- Erythrophobia, the fear of blushing, creates anxiety, which in turn causes more blushing. If this is a serious issue for you, consider seeing a cognitive behavioral therapist to help you overcome the fear. The therapist will work with you to explore the situations that cause the blushing. Then you will work to understand the connection between the situations and the underlying beliefs and thoughts that cause you to react with fear. While severing the connection between the stimulus (the troublesome situation) and the thoughts can be done on your own through relaxation techniques, visualization, meditation, self-affirmation, and self-hypnosis, the most effective and possibly fastest route is to work with a professional in the field.

• As a last resort, and only in severe situations that may be crippling and preventing you from presenting at all, consider consulting a physician, who may prescribe beta blockers or other anxiety-reducing medications.

Please consider that embarrassment is fundamentally a "moral emotion."[2] It arises from a sensitivity to what others think and is a kind of graceful apology to whoever is looking. Blushing is a very human event.

I would like to overcome the occasional situation when my mind goes blank and I forget what I am planning to say.

Anxiety about presenting can have a negative impact on your short-term memory and your ability to concentrate. When you are gripped by performance anxiety, your body produces the natural response of fight or flight. This means that all of your mental resources are diverted to survival. Remembering things is not a priority for the brain at that point. To get you ready to fight or flee, in response to stress, your body releases cortisol into your bloodstream.

Scientists have discovered that human volunteers who are injected with cortisol are temporarily impaired in their learning and recall abilities.[3] Deep breathing and relaxation are therefore of paramount importance when you are anxious.

Practice self-care *before* an important presentation. This includes ensuring that you get adequate sleep for two or three nights before a major presentation; exercise; and relax through yoga, meditation, or any other preferred relaxation regimen.

Remind yourself that only you know what you were going to say next. So if you forget, there is no need to signal to the audience that you are having a memory lapse. They will not notice unless you tell them. What benefit could you possibly derive by saying, "I am sorry, I seem to have a mental block"?

Here are some additional strategies to help you when you experience a memory hiccup.

Say Nothing About It to the Audience
Pause briefly. Take a deep breath. Adjust your posture: stand tall. Consciously focus on your expression and be intentional about controlling your facial muscles so that you don't look anxious (e.g., with a furrowed brow). Stop reading right now and practice control of your facial muscles. Get used to doing this so that you can do it effortlessly when you experience a memory blank.

Don't look down hoping the earth opens up and swallows you, and don't look at the door or window, hoping you can escape. Instead, look at a friendly face in the audience. You know who they are.

Smile. If you have been following the advice in this book of pausing, making eye contact, smiling once in a while, and standing tall, the audience will not perceive any difference in your attitude at the time you experience a memory block.

Repeat Your Last Statement

If you forget what you were going to say, repeat your last statement. If it was an important statement, repeat it exactly. "As I said, our differences matter less." If it was a routine, unimportant point, repeat it by rephrasing. In most case, the repetition is enough to help you calm down and remember what you were planning to say next.

Have a One-Page Outline with You

As a security measure, have a one page outline of your presentation in a spot where you can easily glance at it. This is the skeleton of your speech, showing the key concepts of your talk clearly written in bold, capital letters. If you rehearsed from your outline, rather than your detailed script, this document should be very familiar to you, so that a mere glance at the key word will trigger your memory. Consider, as well, using color to help you: highlight each key word or section in a different color. When the mental freeze occurs, you calmly and briefly glance at your outline sheet, then look up at the audience, pause slightly, and carry on.

It is quite acceptable to look at your notes once in a while, as long as you do it briefly, confidently, and calmly, without signaling panic in your expression. The slight pause, after looking at your outline, gives the audience the impression that you are reflecting on what you will say next. Practice doing this, once in a while in your presentations, even when you do remember your material, so that this becomes one of your natural moves when a mental freeze sets in. Remember to take a discrete deep breath while you look at your outline notes.

Figure 10 shows an example of an outline, which can act as your safety net in the event of a temporary mental lapse. Let's say your talk is about the benefits of using compact fluorescent light bulbs (CFLs).

Outline	Speech
8 (66%)	They increase the lifespan of a bulb. They last 8 times longer! So this will reduce your household lighting costs by up to 66%.
TOO HOT GLOBE	They are safer as they reduce the danger of touching a too hot globe when you replace the bulb.
POLLUTION (450 LB CARBON DIOXIDE)	They reduce pollution. For each CFL that you use instead of an incandescent bulb, you can eliminate up to 450 lbs of carbon dioxide from polluting the environment. It's an easy way to care for the environment.

Figure 10

Have a Glass of Water Nearby
Briefly stop to take a slow sip from a glass of water which you have previously arranged to have nearby. This old trick can work to buy you time to calm down.

Look at a Friendly Face in the Audience
Rest your eyes on an audience member who is friendly. Sometimes this is enough to help you recover from your temporary memory lapse.

Ask the Audience a Question

This can be a planned question or a question about what you just covered before you had the mental block. "Let me interrupt this for a moment to ask a question." And then proceed to ask the question in a confident manner. Again, no one but you knows that this is a tactic to buy time until you calm down. Choose a question that you know your audience will be able to answer so that you turn the focus on them and away from you for a moment.

Or ask a question that might be difficult to answer but for which you have meticulously prepared the answer. It helps, as well, if the question requires a moderately elaborate explanation, perhaps including a well-practiced sketch drawing on the whiteboard or flipchart.

Distribute a Handout

"At this point, I'd like to stop for a moment and have you look at this handout on … after you read it, please let me know if you have any questions." Read your notes while they are reading the handout. Resume your talk by saying something pertinent about the handout and then carrying on.

Start an Activity

If appropriate, give the audience an activity that you have planned. "I'd like you to partner with the person next to you (or in small groups at your table), and discuss what you see as possible solutions to the XYZ issue. Please take five minutes to brainstorm ideas and we will then discuss as a group."

Write Down Your Fears

Before the presentation, write down all of your fears and feelings of worry about the event. Psychologists at the University of Chicago conducted research showing that students who spent just ten minutes writing about their feelings immediately before a test prevented their minds from going blank and scored significantly higher on tests.[4] The same strategy can help you to minimize the anxiety before a presentation.

Writing about your feelings frees memory resources and increases your ability to focus. Research shows that expressing emotion on paper is beneficial even in extreme cases, such as with trauma victims and depression patients. Geoff Cohen of Stanford University said, "Putting your thoughts and feelings down has been shown to increase emotional and even physical well-being."[5] If you can arrange it, find a private place before your presentation to list all of your worries about what might go wrong.

Use a Planned Back-up Slide
To move the focus away from you, you can also have a back-up slide with a complex visual, e.g., a graph, diagram, spreadsheet, or map— anything that is pertinent to your presentation. Show this slide at this time and say something like, "We'll now digress for a moment and go over this spreadsheet to analyze some of the key drivers in this XYZ issue."

I find it difficult to determine the level of detail suitable for the audience when there is a mix of people: specialists and nonspecialists.

A superior presenter is like a gracious host who makes everyone in a social gathering feel comfortable regardless of age, education level, position, or other barometer of status. Approach a presentation to a mixed audience of experts and nonexperts with the same grace and care.

Here are a few tips to get you started.

Explain Technical Terms

Take the time to define all technical terms, acronyms, abbreviations, and industry jargon. For a highly technical presentation that includes nonexperts, consider even distributing a one-page glossary as a handout; briefly refer to it at the start of the presentation. Nonexperts will appreciate your going the extra mile for them.

Provide an Overview

Start with a summary or overview that provides pertinent background information necessary for understanding what follows. Experts in the audience know that this is for the benefit of nonexperts and will not feel patronized. "As we have a mixed audience today, I will start by providing a brief overview of the background on XYZ so that everyone is on the same page. Then I will follow with the technical aspects."

Practice Your Presentation with a Layperson

Go over your explanation of the more complex parts with a person outside your industry and ask them for feedback on your clarity. Make adjustments based on the feedback you receive.

Use Examples to Illustrate Your Points

As much as possible, give analogies related to the audience's everyday life. Consider paraphrasing, using words such as the following:

- "In other words…"
- "By analogy…"
- "To illustrate my point, imagine…"
- "An example of this would be…"

Avoid Math Equations

Even scientists have a tendency to tune out when you present complicated math formulas. Add these as background information in your handouts. As Mark Schoeberl has advised:

> *The problem is that equations are a dense mathematical notation indicating quantitative relationships. People are used to studying equations, not seeing them flashed on the screen for 2 minutes… equations are distracting. People stop listening and start studying the equation. If you have to show an equation— simplify it and talk to it very briefly.*[6]

Use Short Sentences and Common Words

This is particularly important in a highly specialized presentation that includes nonspecialists who will be struggling to keep up with the concepts. Don't make it harder by using obscure language and convoluted sentence structure.

Clarify Your Main Message

Tell them clearly what your main message is. Provide just enough detail to support your message and no more. Any additional detail can be provided in the handout. Conclude with a succinct, crystal-clear summary of your main points.

Follow a Sequential Process

Use verbal markers, such as, "The first point I will cover is ...," "The second point is ...," and "Now I will proceed to the third and final point." Keep the information under each point to a minimum—give the audience only what they need to know, not what is nice to know. Cut out all extraneous information that doesn't support your key message and main points.

Perform Surgery

In deciding what to leave in and what to take out during the preparation process, after each section of your presentation, keep asking yourself, "So what? Why should the audience care about this particular detail? What's in it for them?" If you can't provide a compelling answer, omit this detail. If this causes you some anxiety, include the information in a handout and keep some of it at the ready for questions from the audience.

Provide Interim Summaries

At the end of each major section, provide mini-reviews or summaries.

Check in Periodically

At strategic points, ask questions to make sure you have not left the audience behind: "Is this clear so far?" "Is there anything that I need to clarify before I move on to the next point?"

Use Graphs

Replace tables with graphs, wherever possible, as graphs help people see the relationship between various items more readily.

Add Transitions

Use logical transitions between points to help people follow your train of thought. Use expressions such as

- "Consequently…"
- "In spite of this…"
- "This leads us to…"

(See the Resources section for a list of transitions.)

Stress What Is Important

Stress the importance of various points *during* the presentation, not only at the end. Use expressions such as

- "This is important because…"
- "My next item is particularly crucial."
- "What this means for you is…"

Use Strategic Pauses

After a complex, technical point, pause briefly. Let the information sink in before you move too quickly to the next point.

Keep Variables to a Minimum

Don't introduce too many "variables," as you might do with a highly technical audience. This forces the audience to abandon one train of thought and embark on another. What is only an aside to you may be perceived as a main point; otherwise, why would you mention it? Keep your talk straightforward and uncluttered.

Send Information Ahead of Time

If feasible or appropriate, consider distributing a document containing some detailed background information ahead of time. Ask the audience to read this prior to the presentation.

Don't Assume Everyone Understands

If you are making a technical presentation to sell something to a mixed audience, consider that the decision makers and their entourage will often be in the nonexpert group. The expert group is likely to be a technical person in the organization who has been asked to attend in order to ask the technical questions and to make sure that you are providing valid information. Although these people are technical, they are often not experts in your field. Therefore, although they will be able to absorb the technical aspects more readily than the others, they will not have all of the knowledge that you might assume. So, you will need to ensure that there are no gaps in the necessary information.

The decision maker will also often invite less senior individuals into a meeting or presentation. These people may not have important titles, but they do have influence; that's why they are there, to provide advice and feedback after the presentation. You need to reach these nonexperts as much as the decision makers and the semi-experts in the room. Be mindful of who they are and what prior knowledge, if any, they might have on your topic. Then address any areas that require a more detailed explanation, to help them understand the key messages. A successful presentation will be one that takes into account all three groups without overwhelming everyone with too much detail.

You can break down the level of detail according to the different needs of each group. The decision makers want detail about the return on investment. The nonexperts and non–decision makers need to understand the basics so that they can provide meaningful feedback to the decision makers. The technical attendees are interested in features, bells and whistles, and implementation. Speak about these at a high level; don't include math or explanations of code, and offer to speak separately to this group in a follow-up meeting. Read "Having 'The Talk': Discussing Technology with Managers and Customers" by Nathan Carpenter of RABA Technologies.[7]

How can I best collaborate with other team members to make a good group presentation?

Bear in mind that your presentation must look like a team effort, a musical concert where every player is in tune with the other players and the presentation is a beautifully executed whole and not a series of unconnected parts.

Here are some important tips.

See the Other Presentations Prior to the Event
It is easy to get so enmeshed in your own presentation that you neglect to see the other presentations. This is important to ensure that there is a flow between the various parts.

Set and Observe Ground Rules
How long is the total presentation? How long does each presenter have? What order is best to present the material? Appoint a time keeper and choose a signal to help the speakers stay on track.

Ensure Smooth Transitions

To achieve a sense of unity, each presenter should refer briefly to the key points made by the other presenters, creating a link to the other presentations. As well, each presenter should briefly preview the presentation that follows. This gives the entire presentation a professional feel and helps the audience follow and retain the information more easily. "Briefly" is key here. You don't want to steal each other's thunder; you just want to create flow and unity—recognizing that it is one presentation but that you have elected to divide it into segments, with each segment presented by a different person. The audience should not suffer because of that.

Design for Variety

Think about the audience that will be listening to five or six presenters: are all the presentations using the same format, e.g., lecturing with PowerPoint slides? This could be tedious for the audience. Build some variety into each segment, e.g., questions, rhetorical questions, activities, exercises, video clips, cartoons, interesting visuals or graphics, props, or exhibits. You want to aim for a change of pace, a way to re-engage the audience's attention.

Pay Attention

When another team member is speaking, all the others need to pay close attention and look interested. Please don't forget that: when one team member is speaking, the entire team is "on." Even though the audience is paying attention to the speaker, they do occasionally look at the other members of the team. Look at the speaker and look at the audience to gauge reactions. Stay alert and engaged, and look interested. Don't read your notes, yawn, look at your watch, remove lint from your jacket, look out the window, whisper to your neighbor, glance at your mobile device, or leave the room unnecessarily. All of these have been observed!

Support Each Other

Don't disagree with what another team member is saying. This is not a debate, it is a team presentation. Any disagreements should occur prior to the main event.

Introduce and Wrap Things Up

If there is no moderator or overall team presentation coordinator, and you are the first speaker, then it is your duty to set the right tone by introducing the team presentation and being fully aware of what everyone will be speaking about. Similarly, if you are the last speaker, it is your duty to wrap things up in an upbeat, positive way, perhaps briefly summing up the previous presentations and thanking the audience.

Establish Rules for Q&A

Are questions allowed during the presentation or at the end of the presentation? Make sure your Q&A procedure is announced to the audience at the beginning. Ensure that team members agree on the rules so that everyone does the same thing on the day of the presentation.

EPILOGUE

"A truly good book teaches me better than to read it.
I must soon lay it down, and commence living on its hint…
What I began by reading, I must finish by acting."
—Henry David Thoreau

The measure of success of a book is not how many people buy it but how many people use it to improve themselves. Henry Miller was once asked what makes a book live. His simple response: "A book lives through the passionate recommendation of one reader to another…Like money, books must be kept in constant circulation." I leave you with two wishes: that you use this book actively and thoroughly to enhance your ability to present, and once you have attained this goal and enriched your mind, that you give your copy to someone else as a gift of knowledge. You will be richer twice.

If you liked this book and found it useful, please consider adding a review on Amazon at **http://amzn.com/1935667122**. Thank you.

RESOURCES

For a full listing of the URLs found throughout the book and in the Resources, please visit http://www.clarionenterprises.com/links.

A. Transitions

B. A Speaker's Library

C. Speaking Blogs

D. Other Useful Websites

E. A Compendium of Presentations

F. A Planning Template

TRANSITIONS

"If you've ever ridden in a car with a stick shift you know that smooth transitions are rare. If something is just a little off, the car bucks like a mule. The same thing is true of sentences."[1]
—**Geraldine Woods**

Transitions help your presentation flow smoothly from start to finish. They are the seamless thread that ties everything together and moves the listeners from one point to another without losing your train of thought. Transitions create clarity and boost your credibility as a competent presenter; their presence is the mark of a seasoned speaker.

Here are lists of useful transitions.

To show result or cause:
- As a result
- Consequently, as a consequence
- Because of that
- For this reason
- That's why
- Therefore
- It follows from this

To repeat information:
- In other words
- In essence
- Once again
- To put it another way
- To repeat
- To put it differently

To show a comparison:
- Likewise
- Like
- Also
- While
- Similarly
- By comparison, compared to, in comparison
- In the same manner
- In the same way
- As
- Comparatively
- Coupled with

To show a contrast or difference:
- But
- However
- Unlike
- Yet
- Though, although, even though
- Nevertheless, nonetheless
- Rather than
- In contrast

- In spite of
- Still
- On the other hand
- Otherwise

To illustrate a point:
- For example, for instance, as an example
- As an illustration, to illustrate my point
- By analogy

To state the obvious:
- Of course
- No doubt, without a doubt
- For sure, surely
- Certainly, for certain
- Admittedly
- Granted that
- Naturally

To clarify:
- For example, for instance
- In other words
- That is
- What I mean is
- To be clear
- What this means is

To add information:
- Besides
- In addition
- Again

- Furthermore
- Also
- Next
- Additionally
- Along with
- As well
- Moreover
- Another
- A second, a third
- The next

To show a conclusion:

- Therefore
- To conclude
- Finally
- Lastly
- The final point, the last point
- As a result
- To sum up, in summary
- To wrap up
- Given these facts
- With this in mind

To emphasize a point:

- Again
- For sure
- Especially
- To repeat, to emphasize
- As I said
- In particular
- Specifically

To generalize:
- In general, generally speaking
- As usual
- Ordinarily
- As a rule, as a rule of thumb
- In principle
- For the most part

To show a sequence:
- To begin with
- At first
- First of all
- The second step, the next step
- Later on
- In turn

To show an exception:
- Except, excepting
- Save for
- Aside from
- Outside of

To show importance:
- Equally important
- Most importantly
- Of greater importance
- Of less importance
- Above all

A SPEAKER'S LIBRARY

"A man only learns in two ways, one by reading,
and the other by association with smarter people."
—Will Rogers

Body Language

Goman, Carol Kinsey. *The Silent Language of Leaders: How Body Language Can Help—or Hurt—How You Lead.* San Francisco: Jossey-Bass, 2011.

Communicating with Different Cultures

Prince, Don W. et al. *Communicating Across Cultures.* Greensboro: Center for Creative Leadership, 2000.

Data Visualization

Few, Stephen C. *Show Me the Numbers: Designing Tables and Graphs to Enlighten.* Oakland: Jonathan G. Koomey, 2004.

Tufte, Edward R. *The Visual Display of Quantitative Information.* Cheshire: Graphics Press, 2001.

Yau, Nathan. *Visualize This: The FlowingData Guide to Design, Visualization, and Statistics.* Indianapolis: Wiley Publishing, Inc., 2011.

Eye Contact

Ellsberg, Michael. *The Power of Eye Contact.* New York: HarperCollins, 2010.

Fear

Esposito, Janet E. *In The SpotLight: Overcome Your Fear of Public Speaking and Performing.* Bridgewater: In the Spotlight, LLC, 2000.

Lerner, Harriet. *The Dance of Fear: Rising Above Anxiety, Fear, and Shame to Be Your Best and Bravest Self.* San Francisco: HarperCollins e-books, 2009.

Rutledge, Thom. *Embracing Fear: and Finding the Courage to Live Your Life.* New York: HarperCollins, 2002.

Humor

Antion, Tom. *Wake 'em Up: How to Use Humor and Other Professional Techniques to Create Alarmingly Good Business Presentations.* Landover Hills: Anchor Publishing, 1997.

Inflated Language

Fugere, Brian et al. *Why Business People Speak Like Idiots: A Bullfighter's Guide.* New York: Free Press, 2005.

Introverts

Ancowitz, Nancy. *Self-Promotion for Introverts: The Quiet Guide to Getting Ahead.* New York: McGraw-Hill, 2009.

Cain, Susan. *Quiet: The Power of Introverts in a World That Can't Stop Talking.* New York: Crown, 2012.

Leadership Communication

Baldoni, John. *Great Communication Secrets of Great Leaders.* New York: McGraw-Hill, 2003.

Crossland, Ron. *Voice Lessons: Applying Science to the Art of Leadership Communication.* Amazon Digital Services, 2012.

Crossland, Ron, and Boyd Clarke. *The Leader's Voice.* New York: Select Books, 2008.

Pearce, Terry. *Leading Out Loud: Inspiring Change Through Authentic Communication.* San Francisco: Jossey-Bass, 2003.

Memory

Foer, Joshua. *Moonwalking with Einstein: The Art and Science of Remembering Everything.* London: The Penguin Group, 2011.

Metaphors

Geary, James. *I Is an Other: The Secret Life of Metaphor and How It Shapes the Way We See the World.* New York: HarperCollins, 2011.

Grothe, Mardy. *I Never Metaphor I Didn't Like: A Comprehensive Compilation of History's Greatest Analogies, Metaphors, and Similes.* New York: HarperCollins, 2008.

Miller, Anne. *Metaphorically Selling: How to Use the Magic of Metaphors to Sell, Persuade, & Explain Anything to Anyone.* New York: Chiron Associates, Inc., 2004.

Sommer, Elyse. *Metaphors Dictionary: 6,500 Comparative Phrases, Including 800 Shakespearean Metaphors.* Canton: Visible Ink Press, 2001.

Persuasion`

Cialdini, Robert. *Influence: The Psychology of Persuasion.* New York: William Morrow and Company, Inc., 2006.

Cialdini, Robert. *Influence: Science and Practice.* New York: Prentice Hall, 2008.

Kawasaki, Guy. *Enchantment: The Art of Changing Hearts, Minds, and Actions.* London: Penguin, 2011.

Presentation Design

Atkinson, Cliff. *Beyond Bullet Points: Using Microsoft Office PowerPoint 2007 to Create Presentations That Inform, Motivate, and Inspire.* Redmond: Microsoft Press, 2008.

Duarte, Nancy. *Slide:ology: The Art and Science of Creating Great Presentations.* Sebastopol, CA: O'Reilly Media, 2008.

Reynolds, Garr. *The Naked Presenter: Delivering Powerful Presentations With or Without Slides.* Berkeley: New Riders, 2011.

Reynolds, Garr. *Presentation Zen Design: Simple Design Principles and Techniques to Enhance Your Presentations.* Berkeley: New Riders, 2010.

Reynolds, Garr. *Presentation Zen: Simple Ideas on Presentation Design and Delivery.* Berkeley: New Riders, 2012.

Presentation Skills

Atkinson, Max. *Lend Me Your Ears: All You Need to Know About Making Speeches and Presentations.* New York: Oxford University Press, Inc., 2004.

Berkun, Scott. *Confessions of a Public Speaker.* Sebastopol, CA: O'Reilly Media, Inc., 2010.

Gallo, Carmine. *The Presentation Secrets of Steve Jobs: How to Be Insanely Great in Front of Any Audience.* New York: McGraw-Hill, 2010.

Kawasaki, Guy. *Enchantment: The Art of Changing Hearts, Minds, and Actions.* London: Penguin, 2011.

Rasiel, Ethan M. et al. *The McKinsey Mind: Understanding and Implementing the Problem-Solving Tools and Management Techniques of the World's Top Strategic Consulting Firm.* New York: McGraw-Hill, 2002.

Reimold, Cheryl, and Peter Reimold. *The Short Road to Great Presentations: How to Reach Any Audience Through Focused Preparation, Inspired Delivery, and Smart Use of Technology.* Hoboken: John Wiley & Sons, Inc., 2003.

Weissman, Jerry. *In the Line of Fire: How to Handle Tough Questions… When It Counts.* Upper Saddle River: Pearson Education, Inc., 2005.

Weissman, Jerry. *The Power Presenter: Technique, Style, and Strategy from America's Top Speaking Coach.* Hoboken: John Wiley & Sons, Inc., 2009.

Weissman, Jerry. *Presenting to Win: The Art of Telling Your Story.* Upper Saddle River: FT Press, 2009.

Scientific Presentations

Alley, Michael. *The Craft of Scientific Presentations: Critical Steps to Succeed and Critical Errors to Avoid.* New York: Springer-Verlag, 2003.

Meredith, Dennis. *Explaining Research: How to Reach Key Audiences to Advance Your Work.* New York: Oxford University Press, Inc., 2010.

Self-compassion

Neff, Kristin. *Self-Compassion: Stop Beating Yourself Up and Leave Insecurity Behind.* New York: HarperCollins, 2011.

Storytelling

Denning, Stephen. *The Leader's Guide to Storytelling: Mastering the Art and Discipline of Business Narrative.* San Francisco: Jossey-Bass, 2011.

Heath, Chip, and Dan Heath. *Made to Stick: Why Some Ideas Survive and Others Die.* New York: Random House, 2007.

Simmons, Annette. *Whoever Tells the Best Story Wins: How to Use Your Own Stories to Communicate with Power and Impact.* New York: AMACOM, 2007.

Stress

Klipper, Miriam Z., and Herbert Benson. *The Relaxation Response.* New York: HarperCollins, 2000.

Sapolsky, Robert M. *Why Zebras Don't Get Ulcers: An Updated Guide to Stress, Stress-Related Diseases, and Coping.* New York: W. H. Freeman, 1998.

Stock, Byron. *Smart Emotions for Busy Business People.* Byron Stock & Associates LLC, 2008.

Webinars

Clay, Cynthia. *Great Webinars: How to Create Interactive Learning That Is Captivating, Informative, and Fun.* New York: Punchy Publishing, 2009.

SPEAKING BLOGS

*"Most people have no idea of the giant capacity we can
immediately command when we focus all of our resources on
mastering a single area of our lives."*
—Tony Robbins

There is a wealth of useful presentation skills blogs. Here is a
sampling:

Alltop Speaking
http://speaking.alltop.com/

Bert Decker
http://decker.com/blog/

Beyond Bullet Points
http://beyondbulletpoints.com/blog/

Carmine Gallo
http://gallocommunications.com/articles/

Dave Paradi's PowerPoint Blog
http://pptideas.blogspot.com/

Idea Transplant
http://blog.ideatransplant.com/

Memo to C-Level Speakers
http://memotospeakers.typepad.com/my_weblog/

Note & Point
http://noteandpoint.com/

PowerPoint Ninja
http://www.powerpointninja.com/

PowerPoint Tips Blog
http://www.ellenfinkelstein.com/pptblog/

Power Presentations
http://www.powerltd.com/_blog/Blogs

Presentation Advisors
http://www.presentationadvisors.com/

Presentation Zen
http://www.presentationzen.com

Six Minutes
http://sixminutes.dlugan.com/

Slide:ology
http://www.duarte.com/books/slideology/www

The Slideshop Blog
http://blog.slideshop.com/

Speaking About Presenting
http://www.speakingaboutpresenting.com/

Speak Schmeak
http://coachlisab.blogspot.com/

OTHER USEFUL WEBSITES

*"Whenever we're afraid, it's because we don't know enough.
If we understood enough, we would never be afraid."*
—Earl Nightingale

Body Language

BNET Interview with Dr. Carol Kinsey Goman:
Nonverbal Communication for Leaders (video)
http://www.5min.com/Video/
Non-Verbal-Communication-For-Leaders-517061872

Cartoon Sources

Better Cartoon
http://www.bettercartoon.com/business-cartoons

The Cartoon Bank (New Yorker)
http://www.cartoonbank.com/

Cartoon Resource
http://www.cartoonresource.com/

Dilbert
http://www.dilbert.com/

Graham Harrop
http://www.grahamharrop.com/bio.htm

Chairing a Meeting

Guidelines for Serving As a Session Chair
http://www.eval.org/eval2007/aea07.presenterguidelines.asp

Emotional Intelligence Assessments

Comparison of EQ Tests (Six Seconds)
http://www.6seconds.org/2011/07/18/comparison-of-eq-tests/

Emotional Intelligence Measures (EI Consortium)
http://www.eiconsortium.org/measures/measures.html

Emotional Intelligence Models

The Bar-On Model of Social and Emotional Intelligence
http://www.reuvenbaron.org/bar-on-model/essay.php?i=3

The Emotional Competencies (Goleman) Model
http://www.eiconsortium.org/measures/eci_360.html

The Six Seconds Model of EQ
http://www.6seconds.org/2010/01/27/the-six-seconds-eq-model/

Fillers

Olivia Mitchell: How to Eliminate Filler Words
http://speakingaboutpresenting.com/delivery/obama-eliminate-ums/

First Impressions

Carlin Flora, The First Impression, *Psychology Today*
http://www.psychologytoday.com/articles/200405/the-first-impression

Ice Breakers

Mind Tools: Ice Breakers
http://www.mindtools.com/pages/article/newLDR_76.htm

Images

123RF
http://www.123RF.com

BigStock
http://www.bigstockphoto.com

Flickr
http://www.flickr.com

Fotolia
http://www.fotolia.com

iStockphoto
http://www.istockphoto.com/

Stock.xchng
http://www.sxc.hu/

Inflated Words

David Meerman Scott: Top Gobbledygook Phrases
http://www.webinknow.com/2009/04/top-gobbledygook-phrases-used-in-2008-and-how-to-avoid-them.html

Infographics

Top 10 Infographics Resources
http://blog.braintraffic.com/2010/05/top-10-infographic-resources/

Using Infographics on PowerPoint Slides
http://www.thinkoutsidetheslide.com/articles/using_infographics.htm

Keynotes

eHow: How to Write a Keynote Speech
http://www.ehow.com/how_4966252_write-keynote-speech.html

Ginger Dailey: How to Write a Keynote Speech
http://www.public-speaking-resource.com/2008/09/what-every-aspiring-public-speaker.html

Lecturing

Center for Teaching Excellence, 17 Links on Effective Lecturing
http://cte.umdnj.edu/traditional_teaching/traditional_lecture.cfm

Memory Enhancers

7 Simple Ways to Improve Your Memory, *Psychology Today*
http://www.spring.org.uk/2011/05/7-simple-ways-to-improve-your-memory-without-any-training.php

Metaphors

Business Metaphors, Analogies, and Similes
http://www.metaphorsandsimiles.com/business/metaphors-analogies-similes.aspx

How to Write a Metaphor
http://www.wikihow.com/Write-a-Metaphor

Shakespeare's Metaphors
http://www.shakespeare-online.com/biography/metaphorlist.html

Mind-map Software

Bubbl.us (free, online)
https://bubbl.us/

Buzan
http://www.thinkbuzan.com/intl/

Mindjet
http://www.mindjet.com

MindView
http://www.matchware.com/en/products/mindview/reviews.htm

Movie Clips

Royalty-free Movie Clips
http://www.movieclip.biz/

Murphy's Law

Breaking Murphy's Law
http://www.breakingmurphyslaw.com/

Music Sources

Free Sound Clips and Music for Presentations
http://www.brainybetty.com/soundsforpowerpoint.htm

Royalty-free Music
http://www.royaltyfreemusic.com/corporate-music.html

Objections

Objection Handling from Changing Minds
http://changingminds.org/disciplines/sales/objection/

Persuasive Presentations

Monroe's Motivated Sequence (video)
http://www.youtube.com/watch?v=k0ED3PckYaM

Plagiarism

Reducing Plagiarism, Indiana University (video)
http://www.indiana.edu/~icy/media/de_series/plagiarism.html

Posture

The Power of Posture, Harvard Business School
http://hbswk.hbs.edu/archive/3597.html

PowerPoint

MS Office 2010 Interactive Guide
http://office.microsoft.com/en-us/getting-started-with-office-2010-FX101822272.aspx

Microsoft: PowerPoint 2010
http://office.microsoft.com/en-us/powerpoint/

Using Presenter View in PowerPoint
http://www.microsoft.com/en-us/showcase/details.aspx?uuid=e7318e64-59b1-4188-b22e-51d2efc19536

Three Reasons to Use PowerPoint's Presenter View
http://www.youtube.com/watch?v=Ye3cns5w4yw

Presentation Software

Prezi
http://prezi.com/

SlideBoom
http://www.appappeal.com/app/slideboom/

SlideRocket
http://www.sliderocket.com/

Presentation Trends (Yearly)

Zeitgeist 2011: A Year of Changes in Presentation Trends
http://blog.slideshare.net/2012/01/17/zeitgeist-2011-a-year-of-
changes-in-presentation-trends/

Presenting to C-Level

Microsoft: Present Complex Data to Client Executives
http://office.microsoft.com/en-us/powerpoint-help/present-complex-
data-to-client-executives-HA001171789.aspx

Quotations

Wikiquotes in 10 Languages
http://www.wikiquote.org/

Famous Business Quotations
http://www.businessurge.com/famous-business-quotes/index.htm

Rehearse Timings in PowerPoint

Microsoft: Rehearse and Time the Delivery of a Presentation
http://office.microsoft.com/en-ca/powerpoint-help/rehearse-and-
time-the-delivery-of-a-presentation-HA010007217.aspx

Rhetorical Figures of Speech

American Rhetoric
http://www.americanrhetoric.com/moviespeeches.htm

Sales Presentations

Guy Kawasaki: How To Create An Enchanting Pitch
https://skydrive.live.com/view.aspx/Guy%5E_Kawasaki%5E_
Example%5E_Pitch%5E_Files/Guy%5E_Kawasaki%5E_Pitch%5E_
Outline%5E_Example.pptx?cid=c949daba49265f05&app=PowerPoint

Sales Presentation: m62 Visual Communications (video)
http://www.m62.net/presentation-theory/presentation-messages/
sales-presentations-and-business-strategy/

Scientific Presentations

The Craft of Scientific Presentations
http://www.writing.engr.psu.edu/csp.html

When the Scientist Presents
http://scientific-presentations.com/presentation-tips/

Slide Design

Carmine Gallo: How to Be Insanely Great in Front of an Audience
http://www.slideshare.net/prwalker/
the-presentation-secrets-of-steve-jobs-2814996

Cursor Gaze: Little Notes of a Presentation Designer
http://cursorgaze.com/

Garr Reynolds: Authors@Google Talk on How to Make Presentations (video)
http://www.youtube.com/watch?v=DZ2vtQCESpk&feature=fvw

Garr Reynolds: Sample Slides: Before and After
http://www.slideshare.net/garr/sample-slides-by-garr-reynolds

James Madison University: Solution Screencasts. (Watch all four.)

Home Page As Hyperlink (video)
http://jmutube.cit.jmu.edu/users/communication_center/
presentations/homepage_hyperlink_technique.zip.content/

Assertion-evidence Technique (video)
http://jmutube.cit.jmu.edu/users/communication_center/
presentations/Assertion_Evidence.zip.content/

The Image as Mnemonic Technique (video)
http://jmutube.cit.jmu.edu/users/communication_center/
presentations/Mnemonic.zip.content/

Slide as Flipbook Technique (video)
http://jmutube.cit.jmu.edu/users/communication_center/
presentations/Slide_As_Flipbook.zip.content/

Microsoft PowerPoint Slidefest: Do and Don't and Slide School 101
http://www.microsoft.com/office/powerpoint-slidefest/slide-
school-101.aspx

Penn State University: Assertion-evidence Structure (video)
http://www.writing.engr.psu.edu/slides.html

SlideShare: Presentation Skills for Teachers
http://slideshare.net/jonesy2008/presentation-skills-for-teachers-version-30

Speaking Tips

Forbes.com: Podium Tactics from 28 Public Speaking Pros
http://www.forbes.com/2007/07/31/microsoft-sun-microsystems-
ent sales-ex_fs_0801byb07_publicspeaking_slide_2.html

The Seven Types of Presentations to Avoid
http://www.speakingaboutpresenting.com/content/
seven-types-presentation-avoid/

Five Tips for Exciting Speeches (see "Provide Five Magic Moments")
http://www.lifetoolsforwomen.com/p/5-tips-speeches.htm

Speech Builders

Cengage Learning : Speech Builder Express
http://www.cengage.com/tlconnect/client/product/findProduct.
do?productId=94

Harvard Business School: Elevator Speech Builder
http://www.alumni.hbs.edu/careers/pitch/

Quick Templates for Creating Speeches
http://speeches.com/

Speedy Presentations

Ignite: 5 minutes, 20 slides
http://ignite.oreilly.com/

PechaKucha: 20 images, 20 seconds (6 minutes, 40 seconds)
http://www.pecha-kucha.org/

Storytelling

Storytelling As Best Practice: Andy Goodman (video)
http://video.google.com/videoplay?docid=-289257716014946841

Storytelling: Passport to the 21st Century (Steve Denning's site)
http://www.creatingthe21stcentury.org/Steve.html

Stress

Bio Dots

> Six Seconds
> http://www.6seconds.org/newstore/products/biodots/
>
> Biodots.net
> http://www.biodots.net/contact/

emWave2™

> Institute of HeartMath
> Stress Relief System (formerly Freeze-Framer®): http://www.
> heartmath.com/technology-products/emwave-technology.html
>
> Six Seconds Store
> http://www.6seconds.org/newstore/products/emwave-2/

Interview with Dr. Herbert Benson about the "Relaxation Response" (video)
http://abcnews.go.com/video/playerIndex?id=7392433

A Wealth of Articles on Stress from *Psychology Today*
http://www.psychologytoday.com/basics/stress

TED.com

Making Presentations in the TED Style
http://www.presentationzen.com/presentationzen/2009/05/making-presentations-in-the-ted-style.html

Videos

KeepVid (download streaming videos)
http://www.keepvid.com/

Visualization

Seeing Is Believing: The Power of Visualization from *Psychology Today*
http://www.psychologytoday.com/blog/flourish/200912/
seeing-is-believing-the-power-visualization

Visual Thesaurus

Interactive Dictionary and Thesaurus
http://www.visualthesaurus.com/howitworks/

Voice Hygiene

Washington Voice Consortium for Voice Care
http://www.voiceproblem.org/diagnosistreatments/prevention/model.php

Webinars

The Webinar Blog
http://wsuccess.typepad.com/webinarblog/2009/07/must-your-
webinar-be-interactive.html

You Tube

Post Your PowerPoint Presentation As a Video to YouTube
http://www.ellenfinkelstein.com/pptblog/
post-your-powerpoint-presentation-as-a-video-to-youtube/

A COMPENDIUM OF PRESENTATIONS

"If we all did the things we are capable of doing,
we would literally astound ourselves."
—Thomas Alva Edison

Seth Godin

All Marketers Are Liars
http://www.youtube.com/watch?v=5VJT3D_RzJo&feature=related

Overpowering Your Lizard Brain
http://www.youtube.com/watch?v=XqozprFZ_38&feature=related

Sliced Bread and Other Marketing Delights
http://www.youtube.com/watch?v=xBIVlM435Zg

Steve Jobs

Apple iPad Is an Incredible Experience
http://www.youtube.com/watch?v=ZfnvH2WU8tU

Steve Jobs's 2005 Stanford Commencement Address
http://www.youtube.com/watch?v=UF8uR6Z6KLc

Guy Kawasaki

Creating Enchantment
http://www.youtube.com/watch?v=A3Wyz3k07ls

The Art of the Start
http://www.youtube.com/watch?v=jSlwuafyUUo

Randy Pausch

Last Lecture: Achieving Your Childhood Dreams
http://www.youtube.com/watch?v=ji5_MqicxSo

Daniel Pink

On the Surprising Science of Motivation
http://www.youtube.com/watch?v=rrkrvAUbU9Y

Sir Ken Robinson

Do Schools Kill Creativity?
http://www.youtube.com/watch?v=iG9CE55wbtY

Robert Sapolski (how to lecture naturally behind a podium)

The Uniqueness of Humans
http://www.ted.com/talks/robert_sapolsky_the_uniqueness_of_humans.html

Are Humans Just Another Primate?
http://www.youtube.com/watch?v=YWZAL64E0DI

Depression in U.S.
http://www.youtube.com/watch?v=NOAgplgTxfc

Daniel J. Siegel (how to lecture naturally behind a podium)

Mindsight: The New Science of Personal Transformation
http://www.youtube.com/watch?v=Gr4Od7kqDT8

Victor Antonio

Sales Training: Why Closing Techniques Won't Work
http://www.youtube.com/watch?v=CbawO1eDam8&feature=related

Motivational Speech
http://www.youtube.com/watch?v=slC5L93SjIs&feature=related

Torpedo Your Dream
http://www.youtube.com/watch?v=cAAG3b9kyYs&feature=related

A PLANNING TEMPLATE

"Begin with the end in mind."
—Stephen R. Covey

After you have written your conclusion and you know where you want to end up, retrace your steps and start building the presentation that will take you to that end.

Part I: Start with Your Conclusion

Transition statement (What transition statement will you use to signal that you are nearing the end of your presentation?)	
Briefly summarize your main points.	
1.	2.
3.	4.
5.	
Emphasize the "why."	
Your memorable ending (anecdote, quote, question, sound bite, etc.)	

Part II: The Body (Repeat process for additional points.)

Transition statement (to signal the end of the introduction and start of the main part of presentation)	
First Point	Supporting Evidence
Any *Necessary* Details	What will you show on the slides?
Second Point	Supporting Evidence
Any *Necessary* Details	What will you show on the slides?
Third Point	Supporting Evidence
Any *Necessary* Details	What will you show on the slides?
Fourth Point	Supporting Evidence
Any *Necessary* Details	What will you show on the slides?
Fifth Point	Supporting Evidence
Any *Necessary* Details	What will you show on the slides?

Part III: The Introduction

Write the introduction at the end, after you have written the entire presentation and created all of the slides.

1. Grab their attention with a hook.	2. Briefly tell them what your main topic is. What is the presentation about?
3. Introduce yourself. Give them your credentials; tell them why you are uniquely qualified to speak on this topic, e.g., your experience, qualifications, passion, etc.	4. Tell them what they will gain from listening to your presentation. What are the concrete take-aways?
5. Go over your agenda. List all main points.	

NOTES

"I plan someday to write a scholarly article consisting of a single sentence and a twenty-page footnote."
—Jeffrey L. Staley

Introduction

1. C. I. Hovland and W. Weiss, "The Influence of Source Credibility on Communication Effectiveness," *Public Opinion Quarterly* 15 (1951): 635–650. R. E. Petty et al., "Attitudes and Attitude Change," *Annual Review of Psychology* 48 (February 1997): 609–647.

2. "2011 Edelman Trust Barometer® Key Findings Presentation," *Edelman*, 2011, http://www.edelman.com/trust/2011/.

3. James Kouzes and Barry Posner, *Credibility: How Leaders Gain and Lose It, Why People Demand It* (San Francisco: Jossey-Bass, 2003).

4. James C. McCroskey and Thomas J. Young, "Ethos and Credibility: The Construct and Its Measurement After Three Decades," *Central States Speech Journal* 32, no. 1 (1981).

5. C. I. Hovland and W. Weiss, "The Influence of Source Credibility on Communication Effectiveness," *Public Opinion Quarterly* 15 (1951): 635–650.

6. J. C. McCroskey and J. J. Teven, "Goodwill: A Reexamination of the Construct and Its Measurement," *Communication Monographs* 66 (1999): 90–103.

7. Herbert Kelman and Carl Hovland, "Reinstatement of the Communicator in Delayed Measurement of Opinion Change," *Journal of Abnormal and Social Psychology* 48 (1953): 327–335.

8. D. K. Berlo, J. B. Lemert, and R. J. Mertz, "Dimensions for Evaluating the Acceptability of Message Sources," *Public Opinion Quarterly* 33 (1969): 562–576.

9. Ethan M. Rasiel, *The McKinsey Mind: Understanding and Implementing the Problem-Solving Tools and Management Techniques of the World's Top Strategic Consulting Firm* (New York: McGraw-Hill, 2002).

Chapter 1

1. You can watch a video of Jim Kouzes's lecture on credibility at http://www.youtube.com/watch?v=CrMyOWwbar8&feature=related.

2. "Improving Your Memory," *Ambassadors Caregivers*, http://ambassadorscare.com/Family-Resources/Articles/Strategies-for-Improving-Memory.aspx.

3. Mindsource Technologies, 2009.

4. "7 Simple Ways to Improve Your Memory Without Any Training," *PsyBlog*, May 19, 2001, http://www.spring.org.uk/2011/05/7-simple-ways-to-improve-your-memory-without-any-training.php.

5. Paul Zak, "Sleep Enforces the Temporal Order in Memory" (Department of Neuroendocrinology, University of Lübeck, Germany, 2007).

6. *The Center for New Discoveries in Learning*, http://www.newdiscoveries.org. See also Alistair Smith, *Accelerated Learning in Practice* (London: Network Educational Press, 2007).

7. Joshua Foer, *Moonwalking with Einstein: The Art and Science of Remembering Everything* (London: The Penguin Group, 2011).

8. You can view the video "To Remember Better, Build a Mansion in Your Mind" at http://worldsciencefestival.com/videos/to_remember_better_build_a_mansion_in_your_mind.

9. View the video tour for Google Reader, "Google Reader in Plain English," at http://www.youtube.com/watch?v=VSPZ2Uu_X3Y.

10. The URL for Refdesk is http://www.refdesk.com.

11. To set up Google Alerts, visit http://www.google.com/alerts.

12. Seth Godin, "The Arrogance of Willful Ignorance," *Seth Godin's Blog*, July 7, 2011, http://sethgodin.typepad.com/seths_blog/2011/07/the-arrogance-of-ignorance.html.

13. "'The Art of Woo': Selling Your Ideas to the Entire Organization, One Person at a Time," *Knowledge@Wharton* (October 17, 2007), http://knowledge.wharton.upenn.edu/article.cfm?articleid=1823.

14. Noah J. Goldstein, Steve J. Martin, and Robert B. Cialdini, *Yes! 50 Scientifically Proven Ways to Be Persuasive* (New York: Free Press, 2008).

15. Ashley Floyd Fields, "A Study of Intuition in Decision-Making Using Organizational Engineering Methodology" (dissertation, Wayne Huizenga Graduate School of Business and Entrepreneurship of Nova Southeastern University, 2001).

16. Ron Crossland and Boyd Clarke, *The Leader's Voice: How Your Communication Can Inspire Action and Get Results!* (New York: Select Books, 2008).

17. "List of Cognitive Biases," *Wikipedia*, http://en.wikipedia.org/wiki/List_of_cognitive_biases.

18. Janaé Rubin, "Overcoming Objections," *Folio* (November, 2005): 80–81. Cited in "Objections Are Opportunities to Build Relationships," *Web Books Publishing*, http://www.web-books.com/eLibrary/NC/B0/B67/63MB67.html#ftn.fwk-richmond-fn11_013.

19. Ethan M. Rasiel, *The McKinsey Mind: Understanding and Implementing the Problem-Solving Tools and Management Techniques of the World's Top Strategic Consulting Firm* (New York: McGraw-Hill, 2002).

20. "'The Art of Woo': Selling Your Ideas to the Entire Organization, One Person at a Time," *Knowledge@Wharton* (October 17, 2007), http://knowledge.wharton.upenn.edu/article.cfm?articleid=1823.

21. "'The Art of Woo': Selling Your Ideas to the Entire Organization, One Person at a Time," *Knowledge@Wharton* (October 17, 2007), http://knowledge.wharton.upenn.edu/article.cfm?articleid=1823.

22. "The Illusion of Truth," *PsyBlog*, December 8, 2010, http://www.spring.org.uk/2010/12/the-illusion-of-truth.php.

Chapter 2

1. Ron Ashkenas, "In Presentations, Learn to Say Less," *Harvard Business Review Blog Network*, January 10, 2012, http://blogs.hbr.org/ashkenas/2012/01/in-presentations-learn-to-say.html?utm_source=feedburner&utm_medium=feed&utm_campaign=Feed%3A+harvardbusiness+%28HBR.org%29.

2. William D. Jensen, *The Simplicity Survival Handbook: 32 Ways to Do Less and Accomplish More* (New York: Basic Books, 2003).

3. Daniel J. Siegel, M.D., "Google Personal Growth Series: Mindsight: The New Science of Personal Transformation," video, April 22, 2009, http://www.youtube.com/watch?v=Gr4Od7kqDT8.

4. Gord Hotchkiss, "Scanning Consideration Sets and Their Importance to Search Marketers," *Search Engine Land*, March 23, 2007, http://searchengineland.com/scanning-consideration-sets-and-their-importance-to-search-marketers-10801.

5. "Offer a Third Choice: Boost Sales," *Neuromarketing* (blog), December 15, 2008, http://www.neurosciencemarketing.com/blog/articles/third-option.htm.

6. Guy Kawasaki, "The Importance of a Good Presentation," video, February 19, 2003, http://www.youtube.com/watch?v=QrF9Znu9yVo&feature=related.

Chapter 3

1. John Medina, *Brain Rules: 12 Principles for Surviving and Thriving at Work, Home, and School* (Seattle: Pear Press, 2008).

2. Steven K. Scott, *Mentored by a Millionaire: Master Strategies of Super Achievers* (Hoboken: John Wiley & Sons, Inc., 2004).

3. Richard St. John, "Success Is a Continuous Journey," video, February 2009, http://www.ted.com/talks/richard_st_john_success_is_a_continuous_journey.html.

4. Oliver L. Velez and Greg Capra, *Tools and Tactics for the Master Day Trader* (New York: McGraw-Hill, 2000).

5. Seth Godin, "Seth Godin Live Seminar for Good Causes," video, October 22, 2009, http://www.squidoo.com/daylongseminar.

6. "Identity Theft," *Commonwealth of Massachusetts*, http://www.mass.gov/eopss/crime-prev-personal-sfty/identity-theft/.

7. Meredith Stokke, "Did You Know???," *Food for Thought* (blog), February 11, 2010, http://meredithstokkencc.blogspot.com/2010/02/did-you-know.html.

8. Dave Logan, "David Logan on Tribal Leadership," video, October 2009, http://www.ted.com/talks/david_logan_on_tribal_leadership.html.

9. The URL for "Today in History" is http://www.worldofquotes.com/history/.

10. Also refer to "Famous Proverbs" at http://famous-proverbs.com/.

11. Larry Page, "University of Michigan Commencement Address," video, May 2, 2009, http://www.google.com/intl/en/press/annc/20090502-page-commencement.html.

12. Bryan Dyson, "Speech by Brian Dyson, CEO Coca Cola," *Dankind* (blog), February 1, 2007, http://www.dankind.com/blog/128/speech-by-bryan-dyson-ceo-coca-cola.

13. Ray Zahab, "Ray Zahab Treks to the South Pole," video, February 2009, http://www.ted.com/talks/ray_zahab_treks_to_the_south_pole.html?c=314668.

14. John La Grou, "John La Grou Plugs Smart Power Outlets," video, February 2009, http://www.ted.com/talks/john_la_grou_plugs_smart_power_outlets_1.html.

15. Peter Drucker.

16. Patricia Fripp, "So You've Been Asked to Do Public Speaking," *The Sideroad*, http://www.sideroad.com/Public_Speaking/public_ speaking.html.

17. For ideas on movie quotes, visit "Top 10 Movie Quotes" at http:// www.filmsite.org/topquotes.html.

18. Lord Browne, "Energy and the Environment, 10 Years On," *BP*, April 26, 2007, http://www.bp.com/genericarticle.do?categoryId=9 8&contentId=7032698.

19. Seth Godin, "Quieting the Lizard Brain," video, http://vimeo. com/5895898.

20. "HBS Elevator Pitch Builder," *Harvard Business School Alumni Career Services*, http://www.alumni.hbs.edu/careers/pitch/.

21. To see step-by-step instructions for creating hyperlinked agenda items, view the brief video "How to Create an Agenda Slide to Organize a PowerPoint Presentation" at http://www.youtube.com/ watch?v=oCh4f9Xd0Dc.

Chapter 4

1. Rhonda Abrams, *Winning Presentation in a Day: Get It Done Right, Get It Done Fast* (Palo Alto: The Planning Shop, 2005).

2. Jeremy Gutsche, "Creativity Keynote Speech," video, http://www. youtube.com/watch?v=SJ9f-_2DS4g&feature=relmfu.

3. Elie Wiesel, "The Perils of Indifference," *The History Place*, April 12, 1999, http://www.historyplace.com/speeches/wiesel.htm.

4. Seth Godin, "Standing Out," video, February 2003, http://www.ted. com/talks/seth_godin_on_sliced_bread.html.

5. Elizabeth Lesser, "Take 'the Other' to Lunch," video, December 2010, http://www.ted.com/talks/elizabeth_lesser_take_the_ other_to_lunch.html.

6. Tim Brown, "Creativity and Play," video, May 2008, http://www. ted.com/talks/tim_brown_on_creativity_and_play.html.

7. Neil Pasricha, "The 3 A's of Awesome," video, September 2010, http://www.ted.com/talks/neil_pasricha_the_3_a_s_of_ awesome.html.

Chapter 5

1. Tom Peters, *The Little Big Things: 163 Ways to Pursue Excellence* (New York: HarperCollins, 2010), 448.

2. Lev Grossman, "Person of the Year 2010: Mark Zuckerberg," *Time Magazine* (December 15, 2010), http://www.time.com/time/specials/packages/ article/0,28804,2036683_2037183_2037185,00.html.

Chapter 6

1. Jerry Weissman, *In the Line of Fire: How to Handle Tough Questions... When It Counts* (Upper Saddle River, NJ. Pearson Education, Inc., 2005).

2. Jerry Weissman, *In the Line of Fire: How to Handle Tough Questions... When It Counts* (Upper Saddle River, NJ: Pearson Education, Inc., 2005).

Chapter 7

1. Bill Jensen, "How to Give Executives Less Information and Keep 'Em Happy," *The Simplicity Survival Handbook: 32 Ways to Do Less and Accomplish More* (New York: Basic Books, 2003).

2. Scott Eblin, "How to Get the CEO to Listen to You," *Next Level Blog*, April 6, 2011, http://scotteblin.typepad.com/blog/2011/04/how-to-get-the-ceo-to-listen-to-you.html.

3. Jerry Weissman, *Less Is More: The Proper Use of Graphics for Effective Presentations, Kindle Edition* (Upper Saddle River: FT Press, 2009).

4. Jerry Weissman, *Less Is More: The Proper Use of Graphics for Effective Presentations, Kindle Edition* (Upper Saddle River: FT Press, 2009).

5. Scott Eblin, *The Next Level: What Insiders Know About Executive Success* (Mountain View, CA: Davies-Black Publishing, 2006).

6. Sims Wyeth, "Presentation Skills: Presenting to Senior Executives," *High Stakes Presentations* (blog), January 27, 2010, http://www.simswyeth.com/20100127-presentation-skills-presenting-to-senior-executives/.

Chapter 8

1. Michael Fienen, "The Great Keynote Meltdown of 2009," *.eduGuru* (blog), October 9, 2009, http://doteduguru.com/id3712-the-great-keynote-meltdown-of-2009.html.

2. Michael Fienen, "The Great Keynote Meltdown of 2009," *.eduGuru* (blog), October 9, 2009, http://doteduguru.com/id3712-the-great-keynote-meltdown-of-2009.html.

3. "Keynotes: The Good, the Bad, and the Horrific," *Sourcing Innovation* (blog), October 23, 2007, http://blog.sourcinginnovation.com/2007/10/23/keynotes-the-good-the-bad-and-the-horrific.aspx?view=threaded.

4. You can view Bill Cosby's keynote speech at Carnegie Mellon University at http://www.youtube.com/watch?v=BY-WFfajWq8.

5. To watch the interview between Lisa Nirell and Guy Kawasaki, visit https://www.youtube.com/watch?v=cA2G44xqHWU&feature=player_embedded%23at=202.

6. You can find "A Handbook of Rhetorical Devices" at http://www.virtualsalt.com/rhetoric.htm.

7. You can find "American Rhetoric: Rhetorical Figures in Sound" at http://www.americanrhetoric.com/rhetoricaldevicesinsound.htm.

8. Sir Ken Robinson, "Schools Kill Creativity," video, February 2006, http://www.ted.com/talks/ken_robinson_says_schools_kill_creativity.html.

9. Marc A. Brackett, "Educating the Whole Child (and Adult) with Emotional Literacy," video, June 2011, http://tedxtalks.ted.com/video/TEDxGoldenGateED-Marc-Bracket-2.

10. John Maeda, "The Simple Life," video, March 2007, http://www.ted.com/talks/john_maeda_on_the_simple_life.html.

11. John Chambers, "Haas School of Business: Dean's Speaker Series," video, September 28, 2010, http://www.youtube.com/watch?v=WXPMdaOC3kk.

12. Victor Antonio, "Torpedo Your Dream," video, September 2009, http://www.youtube.com/watch?v=cAAG3b9kyYs&feature=related.

13. Garr Reynolds, "Bill Clinton and the Art of Speaking in a 'Human Voice,'" *Presentation Zen* (blog), October 24, 2006, http://www.presentationzen.com/presentationzen/2006/10/bill_clinton_an.html.

14. Mariah Burton Nelson, "How to Write a Keynote Speech," *Mariah Burton Nelson*, 2003, http://www.mariahburtonnelson.com/Articles/WriteSpeech.htm.

15. Jeremy Gutsche, "Keynotes," *Jeremy Gutsche*, http://www.jeremygutsche.com/keynotes.

16. Sean D'Souza, "Why Do Most Headlines Fail?," *PsychoTactics*, http://www.psychotactics.com/.

17. Mario Cuomo, "A Tale of Two Cities," video, July 16, 1984, http://www.youtube.com/watch?v=kOdIqKsv624.

18. Guy Kawasaki, *Enchantment: The Art of Changing Hearts, Minds, and Actions* (London: Portfolio/Penguin, 2011).

19. You can view Victor Antonio's speech at the University of Phoenix, Raleigh Campus, at http://www.youtube.com/watch?v=slC5L93SjI s&feature=related.

20. You can watch a video of Tom Peters delivering his keynote speech for Drucker Day 2010 at http://www.youtube.com/watch?v=lA09tzoPR4k.

21. Steve Farber, "Extreme Leadership Expert," video, http://www.viddler.com/explore/SpeakersSpot/videos/299/.

22. Barack Obama, "Ebenezer Baptist Church Address," video, January 20, 2008, http://www.americanrhetoric.com/speeches/barackobama/barackobamaebenezerbaptist.htm.

23. "Speech Critiques," *Six Minutes* (blog), http://sixminutes.dlugan.com/video-critiques/.

24. Les Posen, "So Who Are They Trying to Kid? Some Lessons You Won't Learn About Presenting from This Dufus Competition," CyberPsych (blog), March 25, 2007, http://homepage.mac.com/lesposen/blogwavestudio/LH20070403124024/LHA20070325012920/index.html.

Chapter 9

1. Jane McGrath, "Top 5 Worst Corporate Icebreakers," *HowStuffWorks*, http://communication.howstuffworks.com/worst-ice-breaker.htm#mkcpgn=kaw1.

2. Richard L. Sullivan and Noel McIntosh, "Delivering Effective Lectures" (U.S. Agency for International Development, 1996), http://www.reproline.jhu.edu/english/6read/6training/lecture/sp605web.pdf.

3. Donald A. Bligh, *What's the Use of Lectures?* (New York: Jossey-Bass, 2000).

4. David Rock, "Rethinking How We 'Conference,'" *Your Brain at Work* (blog), April 22, 2011, http://www.psychologytoday.com/blog/your-brain-work/201104/rethinking-how-we-conference.

5. David Rock, "Rethinking How We 'Conference,'" *Your Brain at Work* (blog), April 22, 2011, http://www.psychologytoday.com/blog/your-brain-work/201104/rethinking-how-we-conference.

6. John Bobell and Robert Croker (Idaho State University). Mentioned in Dan Bobinski, "Role Play: The 'Love-Hate' Relationship," *The Center for Workplace Excellence* (blog), June 13, 2007, http://www.workplace-excellence.com/role-play-the-love-hate-relationship/.

7. You can learn more about Leadout at http://www.leadout.com.

8. You can learn more about Big Fish at http://www.bigfishinteractive.com.

9. You can learn more about Thiagi at http://www.thiagi.com/games.html.

10. You can learn more about Sneetch Marbles, by Six Seconds, at http://www.6seconds.org/newstore/products/sneetch-marbles-inc-complete-kit/.

11. Kate M. Halverson, http://katehalverson.com.

12. Josh Freedman, "What Makes EQ Learning Work," *Six Seconds* (blog), January 12, 2011, http://www.6seconds.org/2011/01/12/what-makes-eq-learning-work/.

13. "Hot cognition," *Wikipedia*, http://en.wikipedia.org/wiki/Hot_cognition.

14. The engage, activate, and reflect phases are also described in Six Seconds' book on organizational transformation: Joshua Freedman, *Inside Change: Transforming Your Organization with Emotional Intelligence* (San Francisco, CA: Six Seconds Emotional Intelligence Press, 2010).

15. Marilla Svinicki et al., *McKeachie's Teaching Tips: Strategies, Research, and Theory for College and University Teachers* (Belmont, CA: Wadsworth Publishing, 2011).

16. Ronald T. Hyman, *Strategic Questioning* (Upper Saddle River: Prentice Hall, 1979).

17. Stephen D. Brookfield and Stephen Preskill, *Discussion As a Way of Teaching: Tools and Techniques for Democratic Classrooms* (San Francisco: Jossey-Bass, 2005).

18. You can find TEDTalks at http://www.ted.com/talks.

19. Kathryn Schulz, *Being Wrong: Adventures in the Margin of Error* (New York: HarperCollins Publishers, 2010). See also a video of the author's TED presentation, "On Being Wrong," March 2011, http://www.ted.com/talks/kathryn_schulz_on_being_wrong.html.

20. Daniel Goleman, "Social Intelligence for Teachers: Looking for Some Help," *Daniel Goleman* (blog), February 1, 2007, http://danielgoleman.info/2007/02/01/social-intelligence-for-teachers-looking-for-some-help/.

21. Mark Walsh, "Training with Heart," *Integration Training* (blog), January 31, 2011, http://integrationtraining.co.uk/blog/2011/01/training-heart.html.

22. Seth Godin, "Your Smile Didn't Matter," *Seth Godin's Blog*, September 5, 2010, http://sethgodin.typepad.com/seths_blog/2010/09/your-attitude-didnt-matter.html.

23. Arlie Russell Hochschild, *The Managed Heart: Commercialization of Human Feeling* (Berkeley: University of California Press, 2003).

24. Sam Harris, "Science Can Answer Moral Questions," video, February 2010, http://www.ted.com/talks/lang/eng/sam_harris_science_can_show_what_s_right.html.

25. Sam Harris, "The Silent Crowd: Overcoming Your Fear of Public Speaking," *The Blog*, September 12, 2011, http://www.samharris.org/blog/item/the-silent-crowd-overcoming-your-fear-of-public-speaking/.

Chapter 10

1. Guy Kawasaki, "10-20-30 Presentation Rule," video, http://www.youtube.com/watch?v=liQLdRk0Ziw.

2. Edward Tufte, "Powerpoint Is Evil," *Wired* 11, no. 9 (2003), http://www.wired.com/wired/archive/11.09/ppt2.html.

3. "Becoming an Effective Presenter of Engineering and Science," *Penn State College of Engineering*, http://www.engr.psu.edu/speaking/Visual-Aids.html.

4. James Madison University, "Assertion Evidence," *JMUtube*, video, http://jmutube.cit.jmu.edu/users/communication_center/presentations/Assertion_Evidence.zip.content/.

5. Seth Godin, "Where to Find Great Ideas and Arresting Images (for Free)", *Seth Godin's Blog*, March 29, 2008, http://sethgodin.typepad.com/seths_blog/2008/03/where-to-find-g.html.

6. Mason Hipp, "Find the Perfect Image for Any Project in 5 Steps," March 19, 2009, *Freelance Folder* (blog), http://freelancefolder.com/find-the-perfect-image-for-any-project-in-5-steps/.

7. John Medina, *Brain Rules: 12 Principles for Surviving and Thriving at Work, Home, and School* (Seattle: Pear Press, 2008), 240.

8. James Madison University, "Homepage Hyperlink Technique," *JMUtube*, video, http://jmutube.cit.jmu.edu/users/communication_center/presentations/homepage_hyperlink_technique.zip.content/.

9. Visit Cool Infographics at http://www.coolinfographics.com/.

10. Angela Alcorn, "10 Awesome Free Tools to Make Infographics," *MakeUseOf* (blog), October 8, 2010, http://www.makeuseof.com/tag/awesome-free-tools-infographics/.

11. Visit Three D Graphics at http://www.threedgraphics.com/tdg/.

12. Visit SmartDraw at http://www.smartdraw.com/videos/demo/.

13. "PowerTips: Wooing with Color," *PresentationPro*, http://vvv.presentationpro.com/products/pdpresentationtips.asp.

14. "Statistics by Country for Red-Green Color Blindness," RD, http://www.wrongdiagnosis.com/r/red_green_color_blindness/stats-country.htm.

15. "Top Ten Slide Tips," *Garr Reynolds*, http://www.garrreynolds.com/Presentation/slides.html.

16. Mentioned in Susanne Fuhrman, Ph.D., "Credibility," *Usability*, http://www.usability.gov/articles/102009news.html#fonts.

17. "Top Ten Slide Tips," *Garr Reynolds*, http://www.garrreynolds.com/Presentation/slides.html.

18. Visit Identifont at http://www.identifont.com/.

19. Visit What Font is at http://www.whatfontis.com/.

20. Guy Kawasaki, "10-20-30 Presentation Rule," video, http://www.youtube.com/watch?v=liQLdRk0Ziw.

21. "World's Best Presentation Contest Winners Announced," *How to Change the World* (blog), May 7, 2007, http://blog.guykawasaki.com/2007/05/worlds_best_pre.html#axzz1YGdylGey.

22. "Winners of World's Best Presentation Contest," *Holy Kaw!* (blog), September 30, 2009, http://holykaw.alltop.com/winners-of-worlds-best-presentation-contest.

23. "A Collection of Some of the Best SlideRocket Presentations," *SlideRocket*, http://www.sliderocket.com/product/presentation_showcase.html.

24. Visit SlideShare at http://www.slideshare.net/.

Chapter 11

1. Guy Kawasaki and Michele Moreno, *Rules for Revolutionaries: The Capitalist Manifesto for Creating and Marketing New Products and Services* (New York: Harper Paperbacks, 2000), 142.

2. "Attendees Share Webinar Turnoffs: Find Out Which Ones Top the List," *MarketingSherpa*, July 15, 2008, http://www.marketingsherpa.com/article.php?ident=30705&pop=no#.

3. Ken Molay, "Best Practices for Webinars" (white paper).

4. "Conducting a Webinar: A Step-by-Step Guide to Planning and Executing a Successful Webinar," *Communiqué Conferencing, Inc.*, 2003, http://www.communiqueconferencing.com/webseminarwhitepaper.pdf.

5. Patricia Fripp, "15 Tips for Webinars: How to Add Impact When You Present Online," *Patricia Fripp* (blog), September 8, 2009, http://fripp.blogs.com/presentations/2009/09/15-tips-for-webinars-how-to-add-impact-when-you-present-online.html.

6. Julia Young, "5 Surefire Tips for Running an Effective and Engaging Webinar," *Facilitate Proceedings* (blog), June 3, 2009, http://facilitate.com/blog/index.php/2009/06/5-surefire-tips-for-running-an-effective-and-engaging-webinar/. To learn more about *Fresh Air*, visit http://www.npr.org/programs/fa/about/.

7. Ken Molay, "Using PowerPoint Notes to Create a Handout," *The Webinar Blog*, September 28, 2009, http://wsuccess.typepad.com/webinarblog/2009/09/using-powerpoint-notes-to-create-a-handout.html.

Chapter 12

1. I credit Boyd Clarke and Ron Crossland for bringing this quote to my attention.

2. F. John Rey, "Getting Your Point Across," *About.com*, http://management.about.com/cs/communication/a/GetPointOver702.htm.

3. Brian Fugere and Chelsea Hardaway, *Why Business People Speak Like Idiots: A Bullfighter's Guide* (New York: Free Press, 2005).

4. Visit *Fight the Bull* at http://www.fightthebull.com/bullfighter.asp.

5. View the Gobbledygook Manifesto at http://www.webinknow.com/2006/10/the_gobbledygoo.html.

6. Try the Gobbledygook Grader at http://marketing.grader.com/.

7. View "The Complete List of Banished Words" at http://www.lssu.edu/banished/complete_list.php.

8. Ron Crossland and Boyd Clarke, *The Leader's Voice: How Leaders Communicate During Turbulent Times* (New York: Select Books, 2002).

9. To learn more about wax words, read "Clean the Wax from Your Words," ECG, http://ecglink.com/library/ps/wax.html.

10. Seth Godin, "The Best Presentation...," *Seth Godin's Blog*, March 10, 2006, http://sethgodin.typepad.com/seths_blog/2006/03/the_best_presen.html.

11. You can view this list at http://www.plainlanguage.gov/howto/wordsuggestions/simplewords.cfm.

12. View a video of Ira Glass speaking on storytelling at http://www.youtube.com/watch?v=BI23U7U2aUY&feature=relmfu.

13. Michael I. Norton, "People Often Trust Eloquence More Than Honesty," *HBR Blog Network*, video, November 2, 2010, http://blogs.hbr.org/video/2010/11/people-often-trust-eloquence-m.html.

14. Stanley L. Brodsky, Tess M. S. Neal, Robert J. Cramer, and Mitchell H. Ziemke, "Credibility in the Courtroom: How Likeable Should an Expert Witness Be?" *Journal of the American Academy of Psychiatry and the Law* 37:525–532, 2009.

15. "Meet the Masterminds: Robert Cialdini on *Influence*," *Management Consulting News*, http://www.managementconsultingnews.com/interview-robert-cialdini.

16. Keld Widinberg Jensen, "The 15-85% Rule of PowerPoint Presentations," August 9, 2011, http://www.youtube.com/watch?v=bj5lO-HqToE.

17. D. P. McAdams and J. Power, "Themes of Intimacy in Behavior and Thought," *Journal of Personality and Social Psychology* 40 (1981): 573–587.

18. Anthony Pratkanis and Elliot Aronson, *Age of Propaganda: The Everyday Use and Abuse of Persuasion* (New York: Henry Holt, 1992).

Chapter 13

1. James M. Kouzes and Barry Z. Posner, *The Truth About Leadership: The No-Fads, Heart-of-the-Matter Facts You Need to Know* (San Francisco: Jossey-Bass, 2010).

2. D. Joel Whalen, *I See What You Mean: Persuasive Business Communication* (Thousand Oaks, CA: Sage Publications, 1996).

3. James C. McCroskey and Jason J. Teven, "Goodwill: A Reexamination of the Construct and Its Measurement," *Communication Monographs* 66 (March 1999).

4. James M. Kouzes and Barry Z. Posner, *The Leadership Challenge, Third Edition* (San Francisco: Jossey-Bass, 2002), 51.

5. James M. Kouzes and Barry Z. Posner, *The Leadership Challenge, Third Edition* (San Francisco: Jossey-Bass, 2002), 52.

6. "The Six Seconds EQ Model," *Six Seconds* (blog), January 27, 2010, http://www.6seconds.org/2010/01/27/the-six-seconds-eq-model/.

7. Tom Peters, *100 Ways to Succeed/Make Money, Tips #1–25*, compiled from the blog at www.tompeters.com, http://www.tompeters.com/pdfs/TPSuccessTips1-25.pdf.

8. You can view Tom Peters's video "Leadership: The Problem Isn't the Problem" at http://www.youtube.com/watch?v=UFZA2rWUjxI. Or you can download a transcript at http://www.tompeters.com/dispatches/011428.php.

Chapter 14

1. Lea Winerman, "'Thin Slices' of Life" *Monitor on Psychology* 36 (March 2005): 54.

2. Moshe Barr, Maital Neta, and Heather Linz, "Very First Impressions," *Emotion* 6, no. 2 (2006): 269–278. Cited by Harvard Medical School, http://barlab.mgh.harvard.edu/papers/VFI_emotion.pdf.

3. Ian Sample, "Ancient Brain Circuits Light Up So We Can Judge People on First Impressions," *The Guardian*, March 8, 2009, http://www.guardian.co.uk/world/2009/mar/08/human-brain-circuit-impressions.

4. Guy Kawasaki, "Speaking as a Performing Art," *How to Change the World* (blog), June 12, 2007, http://blog.guykawasaki.com/2007/06/speaking_as_a_p.html#axzz1DJs7F4qG.

5. Adam D. Galinsky and Li Huang, "How You Can Become More Powerful by Literally Standing Tall," *Scientific American*, January 4, 2011.

6. "How to Use Your Body to Persuade Your Audience and Get Your Point Across," *World Class Solutions*, http://www.wclass.com/presentation_skills.html.

7. View Mark Walsh's video presentation "Evocative Leadership: Length, Width and Depth" at http://www.youtube.com/watch?v=LtvKZ_Y8J5k&feature=related.

8. Steven A. Bebe, "Eye Contact: A Nonverbal Determinant of Speaker Credibility," *The Speech Teacher* 23, no. 1 (1974).

9. C.L. Kleinke, "Gaze and Eye Contact: A Research Review," *Psychological Bulletin* (July 1986): 78–100. Cited in PubMed.gov, http://www.ncbi.nlm.nih.gov/pubmed/3526377.

10. Jari Hietanen, "A Direct Gaze Enhances Face Perception," Academy of Finland Press Release, August 13, 2008, http://www.aka.fi/en-gb/A/Academy-of-Finland/Media-services/Press-releases/Press-releases-2008/A-direct-gaze-enhances-face-perception/.

11. Scott Berkun, *Confessions of a Public Speaker* (Sebastopol, CA: O'Reilly Media, Inc., 2010), 158.

12. Jane Taber, "Turtle Talk Wins the Race," *The Globe and Mail*, February 22, 2008, http://www.theglobeandmail.com/life/article669604.ece.

13. Mary-Elaine Jacobsen, *The Gifted Adult: A Revolutionary Guide for Liberating Everyday Genius* (New York: Ballantine Books, 2000).

14. "Podium Practices from 28 Public Speaking Pros," *Forbes.com*, http://www.forbes.com/2007/08/01/sun-microsystems-nokia-ent-sales-cx_ll_0801byb07_publicspeaking.html.

15. "Bill Clinton Speaks at Harvard's 2007 Class Day (3/3)," video, June 2007, http://www.youtube.com/watch?v=6GYaArm8tZg.

16. University of Michigan, "Persuasive Speech: The Way We, Um, Talk Sways Our Listeners," *ScienceDaily*, May 15, 2011, http://www.sciencedaily.com/releases/2011/05/110515122507.htm.

17. Yoon-Hee Kwon, "The Influence of Appropriateness of Dress and Gender on the Self-Perception of Occupational Attributes," *Clothing and Textiles Research Journal* 12 (March 1994): 33–39.

18. Gwendolyn S. O'Neal and Mary Lapitsky, "Effects of Clothing as Nonverbal Communication on Credibility of the Message Source," *Clothing and Textiles Research Journal* 9, no. 3 (March 1991): 28.

19. Allan Rollman et al., "Introduction in Non-Verbal Communication," Fort Hays State University, http://bigcat.fhsu.edu/~zhrepic/Teaching/GenEducation/nonverbcom/nonverbcom.htm.

20. B. J. Fogg, Cathy Soohoo, and David Danielson, "How Do People Evaluate a Web Site's Credibility?" *Consumer Reports WebWatch*, November 11, 2002, http://www.consumerwebwatch.org/dynamic/web-credibility-reports-evaluate-abstract.cfm.

21. Guy Kawasaki, *Enchantment: The Art of Changing Hearts, Minds, and Actions* (New York: Penguin Group (USA), Inc., 2011).

22. "Professional Dress Code and Tattoos," *Burleson Consulting*, http://www.dba-oracle.com/dress_code_tattoos.htm.

23. Mary Lorenz, "Do Clothes Make the Manager?: Employers Weigh In," *The Hiring Site* (blog) by *Career Builder*, June 6, 2011, http://thehiringsite.careerbuilder.com/2011/07/06/do-clothes-make-the-manager-employers-weigh-in/.

24. Gini Dietrich, "Attire Not Appropriate for Public Speaking," *SpinSucks* (blog), May 26, 2010, http://www.spinsucks.com/ social-media/attire-not-appropriate-for-public-speaking/.

25. Visit CareerBuilder at http://www.careerbuildcr.com.

26. Robert B. Cialdini, *Influence: The Psychology of Persuasion* (New York: William Morrow and Company, 1993).

Chapter 15

1. Warren Bennis, *On Becoming a Leader* (Philadelphia: Perseus Books Group, 1989). In Rowan Gibson et al., eds., *Rethinking the Future: Rethinking Business, Principles, Competition, Control & Complexity, Leadership, Markets, and the World* (Boston: Nicholas Brealey Publishing Limited, 1998).

2. Visit the Myers & Briggs Foundation online at http://www. myersbriggs.org/.

Chapter 16

1. John Baldoni, "The 3 C's of Leadership," *SmartBlog on Leadership*, July 29, 2011, http://smartblogs.com/leadership/2011/07/29/ the-3-cs-of-leadership/.

2. Scott Berkun, *Confessions of a Public Speaker* (Sebastopol, CA: O'Reilly Media, Inc., 2010), 15.

3. Joseph O'Connor, *Free Yourself from Fears with NLP: Overcoming Anxiety and Living Without Worry* (London: Nicholas Brealey Publishing, 2005).

4. Sharon Begley, *Train Your Mind, Change Your Brain: How a New Science Reveals Our Extraordinary Potential to Transform Ourselves* (New York: Ballantine Books, 2007).

5. Cited in iWise Wisdom on-Demand, http://www.iwise.com/rkYsF.

6. Tiger Woods, *How I Play Golf* (New York: Warner Books, 2001).

7. Tiger Woods, "Dear Tiger: Mental Preparation for Tournaments," *Tiger Woods*, August 21, 2009, http://www.tigerwoods.com/news/article/200908216538960/deartiger/.

8. Clifford N. Lazarus, "Three Keys to Optimum Mental Fitness: How to Exercise Your Psychological Muscles," *Think Well* (blog) on *Psychology Today*, May 21, 2011, http://www.psychologytoday.com/blog/think-well/201105/three-keys-optimum-mental-fitness.

9. John Medina, *Brain Rules: 12 Principles for Surviving and Thriving at Work, Home, and School* (Seattle: Pear Press, 2008).

10. "Six Stress-Busting, Mood Boosting Foods," *CBS News*, January 15, 2011, http://www.cbsnews.com/stories/2011/01/15/earlyshow/saturday/main7249495.shtml.

11. You can find the eHow article "What Foods Are Natural Beta Blockers?" at http://www.ehow.com/list_6459910_foods-natural-beta-blockers_.html.

12. You can view the video "Breathe" from The Energy Project at http://www.youtube.com/watch?v=dEJbDDWzrUs.

13. Herbert Benson, *The Relaxation Response* (New York: William Morrow and Company, 1975).

14. Learn about the relaxation response at Dr. Benson's website, at http://www.relaxationresponse.org/steps/.

15. Learn about HeartMath's biofeedback device emWave2 at http://www.heartmath.com/technology-products/emwave-technology.html.

16. *Biodot Skin Thermometers*, http://www.biodots.net/about/.

17. Sims Wyeth, "Five Ways to Speak Like Obama," *BNET*, April 20, 2009, http://www.bnet.com/article/five-ways-to-speak-like-obama/290100.

18. "How Music Affects Us and Promotes Health,." *eMedExpert.com*, http://www.emedexpert.com/tips/music.shtml.

19. You can watch a video of President Obama's less than perfect speech at a town hall event at http://www.youtube.com/watch?v=-zlh7yfZ-UE.

20. Leonard Koren, *Wabi-Sabi: For Artists, Designers, Poets & Philosophers* (Berkeley: Stone Bridge Press, 1994).

21. Bruna Martinuzzi, *The Leader as a Mensch: Become the Kind of Person Others Want to Follow* (San Francisco: Emotional Intelligence Press, 2009).

22. Albert Bandura, "Self-Efficacy," in *Encyclopedia of Human Behavior* 4: 71–81, ed. V. S. Ramachaudran (New York: Academic Press, 1994). (Reprinted in *Encyclopedia of Mental Health*, ed. H. Friedman (San Diego: Academic Press, 1998). Cited at http://www.des.emory.edu/mfp/BanEncy.html.

23. University of Exeter, "Emotional Support Leads to Sporting Success," *ScienceDaily*, May 1, 2009, http://www.sciencedaily.com/releases/2009/05/090501110212.htm.

24. Bruna Martinuzzi, "Self-Efficacy: The First Requisite for Success," *OpenForum*, November 12, 2010, http://www.openforum.com/idea-hub/topics/the-world/article/self-efficacy-the-first-requisite-for-success-bruna-martinuzzi.

25. Peter Bregman, "How to Teach Yourself to Trust Yourself," *HBR Blog Network*, November 3, 2010, http://blogs.hbr.org/bregman/2010/11/how-to-teach-yourself-to-trust.html.

26. Marshall Goldsmith, "Becoming Who You Want to Be," *Marshall Goldsmith*, http://www.marshallgoldsmithlibrary.com/cim/articles_display.php?aid=873.

27. Joshua Freedman, "The Six Seconds EQ Model," *Six Seconds* (blog), January 27, 2010, http://www.6seconds.org/2010/01/27/the-six-seconds-eq-model/.

28. Daniel Goleman, *The Brain and Emotional Intelligence: New Insights* (Northampton, MA: More Than Sound, 2011).

29. Bruna Martinuzzi, "The Chains of Habit," *OpenForum*, April 27, 2011, http://www.openforum.com/idea-hub/topics/lifestyle/article/the-chains-of-habit.

30. Seymour Segnit, *CTRN: Change That's Right Now*, http://fear-of-public-speaking.changethatsrightnow.com/.

31. You can view Seymour Segnit's video blogs on public-speaking fear at http://fear-of-public-speaking.changethatsrightnow.com/.

32. "Do It Yourself: Body Language," *OpenForum*, video, December 5, 2010, http://www.openforum.com/idea-hub/topics/lifestyle/video/do-it-yourself-body-language.

33. "18 Ways Attention Goes Wrong," *PsyBlog*, April 13, 2009, http://www.spring.org.uk/2009/04/18-ways-attention-goes-wrong.php.

34. Seth Godin, "Lady Gaga and Me," *Seth Godin's Blog*, December 16, 2010, http://sethgodin.typepad.com/seths_blog/2010/12/lady-gaga-and-me.html.

Chapter 17

1. Echo Swinford, "Recover a Corrupt PowerPoint File," Microsoft's *Office* website, http://office.microsoft.com/en-in/powerpoint-help/recover-a-corrupt-powerpoint-file-HA001116878.aspx.

2. You can download the free PowerPoint Viewer at http://www.microsoft.com/download/en/details.aspx?displaylang=en&id=13.

3. "2009 King Day Keynote: Who Plays King in the Age of Obama?," *Bates College*, February 4, 2009, http://www.bates.edu/news/2009/02/04/2009-king-day-keynote/.

4. Lilly Walters, *What to Say When…You're Dying on the Platform: A Complete Resource for Speakers, Trainers, and Executives* (New York: McGraw Hill, Inc., 1995).

5. You can view "Humor for Speakers" at http://halife.com/speakers/.

6. Malcolm L. Kushner, *Presentations for Dummies* (Indianapolis: Wiley Publishing, Inc., 2004).

7. You can learn more about YouSendIt at http://www.yousendit.com.

8. You can learn more about Dropbox at http://www.dropbox.com.

9. View the "Worldwide Electrical Outlet List" at http://electricaloutlet.org/.

10. For a Mac, you will need to purchase a DVI-VGA adapter, which you plug into the DVI port on your laptop; then plug the video cable into the adapter and into the projector.

Chapter 18

1. Peter Reimold and Cheryl Reimold, *The Short Road to Great Presentations: How to Reach Any Audience Through Focused Preparation, Inspired Delivery, and Smart Use of Technology* (Hoboken: John Wiley & Sons, Inc., 2003), 186.

2. Tom Antion, "Preparing for International Presentations: The Humor Perspective," Tom Antion, http://www.antion.com/articles/internat.htm.

3. Roger E. Axtell, *Gestures: The Do's and Taboos of Body Language Around the World* (New York: John Wiley & Sons, Inc., 1998).

Chapter 19

1. Jerry Weissman, *Presenting to Win: The Art of Telling Your Story* (Upper Saddle River, NJ: FT Press, 2009).

2. D. K. Berlo, J. B. Lemert, and R. J. Mertz, "Dimensions for Evaluating the Acceptability of Message Sources," *Public Opinion Quarterly* 33, no. 4 (1970): 563–576.

3. James Kouzes and Barry Posner, *Credibility: How Leaders Gain and Lose It, Why People Demand It* (San Francisco: Jossey-Bass, 2003).

4. G. Theonas, D. Hobbs, and D. Rigas, "The Effect of Facial Expressions on Students in Virtual Educational Environments," *International Journal of Social Sciences* 2 (2007): 1. Cited at http://www.waset.org/journals/ijhss/v2/v2-1-7.pdf.

5. Marianne LaFrance, *Lip Service: Smiles in Life, Death, Trust, Lies, Work, Memory, Sex, and Politics* (New York: W. W. Norton & Company, Inc., 2011), 53.

6. Simone Schnall and James D. Laird, "Keep Smiling: Enduring Effects of Facial Expressions and Postures on Emotional Experience and Memory," *Cognition and Emotion* 17, no. 5 (2003): 787–797. Cited at http://www.psy.plymouth.ac.uk/research/ece/publications/pdf/keep-smiling.pdf.

7. Ron Crossland and Boyd Clarke, *The Leader's Voice: How Your Communication Can Inspire Action and Get Results!* (New York: Select Books, 2008).

8. Garr Reynolds, *Presentation Zen Design: Simple Design Principles and Techniques to Enhance Your Presentations* (Berkeley: New Riders, 2010).

9. Watch a video of John Chambers moving effectively during a presentation at http://www.youtube.com/watch?v=8TH7-muFaH0&feature=related.

10. Watch a video of Guy Kawasaki making effective use of movement as a speaker at http://www.youtube.com/watch?v=xCpViu8kY3o.

11. Mark Suster, "Quick Practical, Tactical Tips for Presentations," *Both Sides of the Table*, May 15, 2011, http://www.bothsidesofthetable.com/2011/05/15/quick-practical-tactical-tips-for-presentations/.

12. Lillian J. Glass, *Talk to Win: Six Steps to a Successful Vocal Image* (New York: Putnam, 1987).

13. Matthew S. McGlone and Barbara Breckinridge, "Why the Brain Doubts a Foreign Accent," *Scientific American*, September 21, 2010, http://www.scientificamerican.com/article.cfm?id=the-brain-doubts-accent.

14. For a list of speech pathologists in the United States, visit http://www.asha.org/findpro/.

15. Visit the website of the Canadian Association of Speech-Language Pathologists and Audiologists at http://www.caslpa.ca/english/index.asp.

16. Visit AccentMaster at http://www.accentmaster.com/Lessons/lessons.htm.

17. Susan Goldin-Meadow, *Hearing Gesture: How Our Hands Help Us Think* (Cambridge, MA: The Belknap Press of Harvard University Press, 2003).

18. Aaron Brehove, *Knack Body Language: Techniques on Interpreting Nonverbal Cues in the World and Workplace* (Gilbert, AZ: Knack Publishing, 2011).

19. Sims Wyeth, "Effective Presentation Skills: Hang 'Em in the Bat Cave," *High Stakes Presentations* (blog), April 3, 2008, http://www.simswyeth.com/20080403-using-your-hands-while-speaking-publicly/.

20. David Wallis, "The Body Politic: From Finger Pointing to Fist Pumps: How Nonverbal Cues Brand the Candidates," *Hand Research*, March 31, 2008, http://www.handresearch.com/news/the-body-politic.htm.

21. You can view Professor Simon Baron Cohen's presentation "Zero Degrees of Empathy" at http://www.youtube.com/watch?v=Aq_nCTGSfWE&feature=player_embedded%23!.

22. D. Joel Whalen, *The Professional Communications Toolkit* (Thousand Oaks, CA: Sage Publications, Inc., 2007).

Chapter 20

1. Wayne Leman, "Eisegeting Hebrew Metaphors and Idioms," *Better Bibles Blog*, November 15, 2005, http://betterbibles.com/2005/11/15/eisegeting-hebrew-metaphors-and-idioms/.

2. James Geary, *I Is an Other: The Secret Life of Metaphor and How It Shapes the Way We See the World* (New York: Harper Collins, 2011).

3. David Brooks, "Poetry for Everyday Life," *The New York Times*, April 11, 2011, http://www.nytimes.com/2011/04/12/opinion/12brooks.html?_r=2.

4. You can view Randy Pausch's last lecture, at Carnegie Mellon University, at http://www.youtube.com/watch?v=ji5_MqicxSo.

5. David LaGesse, "America's Best Leaders: Jeff Bezos, Amazon.com CEO," November 19, 2008, http://www.usnews.com/news/best-leaders/articles/2008/11/19/americas-best-leaders-jeff-bezos-amazoncom-ceo.

6. Warren E. Buffett, "The Greenback Effect," *The New York Times*, August 18, 2009, http://www.nytimes.com/2009/08/19/opinion/19buffett.html?pagewanted=all.

7. Stanford University, "Jack Welch: Create Candor in the Workplace," video, July 27, 2009, http://www.youtube.com/watch?v=PxU6Z0BgyWM.

8. Al Pittampalli, "Death to the Informational Meeting," *Modern Meeting Standard* (blog), July 15, 2011, http://modernmeetingstandard.com/2011/07/death-to-the-informational-meeting/.

9. You can see a video of Al Pacino's speech about winning by inches in Any Given Sunday at http://www.youtube.com/watch?v=9rFx6OFooCs&feature=player_embedded#!.

10. Jaime Henriquez, "10 Common User Questions—And Some Analogies That Help Clear Things Up," *Tech Republic*, December 28, 2009, http://blogs.techrepublic.com.com/10things/?p=1261.

Chapter 21

1. Clive Shepherd, "The Trainer as Storyteller," *Clive on Learning*, November 23, 2005, http://clive-shepherd.blogspot.com/2005/11/trainer-as-storyteller.html#!/2005/11/trainer-as-storyteller.html.

2. Richard Maxwell and Robert Dickman, *The Elements of Persuasion: Use Storytelling to Pitch Better, Sell Faster & Win More Business* (New York: HarperCollins, 2007), 4.

3. "Ira Glass on Storytelling, Part 1 of 4," video, August 18, 2009, http://www.youtube.com/watch?v=loxJ3FtCJJA.

4. Ron Crossland and Boyd Clarke, *The Leader's Voice: How Your Communication Can Inspire Action and Get Results!* (New York: Select Books, 2008).

5. Jeff Bezos, "We Are What We Choose," May 30, 2010, Princeton University, *News at Princeton*, http://www.princeton.edu/main/news/archive/S27/52/51O99/index.xml.

Chapter 22

1. Atul Gawande, "Crimson Tide: What Is Blushing? No One Knows for Sure But It Can Ruin Your Life," *The New Yorker*, February 12, 2001, http://www.newyorker.com/archive/2001/02/12/2001_02_12_050_TNY_LIBRY_000022696?currentPage=all.

2. Atul Gawande, *Complications: A Surgeon's Notes on an Imperfect Science* (New York: Picador, 2002).

3. "Renew: Stress on the Brain," *The Franklin Institute*, http://www.fi.edu/learn/brain/stress.html.

4. Sara Reardon, "Want to Ace Your Test? Share Your Feelings," *Science Now*, January 13, 2011, http://news.sciencemag.org/sciencenow/2011/01/want-to-ace-your-test-share-your.html.

5. Sara Reardon, "Want to Ace Your Test? Share Your Feelings," *Science Now*, January 13, 2011, http://news.sciencemag.org/sciencenow/2011/01/want-to-ace-your-test-share-your.html.

6. Mark Schoeberl and Brian Toon, "Ten Secrets to Giving a Good Scientific Talk," *Climate & Global Dynamics*, http://www.cgd.ucar.edu/cms/agu/scientific_talk.html.

7. Nathan Carpenter, "Having 'The Talk': Discussing Technology with Managers and Customers," *Embarcadero Developer Network*, http://conferences.embarcadero.com/article/32124.

Resource A

1. Geraldine Woods, *Grammar Essentials for Dummies* (Hoboken: Wiley Publishing, Inc., 2010).

INDEX

"A good indexer, like a good editor, serves as the reader's advocate."
—L. F. Radke

A

Abrams, Rhonda, 54
Accent
　rehearsal, coach (usage), 238
　understanding, 236–238
Accent-reduction specialist,
　consultation, 237
Accent-reduction videos, study, 238
Accusatory question, repetition
　(avoidance), 68
Acknowledgment, 184
　variation, 67
Actions, alignment, 160–161
Active voice, usage, 61
Adaptability, 180
Advice, moratorium, 201
Agenda
　design, 51
　entries, creation, 50–51
　key words, usage, 50
　slide, preparation, 50–51
Ailes, Roger, 156
Air quotes, usage, 241
Ali, Muhammad, 40
Altito, Noelie, 39
Ambady, Nalini, 164

American Speech-Language-Hearing
　Association, speech pathologist
　availability, 237
Amygdala, impact, 165
Analogies, 254–256
　consideration of audience, 256
　usage, 60, 255–256
Anaphora, 92
Anecdotes, usage, 41
Annoyance
　hint, 224
　manifestation, 154
Answers, 63–76
　cessation, knowledge, 68
　confirmation, 69
　handouts, preparation, 65
　rehearsal, 66
　short answers, usage, 68
　slides, preparation, 65
Antion, Tom, 223
Antonio, Victor, 96, 100
　Compendium of Presentations, A, 307
Anxiety, 186–205
　creation, blushing (impact), 265–266
　pronouncement, 186
　reduction, 80

Arguments
   simplification, 19
   structural problems, 11–12
Aristotle, xvii
Arrogance, hint, 224
Art of Woo, The (Shell/Moussa), 14, 20
Ashkenas, Ron, 23–24
Assertion, initiation, 37–38
Attention
   grabbing, 31–51
   spans, 32
Attire, importance, 196
Attitude, control, 223–224
Audiences
   age, attention, 34
   aggressiveness, 215
   analogies, considerations, 256
   anxiety, 220
   bad news, impact, 220–222
   body language, 85
   conversations
      appearance, 170
      management, 71
   data, dumping, 24
   details, reduction, 84
   difficulty, 215–224
   distance, eye contact (usage), 169
   distraction, 220
   expectations, 64
   friendly faces
      contact, 269
      location, 171
   goodwill, display, 159
   interest, 31
   introduction of yourself, 48
   listlessness, 220
   memory, usage, 45
   needs, importance, 84
   objectives, clarity, 81
      overwhelming, avoidance, 181
   pauses, 267
   questions, 30
      asking, 270
   recommendations, 21
   strong opinions, impact, 216–220
   trust, earning, 157–158
   understanding, assumption, 276–277
   visualization, 62
Authenticity, xviii, xx, 18, 89, 118,
      146–156, 242
Axtell, Roger E., 223

B

Background documentation, provision,
      183
Background information, usage, 25
Back-up material, availability, 190
Bad news
   delivery, difficulty, 184
   impact, 220–222
Baldoni, John, 186–187
Batteries, provision, 212
Bayne, Stephen, 23
Beginnings
   five-step opening, 32
   importance, 31
Benki, Jose, 175
Bennis, Warren, 185
Benson, Herbert, 194–195
Berkun, Scott, 188
Bezos, Jeff, 248, 260
Biases, familiarity, 18
Big-picture thinking, 182–183
Biodots, 195
Biofeedback device, 195
Blushing, 264–266
   erythrophobia, impact, 265–266
Body calmness, 193–196

Body language
awareness, 71–73, 85
negative body language, 71–72
Other Useful Websites, 296
positive body language, 72–73
receptive body language, 73
Speaker's Library, A, 289
study, 203–204
Body posture, change (impact), 166
Book-end closure, 55
Book of Common Prayer, The, 250
Bottom-line thinking, 183–184
Brain and Emotional Intelligence, The
(Goleman), 202
Brain Rules (Medina), 34, 125
Brains
Brain Rule (Medina), 193
processes, 3f
scans, 165
Branches, creation/drawing, 5
Bregman, Peter, 201
Brehove, Aaron, 238
Brooks, David, 246
Brown, Tim, 57
Browne, Lord, 45
Bruner, Jerome, 257
Buffett, Warren, 39, 248
Bull Composite Index Calculator, 150
Bullets, three (maximum), 27
Business quotations, 39

C

Cain, Susan, 243
Canadian Association of Speech-
Language Pathologists and
Audiologists, website, 237
Card, Orson Scott, 247
Caring, elements, 159
Carlin, George, 36

Carnegie, Dale, 258
Carpenter, Nathan, 277
Cartoons
sources, Other Useful Websites, 296
usage, 47
Chambers, John, 96, 232
Chaplin, Charlie, 167
Churchill, Winston, 64, 246
Cialdini, Robert, 14, 154, 179
Clarke, Boyd, 15–16, 230
C-level, xix, 77–85
presenting, Other Useful Websites,
301
Clinton, Bill (Harvard Class Day
speech), 174
Clinton, Hillary (speech rate), 171
Clipart, avoidance, 82
Clothing, 176–179
advice, 178
shoes, selection, 178
tattoos, coverage, 178
warm clothes, avoidance, 265
wrinkled clothing, avoidance, 178
Coca-Cola (Dyson), 42
Cochran, Johnnie, 15
Cognitive bias, 18, 52
Cohen, Simon Baron, 242–243
Colloquial expressions, replacement, 152
Comfort zone, 89, 169, 180, 182, 185
Comments, acceptance, 201
Commitments, securing, 19–20
Common words, usage, 273
Communication (leadership), A
Speaker's Library, 290–291
Competence, xvii, xviii–xix
perception, 2
proof, 184
Composure (presentation attribute), 187
Concepts, remembering, 9

Conclusions
  planning template, 309
  showing, 287
  templates, 59
Concrete language, usage, 20
Confessions of a Public Speaker (Berkun),
  188
Confidence
  absence, stances (impact), 168
  presentation attribute, 187
Consequential thinking, application, 29
Consultants, template, 28
Content, stress, 275
Contradictory statement, usage, 37
Control (presentation attribute), 187
Conversationalism, 151–153
Conversations, management, 71
Core material, knowledge (audience
      judgment), 2
Corporate database, setup, 66
Corporate non-speak, 152t
Corporate presentation, 66
Corporate vocabulary, 148–149
Covey, Stephen R., 308
Creativity, stimulation, 43
Credentials
  establishment, 48
  non-reliance, 10
Credibility. *See* Terminal credibility
  actions, 242
  aspect of presenting, xv–xix
  postural rigidity, impact, 167
  question-and-answer period,
      importance, 76
  threat, 216
  trustworthiness, 157
Criticism, encounter, 185
Cronkite, Walter, 56
Crossland, Ron, 15, 16, 230, 259–260

Cuddy, Amy, 203–204
Cultures, communication (A Speaker's
      Library), 289
Current events, reference (usage), 43
Custom show, slides (usage), 50–51

D

Data
  analysis, 25
  emphasis, avoidance, 181
  provision, 184
  visualization, A Speaker's Library, 289
Debate, excitement, 184
Decision making, familiarity (biases), 18
Decoy marketing option, 27
Deep breaths, usage, 194
Deep listening, 217
Details
  breakdown, 277
  determination, 271–277
  orientation, 181–182
  reduction, 84
Diana, Princess, 240
Dietrich, Gini, 179
Direct dialogue, usage, 259–260
Direct eye contact, 169
Disappointment, facial expression, 230
Discussion, planning, 78–79
Disraeli, Benjamin, 231, 260
Documentation, provision, 184
Dorsal lateral prefrontal cortex,
      information responsibility, 26
Dress
  quality, 196
  sense, 177
Duck position, 167
Dynamism, 226–244
  components, 227
  energy, 246

expansionist quality, 226
inside-out job, 242
internal manifestation, 227–228
Dyson, Bryan, 42

E

Earned authority, 186–187
Eblin, Scott, 81, 83
Edelman Trust Barometer, xv
"Effects of Clothing As Nonverbal
     Communication on Credibility
     of the Message Source" (O'Neal/
     Lapitsky), 176
Eight-second concentration rule, 3–4
Einstein, Albert, 39, 192, 248
Electrical voltage/outlets, usage, 212
Elevator Pitch Builder, 48
Eliot, T. S., 201
Emerson, Ralph Waldo, 20, 148, 164
Emotional channel, 15–16
Emotional energy, usage, 197–198
Emotional engagement, 227–228
     impact, 241–244
Emotional intelligence (EQ), xx, 28–29,
     118–119, 160–161, 180, 185, 202
     assessments, Other Useful Websites, 297
Emotional question, initiation, 35–36
Emotional states, 199
Emotions, elicitation, 246
Empathy, caring element, 159
emWave2 (HeartMath), 195, 304
Enchantment: The Art of Changing Hearts,
     Minds, and Actions (Kawasaki),
     29, 177
Endings, 52–59
     book-end closure, 55
     memorability, 53–55, 58–59
     movie line, usage, 56
     poem line, usage, 56

question period, 58–59
rhetorical question, usage, 56
signal, 53
songs, usage, 57
speech title, reference, 57
take-away message, slides (usage), 57
templates, 59
trademark sign-off, usage, 56
weakness, 52
Energy Project, 194
Energy saver, deactivation, 213
English-language TV, observation, 238
Enthusiasm, 235
Erudition, attempt, 152
Erythrophobia (blushing fear), impact,
     265–266
"Evocative Leadership: Length, Width
     and Depth" (Walsh), 168
Examples, usage, 60
Executive audiences, understanding,
     77–78
Executives, clothing usage (observation),
     178
Executive summary, usage, 181
Expertise, xvii, xviii, xix, 2–22
     conversations, analysis, 12
     importance, 2
Experts, thoughts/contributions
     (quotation), 13
Explanations, brevity, 19
Expressions, impact, 149t
Eye contact
     breaking, 71
     impact, 168–171
     maintenance, 170
     Speaker's Library, A, 289
     usage
          intelligence, 84–85
          judiciousness, 68

F

Facebook
  members, reference, 62
  pages, usage, 12
Facial expressions, 228–231
  adjustment, 229
  awareness, 72
  dynamism component, 227
Facial feedback theory, 229
Facts
  interpretation, questions (answering),
    65
  reliance, avoidance, 15–18
Factual channel, 15
Fairness, display, 20
Fallacies, impact, 11–12
False alarm, 188–189
Faulty logic, guarding against, 11–12
Fear
  recording, 270–271
  response, function, 187–189
  Speaker's Library, A, 290
Feelings, writing, 271
15/85 percent rule, 155
"Fight or flight" response, 187–189
  misfiring, 189
Fillers, Other Useful Websites, 297
Filler words, elimination, 150–151
Finger pointing, 240
First impressions, Other Useful
    Websites, 297
Five-step opening, 31–32
  flowchart, 33f
Flash drives, usage, 211
Flipchart, usage, 74
Foer, Joshua, 9, 10
Follow-up questions, asking, 218
Ford, Henry, 159
Foreign proverb, usage, 40–41
Franklin, Benjamin, 12

Freedman, Joshua, 112
Frequently asked questions (FAQs),
    264–279
Friendly faces
  contact, 269
  location, 171
Fripp, Patricia, 44
Fugere, Brian, 150
Full-length presentation, slides
    (preparation), 80

G

Gandhi, Mahatma, 14
Gaspworthy characteristic, 61
Gates, Bill, 39
Gaze direction, importance, 169
Geary, James, 245
General Electric (GE), 27, 248
Gestures, 238–241
  hand gestures, 240
  practice, 239
Gestures (Axtell), 223
Gestures, dynamism component, 227
Gifted Adult, The (Jacobsen), 172
Gimmicks, usage, 46
Glass, Ira, 153
Glass, Lillian, 235
Godin, Seth, 13, 37, 46, 56, 120, 125,
    147, 151, 204
  audience attention, 46
  Compendium of Presentations, A, 306
  focus, attention, 204
Goldin-Meadow, Susan, 238
Goldsmith, Marshall, 201
Goleman, Daniel, 202
Goodwill, display, 159
Google Alerts, usage, 13
Google Reader, usage, 12
Google search, 220, 221f
Grammar, correctness, 152

Graphs, usage, 274
Greene, Richard, 240
Green tea, drinking, 193
Gretzky, Wayne, 53–54
Ground rules, setting/observation, 277
Gump, Forrest, 246
Gutsche, Jeremy, 54

H

Hand gestures, 240
Handouts
    advance distribution, 237
    distribution, 270
    provision, 183
    usage, 82
Hard copy, usage, 212
Harris-Lacewell, Melissa, 210
"Having 'The Talk'" (Carpenter), 277
Head, jerking/bobbing, 241
HeartMath, 195
Heisman, John, 64
Hietanen, Jari, 169
Hill, Damon, 40
Hillis, Burton, 11
Historical event, reference (usage), 40
Hitchcock, Alfred, xxi
Hooks, 34–47
Hough, Pat, 167
"How Do People Evaluate a Web Site's Credibility?" (Persuasive Technology Lab), 176
How I Play Golf (Woods), 192
Human speak, 152t
Humor, A Speaker's Library, 290
Humorous quotations, 39
Humorous speech, pauses (usage), 173
Humphrey, Hubert, 146
Hyperlinked agenda entries, creation, 50–51

I

Ice breakers, Other Useful Websites, 297
Idealistic ideas, 182
Ideas
    sale (mistakes), 20
    substantiation, 183
Images, Other Useful Websites, 297–298
Imagine (word), usage, 42
Impatience
    control, 181
    hint, 224
    signal, 72
Importance, showing, 288
Improvisation
    classes, attendance, 205
    usage, 210
Inflated language
    Speaker's Library, A, 290
    usage, avoidance, 148–150
Inflated words, Other Useful Websites, 298
Influence, impact, 14
Influence: Science and Practice (Cialdini), 154
Infographics
    adding, 127
    Other Useful Websites, 298
Information
    adding, 286–287
    appeal, 30
    consolidation, sleep enhancement, 8
    processing
        expectations, 32
        time, 4
    relevance, 30
    remembering, ability (enhancement), 7
    value, assessment, 25
Inner feelings, facial expressions, 230
Inner territory, exploration, 160

Inspiration, 200
 metaphors, usage, 246
 story/metaphor, usage, 22
Intelligence, gathering, 202
Interim summaries, provision, 274
Interpersonal issues, 224
Interruptions, comfort, 74, 79
In the Line of Fire (Weissman), 66
Introduction, planning template, 311
Introversion, preference, 89, 243
Introverted speakers, role models,
 243–244
Introverts, A Speaker's Library, 290
Intuition, source, 15
Ionesco, Eugene, 264
Irrelevant questions, handling, 70

J

Jacobsen, Mary-Elaine, 172
Jargon, presence, 150
Jensen, Bill, 77
Jensen, Keld Widinberg, 155
Jobs, Steve, 28, 55, 251
 Compendium of Presentations, A, 306
Johnson, Lyndon (Martin Luther King
 Jr. meeting), 210
John Wayne stance, 167
Jones, Jim, 14

K

Kaiser, Henry J., 39
Kawasaki, Guy, 29, 91, 100, 122, 130,
 133, 166, 177, 233
 Compendium of Presentations, A, 306
Kenny, Elizabeth, 215
Kernel PowerPoint Repair Software, 207
Keynotes, 86–102
 Other Useful Websites, 298
Key words, usage, 50
King, Billie Jean, 40

King Jr., Martin Luther
 antithesis, 93
 LBJ meeting, 210
 speech rate, 171
King's Speech, The, 194
Knack Body Language (Brehove), 238–239
Koren, Leonard, 198
Kouzes, James, xvi, 157, 160
Kushner, Malcolm L., 211

L

LaFrance, Marianne, 229
LaGesse, David, 248
La Grou, John, 43–44
Language, inflation
 avoidance, 148–150
 Speaker's Library, A, 290
Lapitsky, Mary, 176
Laptop, connection, 213–214
Lazarus, Clifford N., 192
LCD projector, connection, 213
Leadership Challenge, The (Kouzes/
 Posner), 160
Leadership communication, A Speaker's
 Library, 290–291
"Leadership: The Problem Isn't the
 Problem" (Peters), 161
Leader's Voice, The (Crossland/Clarke),
 230, 259–260
Leakage, 223–224
Learning, potential (increase), 8
 sixty-beat-per-minute music, usage, 8
Lecturers, facial expressions, 228
Lecturing, Other Useful Websites, 298
Left frontal lobe, activity, 169
Leman, Wayne, 245
Lennon, John, 42
Lesser, Elizabeth, 56
Likability, 154–156
 behavior characteristics, 155–156

LinkedIn, industry-specific groups (affiliation), 12
Lloyd, Robert, 240
Logan, Dave, 40
Longfellow, Henry Wadsworth, 235
Long pauses, 174–175

M

MAC Studio Fix foundation, 265
Main message, clarification, 273
Main points, anticlimax order, 29
Main topic, usage, 47–48
Major points, examination, 64–65
Malcontents, focus shift, 204
Mansion, building (metaphor), 10
Marketing, rule of three, 27
Mastery experiences, 199
Math equations, avoidance, 273
McCroskey, J. C., xvii
McKinsey Mind, The, xxi, 19
Medina, John, 34
    Brain Rules, 34, 125, 193
Meeting, chairing (Other Useful Websites), 296
Memorable statements, examples, 54–55
Memory
    brain system, importance, 10
    enhancers, Other Useful Websites, 298
    Speaker's Library, A, 291
    usage, 45
Memory-boosting practices, adoption, 3–10
Mental energy, usage, 197–198
Mental rehearsal, 191–192
Mentored by a Millionaire (Scott), 35
Message
    clarification, 273
    focus, 204

Metaphors, 245–254
    creation, 252–254
    development, 249–250
    examples, 247–249
    impact, 60
    library, setup, 251
    location, 250–252
    Other Useful Websites, 299
    power, 246
    Speaker's Library, A, 291
    usage, 22, 245–247
        tendency, avoidance, 183
    usefulness, 249–250
Micro-expressions, 223–224
Miller, Henry, 281
Mind map, 5–7
    contrast, 6, 6f
    software, Other Useful Websites, 299
Mind mapping, 4–7
Miss Goodie Two Shoes stance, 167
Mistakes, admission, 161
Monologue, recognition, 70
Monosodium glutamate (MSG), avoidance, 265
Monotonous tone, avoidance, 235
Moonwalking with Einstein (Foer), 9
Moussa, Mario, 14
Movement, 231–234
    strategic movement, 231–233
Movement, dynamism component, 227
Movies
    clips, Other Useful Websites, 299
    lines, usage, 45, 56
    metaphors, usage, 251–252
Mozart Effect, 8
Multicultural audiences, presentation, 223
Multiple questions, handling, 70–71
Murphy's Law, 206
    Other Useful Websites, 299
Murrow, Edward, R., xv

Music, 8, 114, 197
    sources, Other Useful Websites, 299
Myers-Briggs Type Indicator (MBTI), 185

N

Natural pauses, 175
Navratilova, Martina, 40
Negative body language, 71–72
Negative question, repetition
    (avoidance), 68
Negative reaction, impact, 219
Neural circuitry, impact, 165
Neural pathways, creation, 191, 202
Next Level, The (Eblin), 81, 83
Niacin supplements, usage, 265
Nietzsche, Friedrich, 2
Ning, communities (affiliation), 12
Non-dominant brain activation,
    visualization (usage), 192
Nonverbal language, 218
Norton, Michael I., 153
Notetaking (allowance), pauses (usage),
    173–174
Numbers, visualization, 62

O

Obama, Barack
    anaphora, 92
    Bible parable, 250
    signature gesture, 240
    speaking mistakes, 197
    speech rate, 171
    tricolon, 92
Objections, 18
    Other Useful Websites, 300
Objectives, clarity, 24–25, 81
Objectivity, display, 20
Obvious questions, avoidance, 35
OfficeRecovery, 207

Omega Institute, 56
On Becoming a Leader (Bennis), 185
O'Neal, Gwendolyn S., 176
O'Neal, Shaquille, 202
One-page outline, usage, 268–269
Online service, usage, 212
Online speeches, search, 251
Openings, steps, 33f
OpenOffice, 207
Outline, 268–269
Over-apologizing, avoidance, 210
Overused expressions, usage, 61
Overview
    provision, 272
    usage, 181

P

Page, Larry (commencement speech), 41
Palace method, 9–10
Pasricha, Neil, 57
Passive voice, avoidance, 61
Past events, reference (usage), 45
Pausch, Randy, 147, 247
    Compendium of Presentations, A, 307
Pauses
    frequency, 194
    long pauses, 174–175
    natural pauses, 175
    short pauses, 173–174
    skill, 172
    strategic pauses, usage, 275
    usage, 171–175
Peale, Norman Vincent, 241
PechaKucha, Other Useful Websites, 304
Pedestrian poetry, 246
People person, approach, 184–185
Perfection
    avoidance, 197–199
    obsession, 198

Performance
    anxiety, 186–205
    improvement, emotional support/
        encouragement, 200
    staged performance, 147, 232
Personal anecdote, usage, 41
Personal experience
    mentioning, 10–11
    usage, 49
Personal opinion, questions
        (answering), 65
Personal presence, 164–179
Personal story, 22, 41
Persuasion
    impact, 14
    learning, 14–22
    Speaker's Library, A, 291
    usage, 14
Persuasive presentations, Other Useful
        Websites, 300
Persuasive Technology Lab (Stanford
        University), 129, 176
Peters, Tom, 42, 61, 101, 161, 208, 232
Phrases, rewriting, 62
Physiological reaction, 229
Physiological states, 199
Pictures, usage, 43–44
Pink, Daniel (A Compendium of
        Presentations), 307
Pinker, Steven, 246
Pittampalli, Al, 249
Plagiarism, Other Useful Websites, 300
Plain Language: Improving
        Communication from the Federal
        Government to the Public, 152
Planned back-up slide, usage, 271
PLAN template, 85
Platitudes, usage, 61
Plato, 31

Poems, usage, 56
Poetry, reading, 251
Point of view, clarity, 81
Points
    emphasis, 287
    illustration, examples (usage), 272–273
    pauses, usage, 173
Pop-ups, deactivation, 213
Positive behaviors, practice, 73
Positive body language, 72
Posner, Barry, xvi, 157, 160
Posterior cingulated cortex, impact, 165
Postural rigidity, credibility, 167
Posture, 166–168
    importance, 167
    mindfulness, 168
    Other Useful Websites, 300
    stances, types, 167–168
PowerPoint
    file, corruption/recovery, 206–207
    final slide, 59
    narration, 7
    Other Useful Websites, 300
    Rehearse Timings feature, usage,
        189–190
    templates, 127–128
    timings (rehearsal), Other Useful
        Websites, 301
    viewer, packing, 207–208
Power zone, 240
Preparation, importance, 192
Presence, features, 165–166
Presentations
    analogies, usage, 254–256
    arrival, timing, 196
    attributes of a presenter, 187
    batteries, provision, 212
    beginnings, importance, 31
    benefits, emphasis, 21, 53

big-picture implications, 79
cartoons, usage, 47, 116
checklist, availability, 196
compendium, 306–307
conclusion, 52–59
concrete language, 20
contradictory statements, usage, 37
design, A Speaker's Library, 291–292
discussion, preparation, 78–79
dress code, 177
editing, 60–62, 274
embarrassment, 60
emotion, impact, 16
fairness/objectivity, display, 20
15/85 percent rule, 155
flipchart, usage, 74
folder, shortcuts, 212
foreign proverb, usage, 40–41
forgetfulness, 266–271
gaspworthy characteristic, 61
gimmick, usage, 46
goal, 48, 64, 75, 80
ground rules, setting/observation, 277
habits, consideration, 4
hooks, 34–47
improvement, 243
improvisation, usage, 210
initiation, pauses (usage), 173
know/feel/do, impact, 16, 24
last-minute changes, avoidance, 208
lengthening, 190
main points, anticlimax order, 29
main topic, usage, 47–48
major points, examination, 64–65
movie line, usage, 45, 56
non-sequential method, 127, 182
nourishment, 193–194
objectives, clarity, 24–25, 81
one-page outline, usage, 268–269
order, 83

past event, reference, 45
personal anecdote, usage, 41
persuasion, model, 15–17
pictures, usage, 43–44
planning template, 308–311
PLAN template, usage, 85
practice with a layperson, 272
precautions, 211–213
preparation, 25, 203–204
proofreading, 81
purpose
    clarification, 82–83
    emphasis, 53–54
question-and-answer period, 58–59,
    69–70
quotations, usage, 38–40
recitation, avoidance, 61
rehearsal, 234
repetition, importance, 21–22
review for corporate non-speak, 152
rewriting, 62
shortness, 80
skills, A Speaker's Library, 292
software, Other Useful Websites,
    300–301
songs, usage, 46–47, 57
sound, testing, 214
speed, Other Useful Websites, 304
startling fact, initiation, 37–38
subject, 64
technology glitches, 208–209
topic, writing, 5
tragedy, comedy conversation, 210–211
trends, Other Useful Websites, 301
turnout problems, control, 208
vagueness, avoidance, 21
video, usage, 46, 116
visual aids, absence, 214
visualization, 190–193
wow factor, 61

Presentations for Dummies (Kushner), 211
Presenter View, usage (consideration), 234
Presenting to Win (Weissman), 226
Prezi, Other Useful Websites, 300
Princess Diana, 240
Problem Liabilities Actions Necessary
    (PLAN) template, 85
Process, emphasis, 181
Professional Communications Toolkit, The
    (Whalen), 243
Projector, laptop (connection), 213–214
Proofreading, 81
Proposals, failure, 19–20
Provocative questions, initiation, 36
Public speaking
    anxiety, management through dress,
        196
    fear, 190–191
        management, 188–189
    gestures, 238–241
Purpose
    clarification, 82–83
    emphasis, 53–54
Pushback, encounter, 185

Q

Questions and answers (Q&A)
    closing, control, 75
    period, 58–59
        handling, importance, 76
    problems, 79
    rules
        establishment, 279
        setup, 69–70
    session
        negative body language, 71–72
        time allotment, 75
Questions
    absence, preparation, 73–74
    acknowledgment, variation, 67

answering, 66–76
    preparation, 63–66
answers
    confirmation, 69
    preparation, 190
asking, 270
    methods, alternatives, 76
dodging, avoidance, 153–154
emotional question, 35–36
initiation, 35–36
irrelevant questions, handling, 70
linking, 35
multiple questions, handling, 70–71
preparation, 63–66
    method, 63–64
provocative question, 36
rephrasing/repetition, 67–68
rhetorical question, 36
trigger word, focus, 67
trite/obvious questions, avoidance, 35
Quiet: The Power of Introverts (Cain), 243
Quotations
    Other Useful Websites, 301
    selection, 39
    usage, 38–40, 60

R

Rapport builder, 183
Reading, breadth, 250
"Really Achieving Your Childhood
    Dreams" (Pausch), 247
Recency effect, 52
Receptive body language, 73
Refdesk, usage, 13
Rehearsal
    repetition, 189
    sleep, 8
    timings, 189–190
Rehearse Timings feature, usage, 190
Re-imagine! (Peters), 42

Reimold, Peter/Cheryl, 219
Rejection, fear, 21, 53–54
Relaxation response (Benson), 194–195
Remarks, controversy/inappropriateness
　　(avoidance), 222–223
Resources, 283–311
Responsiveness (caring element), 159
Revelations, avoidance, 19
Reynolds, Garr, 51, 97, 129, 231
Rhetorical figures of speech, Other
　　Useful Websites, 301
Rhetorical questions
　　initiation, 36
　　pauses, usage, 174
　　usage, 56
Right brain activation, visualization
　　(usage), 192
Right frontal lobe, activity, 169
Robbins, Anthony, 180, 294
Robinson, Sir Ken, 94, 147
　　Compendium of Presentations, A, 307
Roche, Arthur Somers, 186
Rogers, Carl, 198
Rogers, Will, 289
Role models, 243–244
Rule of three, following, 26–29

S

Sales presentation
　　focus, 84
　　Other Useful Websites, 301–302
Schiller, Daniela, 165
Scientific presentations
　　Other Useful Websites, 302
　　Speaker's Library, A, 293
Scott, David Meerman, 150
Scott, Steven K., 35–36
Screen saver, deactivation, 213
Scriptures, reading, 250
Seabury, David, 241

Segnit, Seymour, 203
Self-acceptance, practice, 198
Self-assuredness, 166
　　telegraphing, pauses (usage), 171
Self-awareness, 160, 180, 185, 202, 224,
　　228, 244
　　increase, 180
　　self-management, relationship,
　　　228–229
Self-care, practice, 267
Self-compassion
　　practice, 201–203
　　Speaker's Library, A, 293
Self-criticism, habit, 201–202
Self-efficacy
　　increase, 199–200
　　undermining, 200
Self-knowledge, 161
Self-management, self-awareness
　　(relationship), 72, 228–229
Self-questions, 203
Self-sabotage, 198
Sellers, Peter, 52
Sequence, 288
Sequential process, following, 274
Shakespeare, William, 26, 246
Shell, Richard, 14
Shoes, selection, 178
Short answers, usage, 68
Short pauses, usage, 173–174
Short Road to Great Presentations, The
　　(Reimold), 219
Short sentences, usage, 273
Siegel, Daniel J., 26
　　Compendium of Presentations, A, 307
Silent observer, 201
Simpson, O. J., 15
Simulation, 7
Simulation games, 110
Sine cera words, 151t

Six Seconds
    Emotional Intelligence Model,
        components, 28–29
    Model of EQ (emotional
        intelligence), 160–161
    simulation game, 110
    training, 112–113
Sixty-beat-per-minute method, 8
Sleep
    impact, 8
    quantity, importance, 193
SlideRocket, 128, 132
Slides
    agenda, 50–51
    assertion evidence, 123–124
    custom show, 50–51
    design, Other Useful Websites,
        302–303
    display, pauses (usage), 173
    minimum, 79–80
    planned back-up slide, usage, 271
    points, addition, 236
    preparation, 65, 80
    take-away message, 57
Smiling, 229–230
    trigger, 229
Social networking, consideration, 12
Songs, usage, 46–47, 57
Sound, testing, 214
Speaker Notes, 234
Speakers
    appeal, 17–18
    library, 289–293
    presence, features, 165–166
    video, observation, 147–148
Speaking
    blogs, 294–295
    deceleration, 238
    engagement, metaphors (usage),
        249–250

    monotonous voice, avoidance, 235
    notes, packing, 213
    public speaking, fear (management),
        188–189
    rate, 171–172
    tips, Other Useful Websites, 303
    voice, 235–238
Speeches
    builders, Other Useful Websites, 303
    quotes, usage, 38–39
    rate, determination, 171–172
    titles, reference, 57
Sports quotations, 40
Staged performance, 147, 232
Stances, types, 167–168
StarOffice, 207
Statement
    contradiction, 37
    repetition, 268
Statistics
    emphasis, avoidance, 181
    usage, 37, 44, 139
Stellar Phoenix PowerPoint Recovery,
    207
Sting, removal, 218–220
St. John, Richard, 36
Stories
    authenticity, 258
    cultural appropriateness, 260
    detail, 259
    direct dialogue, usage, 259–260
    effectiveness, characteristics,
        258–260
    example, 260–262
    kindness, 260
    "lean in" quality, 259
    relevance, 259
    suspense, 259
    theme, 259
    usage, 22, 60

Storytelling, 153, 257–258
  hardwiring, 257
  Other Useful Websites, 304
  Speaker's Library, A, 293
Strategic movement, 231–233
Strategic pauses, usage, 275
Stress
  Other Useful Websites, 304
  Speaker's Library, A, 293
Stress dots, 195
Summarization, brevity, 53
Superiority, hint, 224
Swinford, Echo, 206–207
Symbolic channel, 15
Symbols, usage, 60

T

Take-aways
  message, slides (usage), 57
  provision, 183
Talk to Win (Glass), 235
Talmud, exploration, 251
Tattoos, coverage, 178
Team members
  attention, 278–279
  collaboration, 277–279
Technical terms, explanation, 272
Technology glitches, 208–209
TEDTalk
  La Grou, John, 43–44
  Lesser, Elizabeth, 56
  Logan, Dave, 40
  Other Useful Websites, 304
  Pasricha, Neil, 57
  Sapolski, Robert, 307
  St. John, Richard, 36
10-20-30 Rule, 130
Terminal credibility, 52
Teven, Jason J., xvii
Thermodynamics, Murphy's law, 206
Thinking, presentation (embodiment), 25

This American Life (Glass), 153
Thoreau, Henry David, 281
Throat, clearing (avoidance), 241
Tinted glasses, avoidance, 178
Toastmasters, 205
Toes, elevation, 241
Tomlin, Lily, 39
Topic
  coverage, 50–51
  emotional engagement, 227–228
  example, 6f
  executive summary, usage, 181
  nature, control, 74
  selection, 49–50
  usage (*See* Main topic)
Trademark sign-off, usage, 56
Tragedy, comedy conversation,
    210–211
Transitions, 284
  addition, 275, 286–287
  clarification, 286
  comparison, 285
  contrast/difference, 285–286
  information, repetition, 285
  result/cause, showing, 284
  smoothness, 278
Transition words/phrases, usage, 18
Trends, changes, 12–13
Tricolon, 92
Trigger word, focus, 67
Trite questions, avoidance, 35
Trust, earning, 157–158
Trustworthiness, 157–161
Tufte, Edward, 122
Twain, Mark, xv
20-20-20 rule, 4

U

Understanding (caring element), 159
Unistal Quick Recovery, 207
Upbeat music, listening to, 197

V

Vagueness, avoidance, 21
Values, actions (alignment), 160–161
Variables, minimum, 275
Vaynerchuk, Gary, 232
Verbal persuasion, 199
Vicarious experiences, 199
Video
    Other Useful Websites, 305
    usage, 46
Vision, explanation, 182
Visnjic, Goran, 236
Visual aids, absence, 214
Visualization
    impact, 192
    mental rehearsal, 191–192
    Other Useful Websites, 305
    success, 191
Visual thesaurus, Other Useful Websites,
    305
Vocal variety, dynamism component,
    227
Voice, 235
    enthusiasm, 235
    hygiene, Other Useful Websites, 305
Vulnerability, risk, 16

W

Walsh, Mark, 119, 168
Wax words, 151t
Wayne, John (stance), 167
"We Are What We Choose" (Bezos),
    260–262
Webinars, 133–144
    Other Useful Websites, 305
    Speaker's Library, A, 293
Weissman, Jerry, 66, 72, 82, 226
Welch, Jack, 39, 248
    rule of three, 27–28
Whalen, D. Joel, 159, 243

*What to Say When… You're Dying on the
    Platform* (Waters), 211
Why Business People Speak Like Idiots
    (Fugere), 150
Wiesel, Elie, 55
Wilson, Orvel Ray, 38
Winning Presentation in a Day (Abrams),
    54
Woods, Geraldine, 284
Woods, Tiger, 192
Words
    inflation, Other Useful Websites, 298
    listener processing, 151
    personalization, 153
Wow factor, 61
Wrinkled clothing, avoidance, 178
Written language, replacement, 152
Wyeth, Sims, 195

Y

*Yes! 50 Scientifically Proven Ways to Be
    Persuasive* (Cialdini), 14–15
YouTube
    downloading, 46
    Other Useful Websites, 305

Z

Zahab, Ray, 43
"Zero Degrees of Empathy" (Cohen), 242
Ziglar, Zig, 14, 226